The
Reference Shelf®

U.S. National Debate Topic: 2018-2019

Immigration

The Reference Shelf
Volume 90 • Number 3
H.W. Wilson
A Division of EBSCO Information Services, Inc.

Published by
GREY HOUSE PUBLISHING
Amenia, New York
2018

The Reference Shelf

The books in this series contain reprints of articles, excerpts from books, addresses on current issues, and studies of social trends in the United States and other countries. There are six separately bound numbers in each volume, all of which are usually published in the same calendar year. Numbers one through five are each devoted to a single subject, providing background information and discussion from various points of view and concluding with an index and comprehensive bibliography that lists books, pamphlets, and articles on the subject. The final number of each volume is a collection of recent speeches. Books in the series may be purchased individually or on subscription. Printed in Canada.

Publisher's Cataloging-In-Publication Data
(Prepared by The Donohue Group, Inc.)
Names: Grey House Publishing, Inc., compiler.
Title: U.S. national debate topic, 2018-2019. Immigration / [compiled by] Grey House Publishing.
Other Titles: US national debate topic, 2018-2019. Immigration | United States national debate topic, 2018-2019. Immigration | Immigration | Reference shelf ; v. 90, no. 3.
Description: Amenia, New York : Grey House Publishing, 2018. | Includes bibliographical references and index.
Identifiers: ISBN 9781682178669 (v. 90, no. 3) | ISBN 9781682177471 (volume set)
Subjects: LCSH: United States--Emigration and immigration--Government policy--History--21st century. | Emigration and immigration law--United States--History--21st century. | Illegal aliens--Government policy--United States--History--21st century. | Deportation--Government policy--United States--History--21st century. | Asylum, Right of--Government policy--United States--History--21st century. | Border security--Mexican-American Border Region.
Classification: LCC JV6483 .U8 2018 | DDC 325.73--dc23

Contents

3

The Census

4

Border Wall

5

Sanctuary

Preface

The Problem with Immigrants

Immigration is a process through which foreign-born individuals travel to a new country in the hopes of remaining on a long-term basis. Migration, by contrast, is the process by which individuals travel to another country on a temporary basis. Both immigration and migration have been among the most controversial issues in American history from the beginning and every nation around the world struggles with how to monitor, control, and conceptualize the movement of individuals across their borders.

Throughout history, politicians often claim that immigration policies are based on economic concerns and the welfare of the population. It is commonly argued by anti-immigration advocates, for instance, that reducing or limiting immigration is about putting Americans first, and that immigration policies, therefore, help to preserve and protect the resources of the nation for the benefit of citizens. However, the history of immigration policies reveals that it is the effort to preserve cultural identity, and not the economic welfare of the American people, that takes center stage in the immigration policy debate. Members of a society's majority are typically more willing to accept immigrants who are similar to themselves in terms of race, ethnicity, and religion. So, white Americans have always been far more willing to accept white, Christian immigrants from Europe than to accept immigrants of other races, ethnicities, or religions.

Arguments for and against immigration have not changed significantly in over 200 years. The nation's first national immigration debate came thanks to an anti-immigration movement led by Alexander Hamilton who used fear of a war with France to promote a strict, anti-French, anti-immigrant policy. Hamilton and the other Federalists were what would today be called "issue entrepreneurs," exaggerating the threat and detrimental effects of immigrants to incite public outrage, which they used to build political power to further their own goals. All anti-immigration advocates since have essentially made the same arguments in much the same way and have used the immigration policy debate as a stand-in for deeper issues like poverty, income inequality, and the gradual erosion of traditional ways of life.

In the 1790s, the Federalists warned that immigrants would take American jobs, would drain governmental reserves and resources, would erode American values, and might act as spies and saboteurs, holding allegiance to the countries and cultures of their birth, rather than to the United States. In 2018, the concerns of the American people are largely the same. Income and wealth inequality, the threat of radical violence, the effort to control illicit black markets for controlled substances and weapons, and overall insecurity about the ways in which the United States has and continues to evolve culturally, remain the scaffolding upon which all anti-immigration arguments are based.

Who Are Immigrants?

The Migration Policy Institute (MPI), a nonprofit think tank that studies immigration, estimated in 2016 that there were 43.7 million immigrants in the United States, constituting a full 13.5 percent of the US population (323 million). Immigrants and their US -born children together account for 27 percent (86.4 million) of the nation's people. In 1850, the first year in which the Census Bureau attempted to measure the immigrant population, immigrants constituted 10 percent of the population. The share of immigrants rose to 14.8 percent in 1890, the highest percentage ever registered, and thereafter began to decline. The lowpoint in immigration history came in 1970, when immigrants constituted just 4.7 percent of the population. Immigration rates rose sharply in the 1980s and 90s, with immigrants constituting a full 13 percent of the population by 2016.[1]

Data from the Census Bureau, immigration and border control authorities, and other academic sources indicate that the immigrant population of the United States is declining. This is occurring for a number of reasons, including falling birth rates, the growth of foreign economies, and more aggressive border enforcement. The foreign-born population increased by 449,000 (1 percent) between 2015 and 2016, which was less than half the rate of growth between 2014 and 2015 (2.1 percent). Immigration experts have found that the immigration rates have been declining since 2008–2009.

All-together, immigrants constitute 17 percent of the American workforce, while making up only 13 percent of the population and thus immigrants are more likely to be employed than native-born Americans. Immigrants do not constitute a majority in any single occupation, though it is often believed that immigrants make up the majority in stereotypical occupations like taxi drivers, domestic servants, or agricultural workers. However, 37 percent of lawful immigrants are in management, business, finance, or other professional fields, while undocumented migrants tend to work in service or construction. [2]

It has often been claimed that immigrants do not "assimilate" into US culture, and remain more connected to their places of birth and native cultures than to US culture. This claim is not based on data or research, but rather is a stereotype that has long been favored by individuals who feel that immigrants never really become "American." However, it is unclear what assimilation means and how to measure whether or not someone assimilates to American culture. Some suggest that English-language fluency is a good measure and, if this measure is used, then American immigrants tend to assimilate linguistically at high rates, much higher than in many other nations with large immigrant populations.[3] Others have suggested that assimilation is based on adopting "American values," and yet, there is little agreement among native-born Americans as to what American values are or should be. For instance, consider whether aversion to racism, or gender equality, should be American values? Some might enthusiastically embrace gender equality as a core

American value and yet, there are many Americans who would not agree. In truth, the United States does not have a single set of core values or cultural characteristics and the belief that there is a core system of uniquely American values is, itself, an inaccurate and highly prejudiced view of American society.

The Illegal Immigrant Population

The vast majority, 76 percent, of immigrants in the United States are legal residents and 44 percent of them are naturalized citizens. There are approximately 11 million unauthorized immigrants in the United States, constituting 24.5 percent of the immigrant population and 3.4 percent of the nation's population overall. Between the 1950s and 2010s, most American immigrants and most unauthorized migrants and immigrants in the United States came from Mexico. For this reason, Mexican immigrants and immigration have been the key issues in the immigration debate.

The danger of Mexican immigration was a cornerstone of Donald Trump's 2016 presidential campaign and has been the key immigration issue for the Republican Party throughout the twenty-first century. The number of unauthorized migrants from Mexico grew rapidly in the 1990s and 2000s, reaching a peak of 6.9 million in 2007. However, immigration from Mexico is also declining and has been declining throughout the 2010s.[4]

Between 2009 and 2014, 1 million Mexicans and their families left the United States for Mexico, while US Census Bureau data indicated that 870,000 left Mexico for the United States. By 2014, the last year for which data was available, Pew Research found that the unauthorized Mexican migrants and immigrant population had fallen to 5.8 million, the lowest since the early 1990s. In 2015, the rate of immigration from Mexico reached its lowest levels since the 1980s. For this reason, immigration experts and researchers have questioned Donald Trump's assertion that the United States needs to step up border control, or to build a wall across the US-Mexican border. For instance, speaking on Wisconsin Public Radio in February of 2017, US Representative Ron Kind opined, "To build a wall now would be locking them in this country."[5]

Immigrants and the Economy

The effect of immigration on the economy is and has always been one of the key issues in immigration debates. Critics of immigration generally argue that all or most of America's resources should be preserved for native-born Americans and thus that immigrants compete for jobs and take resources that would otherwise benefit the native-born.

Harvard economist George Borjas and partner Lawrence Katz are the leading figures behind this argument and conducted research suggesting that, between 1980 and 2000, immigration reduced wages for low-skill workers and non-high-school graduates by as much as 3.4 percent. This research is the core of all fact-based arguments against immigration, but, Borjas and Katz' research is controversial and has been widely disputed. This is because Borjas and Katz compare immigrants and US workers directly, assuming that these workers compete for the same jobs. This assumption then created the impression that immigrants outcompete native workers and take opportunities and resources directly from them. Critics argue that this is not the case. A 2015 study from the Urban Institute, for instance, found that immigrants and native workers of the same general educational and skill levels nevertheless prefer different jobs and so rarely compete directly.[6]

A 2010 paper for the National Bureau of Economic Research by economist Gianmarco Ottaviano, Giovanni Peri, and Greg Wright found that immigration, overall, increases opportunities for native workers through the creation of new jobs and the expansion of both the economy and the consumer base. Consider that each immigrant living in the United States also spends money within the United States—renting property, purchasing food and consumer goods, and paying taxes through wages and spending—and thus the immigrant population spreads revenue throughout the system.[7] University of California Davis researcher Giovanni Peri then found, in a study published in June 2010, that immigration has increased real wages for native workers by 2.86 percent between 1990 and 2006.[8]

The debate regarding the economic impact of immigration is unresolved and all academics working in the field typically say that more data is desperately needed. However, the general consensus given what data exists and decades of studies is that overall, immigration is good for American workers and has a negligible effect on wages and job availability on the longer term. However, evidence indicates that, in certain circumstances, workers in specific fields may suffer from short-term losses in employment opportunities.

Legal and illegal immigration is fueled by demand. Throughout American history, US companies and individuals have been willing to hire immigrant workers, both legal and unauthorized, because doing so increases profits and fills labor shortages. In the 1940s and 50s, guest worker programs allowed millions of Mexican migrants to temporarily work in the United States. However, US companies and individuals began hiring unauthorized migrants instead, because they would work for less and weren't protected by bilateral guest worker agreements that ultimately increased the cost of hiring them. This is how the US unauthorized immigration problem began, with US companies and farm owners creating the problem by courting unauthorized migrants to increase profits. The problem still exists today.

However, not all economists believe that the movement of labor is something that countries need to be concerned about. For instance, a 2009 paper from the Center for Global Trade Analysis of Purdue University found that full deportation of all unauthorized Mexican immigrants would not help the US workforce or economy and, instead, would reduce the US Gross Domestic Product by 0.61 percent. By contrast, full legalization of immigrant workers, with border control still in place, would increase the GDP by 0.17 percent, while legalization without border control of any kind would increase the GDP by 0.53 percent.[9] Harvard University researcher Lant Pritchett argued further that completely open borders—allowing free movement of laborers into and out of all nations around the world—would increase the global GDP by $65 trillion. Pritchett's findings, if correct, indicate that open borders would be more effective at creating economic growth than any other method ever studied or attempted in the history of the world.[10]

Immigrants and Crime

During his campaign for president, Donald Trump claimed,

> When Mexico sends its people, they're not sending their best. They're not sending you. They're not sending you. They're sending people that have lots of problems, and they're bringing those problems with us. They're bringing drugs. They're bringing crime. They're rapists. And some, I assume, are good people.[11]

Donald Trump's statement contains several concepts that might confuse those seeking to understand the immigration issue. First, the statement suggests that Mexico "sends" immigrants to the United States. Migrants and immigrants are not, "sent" from their native country, but leave seeking work and a better life for themselves or their families. Some migrate or immigrate for education, some to earn money to send back home, some to escape poverty, violence, and instability, and others to find better homes for themselves and their families. Migrating illegally is dangerous and difficult and those who choose to do it typically do so because they see few options to improve their lives in their current environments.

Trump's statement also indicates a belief that immigrants bring drugs and crime to the United States and this belief is common, but not supported by research. A September 2017 study released through the American Public Health Association found no evidence that undocumented migrants increase drug trafficking rates, driving under the influence (DUI) arrests, overdose deaths, drug arrests or any other factor related to drug and alcohol abuse.[12]

Experts in the field, on both sides of the debate, readily admit that there is insufficient data to make broad conclusions about immigration and crime. As of April 2018, the best research-based data on immigration and crime comes from the 2015 report "The Integration of Immigrants into American Society," from the National Academy of Sciences. According to the report, increased immigration rates do not lead to higher crime rates and, in fact, areas with high levels of immigration have lower crime rates overall.[13] The study's authors speculate that the misperception that immigrants are more likely to commit crimes is the result of politicians and other anti-immigration activists spreading false claims as part of various political campaigns against immigration and immigrants.

Finally, the 19 people who conducted the September 11, 2001 terrorist attacks in the United States were legal immigrants and the threat of terrorism has thus been one of the major factors in anti-immigration debates since 2001. Security experts agree that the nation's borders constitute a potential hazard with regards to radical violence but have also found that most radical attacks in the United States have been conducted by individuals who were radicalized while living in the United States, rather than by terrorists who were radicalized elsewhere and then came to the United States for the express purpose of launching an attack.[14] That individuals are turning to radicalism through radicalization within the United States and western European nations demonstrates a growing problem for which there are few current solutions. Writing for *Brookings Institution* in 2016, Michael O'Hanlon and Raymond Odierno suggest that the best way to combat radicalism is by assimilating immigrants into society and that the best way to do this is to find ways to make it possible for immigrants to develop a sense of belonging and allegiance to their adopted society without feeling that they need to abandon all links to their birth-culture to do so.[15] Law enforcement data supports this idea, with Federal Bureau of Investigation (FBI) reports indicating that immigrants have been among the greatest assets in the United States when it comes to fighting terrorism. With links to individuals in communities that might be vulnerable to radicalism, many Muslim Americans have informed police or the FBI about potential attacks, enabling law enforcement to prevent what might otherwise have been devastating attacks like those seen in France and the United Kingdom in 2015.

The Perennial Debate

The immigration debate never abates and hardly changes from decade to decade. President Trump's claims about Mexican immigrants in 2018 are similar in tone and veracity to the claims made by Alexander Hamilton and allies about French immigrants in 1798. Then, as now, the debate was clouded by misinformation and politicians and activists, on both sides, often based their claims on insufficient, misleading, or false information chosen to support their view rather than to inform the public. Data suggests that immigrants provide benefits to American society, but also create challenges and there are therefore cogent arguments that can be made for maintaining and restricting immigration in every generation. Immigration is not even remotely as dangerous or harmful as Donald Trump or the nation's most vehemently anti-immigrant advocates claim, but neither is immigration an entirely benign and beneficial system without complications, challenges, and dangers.

Ultimately, immigration policy is about what Americans want the nation to become and how Americans see fit to use the resources of US society with regard to the rest of the world. Immigration can be a tool to ease global suffering and to further human rights, or it can be a tool to recruit, from the multitudes around the world, only those individuals seen as having qualities that will provide more immediate benefits. Throughout American history, immigration policies have been used to preserve America's racial and ethnic identity and to build the nation's industry and defensive capabilities. There is no absolutely right or wrong way to handle immigration, but each strategy has different moral and ethical implications, not only for American culture, but for the increasingly connected global culture of the present and the future.

Works Used

Aguiar, Angel and Terrie Walmsley. "Economic Analysis of U.S. Immigration Reforms." 2009. *Center for Global Trade Analysis*. Purdue University. http://ageconsearch.umn.edu/bitstream/49302/2/Aguiar_AAEA.pdf.

Gonzalez-Barrera, Ana. "More Mexicans Leaving Than Coming to the U.S." *Pew Research*. Pew Research Center. Nov 19, 2015. Web. http://www.pewhispanic. org/2015/11/19/more-mexicans-leaving-than-coming-to-the-u-s/.

Light, Michael T., Miller, Ty, and Brian C. Kelly. "Undocumented Immigration, Drug Problems, and Driving Under the Influence in the United States, 1990-2014." *AJPH*. American Public Health Association. Apr 23, 2017. https://ajph. aphapublications.org/doi/abs/10.2105/AJPH.2017.303884.

Litke, E. "Yes, We Are Experiencing a Net Outflow of Illegal, Undocumented Workers from America Back to Mexico." *Politifact*. Politifact. Apr 26, 2017. Web. http://www.politifact.com/wisconsin/statements/2017/apr/26/ron-kind/yes-experiencing-net-outflow-illegal-undocumented-/.

López, Gustavo and Kristen Bialik. "Key findings about U.S. immigrants." *Factank*. Pew Research Center. May 3, 2017. Web. http://www.pewresearch.org/fact-tank/2017/05/03/key-findings-about-u-s-immigrants/.

Misra, Tanvi. "Immigrants Aren't Stealing American Jobs." *The Atlantic*. The Atlantic Monthly Group. https://www.theatlantic.com/politics/archive/2015/10/immigrants-arent-stealing-american-jobs/433158/.

O'Hanlon, Michael E. and Raymond Odierno. "Assimilation Is Counterterrorism." *Brookings Institution*. Apr 19, 2016. Web. https://www.brookings.edu/blog/order-from-chaos/2016/04/19/assimilation-is-counterterrorism/.

Ottaviano, Gianmarco I.P., Peri, Giovanni, and Greg C. Wright. "Immigration, Offshoring and American Jobs." *NBER*. The National Bureau of Economic Research. Working Paper No. 16439. Oct 2010. http://www.nber.org/papers/w16439#fromrss.

Peri, Giovanni. "The Impact of Immigrants in Recession and Economic Expansion." *MPI*. Migration Policy Institute. Jun 2010. https://www.migrationpolicy.org/research/impact-immigrants-recession-and-economic-expansion.

Preston, Julia. "Newest Immigrants Assimilating as Fast as Previous Ones, Report Says." *The New York Times*. The New York Times Co. https://www.nytimes. com/2015/09/22/us/newest-immigrants-assimilating-as-well-as-past-ones-report-says.html.

Pritchett, Lant. "The Cliff at the Border." In Ravi Kanbur and Michael Spence, *Equity and Growth in a Globalizing World*. Washington, DC: Commission on Growth and Development/World Bank, 2010, 263.

"U.S. Immigrant Population and Share over Time, 1850-Present." *MPI*. Migration Policy Institute. 2016. Web. https://www.migrationpolicy.org/programs/data-hub/charts/immigrant-population-over-time.

Valverde, Miriam. "Donald Trump's Team Misleads in Tying International Terrorism Report to Immigration." *Politifact*. Politifact. Jan 22, 2018. http://www.politifact. com/truth-o-meter/article/2018/jan/22/donald-trumps-team-misleads-tying-international-te/.

Waters, Mary C. and Marisa Gerstein Pineau. "The Integration of Immigrants into American Society." *National Academies of Sciences*. The National Academies Press. 2015. https://www.nap.edu/download/21746.

Wolf, Z. Byron. "Trump Basically Called Mexicans Rapists Again." *The Point*. CNN. Apr 6, 2018. Web. https://www.cnn.com/2018/04/06/politics/trump-mexico-rapists/index.html.

Notes

1. "U.S. Immigrant Population and Share over Time," *MPI*.
2. López and Bialik, "Key Findings about U.S. Immigrants."
3. Preston, "Newest Immigrants Assimilating as Fast as Previous Ones, Report Says."
4. Gonzalez-Barrera, "More Mexicans Leaving Than Coming to the U.S."
5. Litke, "Yes, We Are Experiencing a Net Outflow of Illegal, Indocumented Workers from America Back to Mexico."
6. Misra, "Immigrants Aren't Stealing American Jobs."
7. Ottaviano, Peri, and Wright, "Immigration, Offshoring and American Jobs."
8. Peri, "The Impact of Immigrants in Recession and Economic Expansion."
9. Aguiar and Walmsley, "Economic Analysis of U.S. Immigration Reforms."
10. Pritchett, "The Cliff at the Border."
11. Wolf, "Trump Basically Called Mexicans Rapists Again."
12. Light, Miller, and Kelly, "Undocumented Immigration, Drug Problems, and Driving Under the Influence in the United States, 1990-2014."
13. Waters and Pineau, "The Integration of Immigrants into American Society."
14. Valverde, "Donald Trump's Team Misleads in Tying International Terrorism Report to Immigration."
15. O'Hanlon and Odierno, "Assimilation Is Counterterrorism."

1
Immigration
Then and Now

Elisabeth Volmar, orginally from Haiti, becomes an American citizen during a U.S. Citizenship & Immigration Services naturalization ceremony at the Hialeah Field Office on January 12, 2018 in Hialeah, Florida. 150 people from different countries around the world took part in the Oath of Allegiance.

Letting Them In: America's Turbulent Immigration History

The nation's first immigration law, the Uniform Rule of Naturalization (signed into law in 1790), provided a comparatively easy road to immigration and naturalization than would be familiar to those attempting to navigate America's complex immigration terrain in the twenty-first century. As a small, fledgling nation, few saw the need for detailed immigration restrictions in 1790 and many politicians favored liberal immigration as a way to build the nation's workforce and to bolster the nation's defensive forces. The nation's first law was therefore rudimentary, requiring only that a person live in the nation for two years, be white and not a slave, and to declare an oath of allegiance in any official court. However, there were some who felt the new law would lead to a rapid influx of undesirables. Among these was James Madison, who said in a February 1790 debate on the topic:

> When we are considering the advantages that may result from an easy mode of naturalization, we ought also to consider the cautions necessary to guard against abuses; it is no doubt very desirable, that we should hold out as many inducements as possible, for the worthy part of mankind to come and settle amongst us and throw their fortunes into a common lot with ours. But, why is this desirable? Not merely to swell the catalogue of people. No, sir, 'tis to encrease the wealth and strength of the community, and those who acquire the rights of citizenship, without adding to the strength or wealth of the community, are not the people we are in want of...[1]

Conservative *National Review* columnist Michelle Malkin used Madison's speech over the 1790 Uniform Rule of Naturalization to argue that the perceptively liberal immigration attitudes of Barack Obama were contrary to what the oft-called "Founding Fathers" envisioned for the evolution of America. The goals of her essay are demonstrated by her final argument: "Put simply, unrestricted open borders are unwise, unsafe, and un-American. A country that doesn't value its own citizens and sovereignty first won't endure as a country for long."[2]

Malkin's essay provides a prime example of a flawed historical argument, not because her underlying opinions are necessarily incorrect, but because she suggests that the view of immigration held by Madison is more valuable than that held by former President Barack Obama, or that Madison's view of "American values" has more merit than the more progressive views favored by those with whom the author disagrees.

Consider that Madison was a dedicated slave owner who defended the institution and industry of slavery during his political career. It has been argued that the slave-owning politicians of the era, including the famed Founding Fathers, were products of their time and cannot be judged by the morality of the modern world, but this is not entirely correct. The idea that slavery was immoral and violated principles of human rights and welfare was well established in 1790. There were many prominent abolitionist activists across the nation, and in Europe, whose views on the institution were well known to the founding fathers and reflected what today would be considered a more modern view of slavery. Madison and the Founding Fathers also knew that slavery provided a massive economic benefit and they were also privy to the views and desires of those seeking to justify the institution of slavery so as to protect the economic benefits it provided. In short, the Founding Fathers participated in this institution despite knowing the moral issues at play. Few Americans outside the Alt-Right and America's white nationalists would promote Madison's view of slavery as an appropriate way to build the nation's wealth in the 2010s and so, is it appropriate to ask why Madison's ideas about immigration should be any more relevant to the modern debate than his ideas about slavery?

The Economics of Immigration Reform

Madison's thoughts on immigration also encapsulate the basic approach to immigration policy since; viewing residency in the United States as a privilege that should be offered primarily to those who have qualities seen as beneficial to the nation. While this approach may seem intuitively correct to many Americans, there is little agreement about which immigrants improve the nation. Madison imagined choosing from among the population of Europe only those with skills and beneficial qualities and yet Madison, like most of the Founding Fathers, wasn't an average person. He and most of the other founding fathers were wealthy elites whose social circles included the nation's wealthiest entrepreneurs. George Washington, for instance, was the richest person in the United States when he was elected president.[3] What this means is that the priorities of the Founding Fathers might have been quite different from those of a local tinsmith living in the era. Throughout the history of immigration reform, the policies that have been put in place, in many cases, are driven by the perspectives of this elite class.

Until 1921, there were few restrictions placed on immigration from Europe and this led to what is called the "golden age of immigration," from around 1880 to the 1930s. It is a commonly accepted myth that immigrants came to the nation because of the allure of US society and the freedom of US culture, but this has rarely been the case. The United States, at its inception, was a country with vast, largely unexploited and unclaimed material wealth and it is precisely this wealth that drew immigrants to the country in the 1700s and continued to draw them in the 2010s. The goal for immigration activists, from the very beginning, was to restrict immigration in such a way as to maintain their own power and position in society.

In the early 1800s, American politics was dominated by white, Protestant men from western and northern Europe. These men led an anti-immigration movement that targeted Catholics and especially Irish Catholics, reflecting ancient European prejudices and the fear that the influx of persons of the Catholic faith would erode the power of the nation's Protestant elite. To popularize the idea that Catholics and the Irish were a threat, powerful politicians and pundits spread fantastic stories about Catholic blood cults, child sex-rings, and other immoral atrocities. Many in the public embraced this view to the point that there were violent riots in America's cities, with mobs of Protestants attacking Irish or Catholic immigrants or churches. The famous 1844 anti-Catholic riots provide one example, fueled largely by un-substantiated claims about Catholic immorality spread through the then Protestant mayor who feared the loss of his support base with waves of Catholic immigrants arriving in the city.[4]

The upper class also, at times, has determined immigration policy; the nation's second major anti-immigration movement, which targeted Chinese laborers, grew out of the tensions created when America's wealthy industrialists began bringing in Chinese laborers to fuel the construction of the railroad and westward expansion. White laborers, who saw themselves as "real" Americans, because they were white and born in the United States, were exploited by the elite class and many were an-gry about the state of the nation's economy and their inability to climb the economic ladder. Because of racial and ethnic prejudice, white laborers turned their anger on the Chinese and Irish laborers who they saw as competing with them for the same jobs. From the 1840s to the 1880s, the anti-Chinese movement became the nation's leading immigration issue, ultimately resulting in Congress deciding to prohibit all Chinese (and later all Asian) immigration to the country.

The Chinese Exclusion Act did not improve the plight of American workers, however, and in each generation new groups of immigrants were targeted for expul-sion or as scapegoats for the economic ills of the time. In the 1930s, for instance, as the Great Depression led to vast unemployment and poverty, a lobby of white labor-ers and western politicians turned against Mexican migrants, immigrants, and their children. Over a million persons of Mexican descent were rounded up and expelled from the United States in the 1930s, about 60 percent of whom were born in the United States and so were American citizens. This "repatriation movement," as it was called, was illegal and unconstitutional and occurred only because the nation's economic elite used Mexican-Americans and immigrants as a scapegoat for the un-derlying economic tensions of the time.[5]

America's immigration history is and has always been a contest between eco-nomic interest groups. At times, anti-immigrant movements are fueled by laborers fearing that immigrants will take their jobs or reduce wages and, at other times, anti-immigrant movements are fueled by elite social leaders who fear that the influx of immigrants will weaken their position in society. Frequently, claims about the negative economic impact of immigration are overstated and based more on fear than fact, but these claims remain a cornerstone of anti-immigration movements into the modern age.

Immigration and Identity Preservation

The history of immigration to the United States is also about the preservation of American identity. Most of the nation's anti-immigration movements have come about because of racial, ethnic, or religious prejudice and the fear that an influx of non-white, non-Christian, or non-western/northern European persons would change the nature of American society. Over the years, there have been anti-Catholic, anti-Asian, anti-Jewish, anti-Mexican, anti-Russian, anti-Socialist, anti-Communist, anti-disabled people, and even anti-poor immigration movements. In each case the core issue is identity, with those actively working to restrict immigration fearing that an influx of immigrants will change American society in unwanted ways.

From 1921 to 1965, US immigration policy was based on a quota system that provided a certain number of visas to people from each country. The number of visas allotted to each country was based on the proportion of people from that country living in the nation. The purpose of these laws was to preserve the nation's ethnic and religious composition. This system remained in place until a wave of liberal policies swept across the United States, fueled by the youth and student activists' movements, and the Civil Rights Debate. In 1965, the nation adopted a new policy that abandoned national quotas, opening up immigration, for the first time, to people of all races, religions, and ethnicities. When this occurred, opponents argued that the change was unfair, because it didn't prioritize the immigration of persons from countries that had "contributed" to the founding of the United States. Senator Sam Ervin of North Carolina thus argued,

> The people of Ethiopia have the same right to come to the United States under this bill as the people from England, the people of France, the people of Germany, and the people of Holland. With all due respect to Ethiopia, I don't know of any contributions that Ethiopia has made to the making of America.[6]

While Ervin might have been correct in claiming that few Ethiopian immigrants had then participated in the foundation of America, his views are clearly based, primarily, on racial prejudice. Consider that, even as Ervin spoke before Congress, there were more than 11 million descendants of African slaves living in the United States whose ancestors had also contributed to the foundation of America that Ervin attributed primarily to white, western and northern Europeans. What Ervin actually wanted was to preserve his own view of American culture, a society dominated by the culture he associated with white Europeans and their descendants. For an African American living in 1965, the arrival of Ethiopian immigrants would likely have appeared far less of a threat.

The end of the quota system did bring Ethiopians to the United States and, in fact, vastly increased the overall diversity of America. Waves of Asian, Arab, Polynesian, Latino, and African immigrants came from around the world, most settling in America's cities. To some, this increasing diversity was a good thing, enriching America's environment by providing new experiences and perspectives and adding to the unique cultural wealth of the nation. Others do not believe that diversity has made America a better place to live and there are some who are still fighting to maintain the dominance of America's white majority against what they see as the increasingly un-American influence of foreign arrivals. For every American like Sam Ervin who feared that Ethiopian immigrants would change the nation he had come to see as his, there is an American eating a meal in one of the nation's Ethiopian restaurants who, at least in the most basic sense, is enjoying the fruits of the nation's 1960s liberalization.

When it comes to immigration and identity, there are no right and wrong answers, only perspectives. Barack Obama's position, that immigration and diversity strengthen American society, can be bolstered by data on the impact of various immigrant groups or through evidence of the many cultural innovations that have come about because of America's unique mix of races and cultural elements, but it is still a matter of perspective. Similarly, President Donald Trump and many other politicians in the same ilk throughout history, have proposed that immigration is a danger to American society and have downplayed or even rejected the idea that diversity and cultural blending is a positive force in American culture. This too is a matter of belief and perspective and not something that can be justified with data or evidence. The United States is a nation of immigrants and, though Americans have resisted immigration at every stage and in every era, American society as it exists is a product of this tense, turbulent blending of cultures, ideas, and perspectives. Whether America has become stronger and better over time, or has been degraded by this process, is something that each American decides for him or herself and that decision is fueled by each person's unique identity and imagined view of what their country is and should be.

Works Used

"2016 Campaign: Strong Interest, Widespread Dissatisfaction." *Pew Research*. Pew Research Center. Jul 7, 2016. Web. http://www.people-press.org/2016/07/07/2016-campaign-strong-interest-widespread-dissatisfaction/.

Gjelten, Tom. "The Immigration Act That Inadvertently Changed America." *The Atlantic*. The Atlantic Monthly Group. Oct 2, 2015. Web. https://www.theatlantic.com/politics/archive/2015/10/immigration-act-1965/408409/.

Hingston, Sandy. "Bullets and Bigots: Remembering Philadelphia's 1844 Anti-Catholic Riots." *Philly Mag*. Philadelphia Magazine. Dec 17, 2015. Web. https://www.phillymag.com/news/2015/12/17/philadelphia-anti-catholic-riots-1844/.

Kertscher, Tom. "Were the Founding Fathers 'Ordinary People'?" *Politifact Wisconsin*. Politifact. Jul 2, 2015. Web. http://www.politifact.com/wisconsin/article/2015/jul/02/founding-fathers-ordinary-folk/.

Malkin, Michelle. "Immigration and the Values of Our Founding Fathers." *National Review*. Dec 11, 2015. Web. https://www.nationalreview.com/2015/12/immigration-founding-fathers-view-michelle-malkin/.

Matthews, Dylan. "The Republican Tax Bill Got Worse: Now the Top 1% Gets 83% of the Gains." *Vox*. Vox Media. Dec 18, 2017. Web. https://www.vox.com/policy-and-politics/2017/12/18/16791174/republican-tax-bill-congress-conference-tax-policy-center.

"Naturalization, [3 February] 1790," *Founders Online*. National Historical Publications & Records Commission." 2002. Web. https://founders.archives.gov/documents/Madison/01-13-02-0018.

Nichols, Alex. "You Should Be Terrified That People Who Like 'Hamilton' Run Our Country." *Current Affairs*. Current Affairs. Jul 29, 2016. Web. https://www.currentaffairs.org/2016/07/you-should-be-terrified-that-people-who-like-hamilton-run-our-country.

Stagg, J.C.A. "James Madison: Life Before the Presidency." *Miller Center*. UVA. Miller Center. 2017. Web. https://millercenter.org/president/madison/life-before-the-presidency.

Wagner, Alex. "America's Forgotten History of Illegal Deportations." *The Atlantic*. The Atlantic Monthly Group. Mar 6, 2017. Web. https://www.theatlantic.com/politics/archive/2017/03/americas-brutal-forgotten-history-of-illegal-deportations/517971/.

Notes

1. "Naturalization, [3 February] 1790," *Founders Online*.
2. Malkin, "Immigration and the Values of Our Founding Fathers."
3. Kertscher, "Were the Founding Fathers 'Ordinary People'?
4. Hingston, "Bullets and Bigots: Remembering Philadelphia's 1844 Anti-Catholic Riots."
5. Wagner, "America's Forgotten History of Illegal Deportations."
6. Gjelten, "The Immigration Act That Inadvertently Changed America."

US Has Long History of Restricting Immigrants

By Kelly Jean Kelly
VOA, January 30, 2017

WASHINGTON—President Donald Trump's executive orders last week limiting immigration to the U.S. may be the first such directives in recent years, but they are hardly the first time the U.S. government has sought to restrict immigration.

The U.S. Constitution, which went into effect in 1789, gave Congress "absolute authority" over immigration law, says Linda Monk, who wrote a book about the Constitution called *The Words We Live By*. The president executes those laws through regulations.

For about the first 100 years of American history, Congress did not place any federal limits on immigration.

During those years, Irish and German immigrants came to the U.S. in large numbers. Many Chinese immigrants did, too. In the 1860s, they came to work as laborers on the continental railroad and stayed.

Members of the American public disapproved of these groups. They did not like the Catholic religion that many Irish and German immigrants practiced. And they did not like Asian immigrants, whom they viewed as convicts, prostitutes, or competition for jobs.

So, in the late 1800s, Congress moved for the first time to limit the number of immigrants. Lawmakers targeted Asians, especially Chinese. The Page Act and the Chinese Exclusion Act banned most Chinese women and workers.

Restrictions on Other Nationalities

By the turn of the 20th century, the U.S. federal government had increased its role in immigration. It established Ellis Island in New York as the entry point for immigrants. And it oversaw a dramatic increase in the number of immigrants, especially from Italy and Eastern Europe. Many of the new arrivals were uneducated and had little money.

Once again, some people opposed the number and kind of immigrants entering the country. A group called the Immigration Restriction League was formed. They petitioned Congress to require immigrants to show that they could at least read.

The Supreme Court has historically permitted the president and Congress a good deal of authority to regulate immigration.

Both Presidents Grover Cleveland and President Woodrow Wilson opposed the requirement. But in 1917, Congress approved the measure over Wilson's objections. People who wished to settle in the U.S. now had to pass a literacy test.

In the 1920s, restrictions on immigration increased. The Immigration Act of 1924 was the most severe: it limited the overall number of immigrants and established quotas based on nationality. Among other things, the act sharply reduced immigrants from Eastern Europe and Africa. And it completely restricted immigrants from Asia, except for Japan and the Philippines.

At the same time, the historian's page at the State Department notes that the act made more visas available to people from Britain and Western Europe.

"In all of its parts, the most basic purpose of the 1924 Immigration Act was to preserve the ideal of U.S. homogeneity," the State Department history page concludes.

Major Change

During the 1940s and 50s, the U.S. made some policy changes that increased—however slightly—the number and nationalities of immigrants.

Then, in 1965, a major change happened. Under pressure in part from the civil rights movement, Congress passed the Immigration and Nationality Act. President Lyndon Johnson signed it.

The act eliminated the quota system based on nationality. Instead, it prioritized immigrants who already had family members in the U.S. It also sought to offer protection to refugees from areas with violence and conflict.

Even though the act kept some limits in place, the origins of immigrants changed dramatically. Instead of being from Western Europe, most immigrants to the U.S. by the end of the 20th century were originally from Mexico, the Philippines, Korea, the Dominican Republic, India, Cuba and Vietnam.

So, What about Trump's Order?

Kunal Parker, a professor at the University of Miami School of Law, says the 1965 law ended "overt discrimination" in U.S. immigration policy. Parker is also the author of a book called *Making Foreigners: Immigration and Citizenship Law in America.."*

Parker says that people who are protesting Trump's executive order probably "perceive what is happening as contrary to U.S. tradition since 1965."

The order bans refugees and people from seven Muslim-majority countries from entering the United States. The countries are Iran, Iraq, Libya, Somalia, Sudan, Syria and Yemen.

Protesters argue that Trump's order discriminates against Muslims and defies the American tradition of welcoming immigrants.

But Parker cautions against seeing Trump's action as illegal. He points out that the Supreme Court has historically permitted the president and Congress a good deal of authority to regulate immigration.

And, he notes, President Obama also signed an executive order related to immigration. That order aimed to protect the families of undocumented immigrants with U.S.-born children.

However, Parker says, "Something that is legal might be very problematic."

Both Parker and legal scholar Linda Monk also note the Constitution requires both Congress and the president follow certain procedures when regulating immigration. Those procedures protect against discrimination.

"The highest law says that these actions have to be carried out fairly," says Monk.

Print Citations

CMS: Kelly, Jean Kelly. "US Has Long History of Restricting Immigrants." In *The Reference Shelf: The National Debate Topic 2018–2019 Immigration*, edited by Betsy Maury, 9-11. Ipswich, MA: H.W. Wilson, 2018.

MLA: Kelly, Jean Kelly. "US Has Long History of Restricting Immigrants." In *The Reference Shelf: The National Debate Topic 2018–2019 Immigration*. Ed. Betsy Maury. Ipswich: H.W. Wilson, 2018. 9-11. Print.

APA: Kelly, J.K. (2018). US has long history of restricting immigrants. In Betsy Maury (Ed.), *The reference shelf: The national debate topic 2018–2019 immigration* (pp. 9-11). Ipswich, MA: H.W. Wilson. (Original work published 2017)

The U.S. Immigration Debate

By Claire Felter and Danielle Renwick
Council on Foreign Relation, March 13, 2018

Introduction

Immigration has been a touchstone of the U.S. political debate for decades, as policymakers must weigh competing economic, security, and humanitarian concerns. Congress has been unable to reach an agreement on comprehensive immigration reform for years, effectively moving some major policy decisions into the executive and judicial branches of government, and fueling debate in the halls of state and municipal governments.

Shortly after taking office, President Donald J. Trump signed executive orders on border security, interior enforcement, and refugees. In mid-2017, Trump rescinded two programs created by President Obama to shield undocumented children and their parents from deportation. Some American cities, states, and individuals have challenged the president's actions in court.

What Is the Immigrant Population in the United States?

Immigrants comprise about 14 percent of the U.S. population: more than forty-three million out of a total of about 323 million people, according to Census Bureau data. Together, immigrants and their U.S.-born children make up about 27 percent of U.S. inhabitants. The figure represents a steady rise from 1970, when there were fewer than ten million immigrants in the United States.

But there are proportionally fewer immigrants today than in 1890, when foreign-born residents comprised 15 percent of the population.

Illegal immigration. The undocumented population is about eleven million and has leveled off since the 2008 economic crisis, which led some to return to their home countries and discouraged others from coming to the United States. In 2017, Customs and Border Protection reported a 26 percent drop in the number of people apprehended or stopped at the southern border from the year before, which some attribute to the Trump administration's policies. At the same time, arrests of suspected undocumented immigrants jumped by 40 percent.

More than half of the undocumented have lived in the country for more than a decade; nearly one third are the parents of U.S.-born children, according to the *Pew Research Center*. Central American asylum seekers, many of whom are minors who have fled violence in their home countries, make up a growing share of those who cross the U.S.-Mexico border. These immigrants have different legal rights from Mexican nationals in the United States: under a 2008 anti–human trafficking law, minors from noncontiguous countries have a right to a deportation hearing before being returned to their home countries.

Though many of the policies that aim to reduce unlawful immigration focus on enforced border security, individuals who arrive to the United States legally and overstay their visas comprise a significant portion of the undocumented population. According to the Center for Migration Studies, individuals who overstayed their visas have outnumbered those who arrived by crossing the border illegally by six hundred thousand since 2007.

Legal immigration. The United States granted nearly 1.2 million individuals legal permanent residency in 2016, more than two-thirds of whom were admitted based on family reunification. Other categories included: employment-based preferences (12 percent), refugees (10 percent), diversity (4 percent), and asylees (3 percent). In late 2017 there were more than four million applicants on the State Department's waiting list for immigrant visas.

> **Comprehensive immigration reform has eluded Congress for years, moving controversial policy decisions into the executive and judicial branches of government.**

Hundreds of thousands of individuals work legally in the United States under various types of nonimmigrant visas. In 2017, the United States granted close to 180,000 visas for high-skilled workers, known as H1B visas, and nearly 250,000 visas for temporary workers in agriculture and other industries. H1B visas are capped at 85,000 per year, with exceptions for certain fields.

Immigrants made up roughly 17 percent of the U.S. workforce in 2014, according to *Pew Research Center*; of those, around two-thirds were in the country legally. Collectively, immigrants made up 45 percent of domestic employees; they also comprised large portions of the workforce in U.S. manufacturing (36 percent), agriculture (33), and accommodation (32). Another *Pew* study found that without immigrants, the U.S. workforce is expected to decline from 173.2 million in 2015 to 165.6 million in 2035; the workforce is expected to grow to 183.2 million if immigration levels remain steady, according to the report.

How Do Americans Feel about Immigration?

A 2017 *Gallup* poll found that 71 percent of Americans considered immigration a "good thing" for the United States. A year earlier, as many as 84 percent supported a path to citizenship for undocumented immigrants if they meet certain requirements. A separate *Gallup* poll found that among Republicans, support for a path to citizenship (76 percent) was higher than support for a proposed border wall (62 percent).

What Legislation Has Congress Considered in Recent Years?

Congress has debated numerous pieces of immigration reform over the last two decades, some considered "comprehensive," others piecemeal. Comprehensive immigration reform refers to omnibus legislation that attempts to address the following issues: demand for high-skilled and low-skilled labor, the legal status of the millions of undocumented immigrants living in the country, border security, and interior enforcement.

The last time legislators came close to significant immigration reform was in 2013, when the Democrat-led Senate passed a comprehensive reform bill that would have provided a path to citizenship for undocumented immigrants and tough border security provisions. The bill did not receive a vote in the Republican-controlled House of Representatives.

What Actions Have Presidents Taken in Recent Years?

Barack Obama. President Obama took several actions to provide temporary legal relief to many undocumented immigrants. In 2012, his administration began a program, known as Deferred Action for Childhood Arrivals (DACA), that offers renewable, two-year deportation deferrals and work permits to undocumented immigrants who had arrived to the United States as children and had no criminal records. Obama characterized the move as a "stopgap measure" and urged Congress to pass the Dream Act, legislation first introduced in 2001 that would have benefited many of the same people. As of March 2017, nearly eight hundred thousand people had taken advantage of DACA.

In 2014, Obama attempted to extend similar benefits to as many as five million undocumented parents of U.S. citizens and permanent residents. However, more than two dozen U.S. states sued the administration, alleging that the program, known as Deferred Action for Parents of Americans (DAPA), violated federal immigration law and the U.S. Constitution. A Texas federal judge blocked the program in 2015, and the Supreme Court effectively killed it in 2016.

Donald J. Trump. Trump has signed several executive orders affecting immigration policy. The first, which focused on border security, instructed federal agencies to construct a physical wall "to obtain complete operational control" of the U.S. border with Mexico. Additionally, it expanded the application of "expedited removal" to anyone who cannot prove they have been in the United States for two years, allowing them to be removed without a court hearing. The second, which focused on interior enforcement, broadened definitions of those unauthorized immigrants prioritized for removal and ordered increases in enforcement personnel and removal facilities. It also moved to restrict federal funds from so-called sanctuary jurisdictions, which in some cases limit their cooperation with federal immigration officials. The third, which focused on terrorism prevention, banned nationals from Iran, Iraq, Libya, Somalia, Sudan, and Yemen from entering the United States for at least ninety days; blocked nationals from Syria indefinitely; and suspended the U.S. refugee program for 120 days.

The actions, particularly the ban on travelers from seven Muslim-majority countries, drew widespread protests and legal challenges from individuals, cities, and states.

> **Together, immigrants and their U.S.-born children make up about 27 percent of U.S. inhabitants.**

In February 2017, a federal judge in Washington State imposed a nationwide restraining order on the so-called travel ban. The Trump administration revised the order to remove some of its most criticized provisions, but a federal judge in Hawaii subsequently imposed a temporary restraining order on it. In December, the U.S. Supreme Court allowed a third iteration of the travel ban to go into effect.

Trump more than halved the annual cap of refugees admitted to the United States to fifty thousand, and his orders could make it more difficult for individuals to seek asylum; more than 180,000 applied for asylum in 2016. In 2017, the administration ended temporary protected status (TPS) for thousands of Nicaraguans and Haitians who were allowed into the United States after environmental disasters in their home countries in 1999 and 2010, respectively. Beneficiaries of TPS are permitted to live and work in the United States for up to eighteen months, a period that can be extended at the president's discretion. In 2018, Trump ended the same relief program for nearly two hundred thousand Salvadorans who came after a 2001 earthquake.

Trump promised during his campaign to revoke both the DAPA and DACA programs, calling them "illegal executive amnesties." In June 2017, he rescinded President Obama's memo creating DAPA, which had never been implemented due to sustained legal challenges. In September, Trump announced his plans to phase out DACA, but said current beneficiaries would be allowed to renew their status up to March 2018. In January 2018, as lawmakers negotiated a potential deal with Trump to extend legal protections for those covered by DACA, a federal judge in San Francisco ruled that the program must remain open as long as legal challenges to its termination continue.

How Are State and Local Authorities Handling These Issues?

States vary widely in how they treat unauthorized immigrants (or anyone suspected of being unauthorized). Some states, such as California, allow undocumented immigrants to apply for drivers' licenses, receive in-state tuition at universities, and obtain other benefits. At the other end of the spectrum, states such as Arizona have passed laws permitting police to question people about their immigration status.

The federal government is generally responsible for enforcing immigration laws, but it may delegate some immigration-control duties to state and local law enforcement. However, the degree to which local officials are obliged to cooperate with federal authorities is a subject of intense debate. Proponents of tougher immigration enforcement have labeled state and local jurisdictions that limit their cooperation with federal authorities as "sanctuary cities." There is no official definition or count of sanctuary cities, but the Immigrant Legal Resource Center identifies more than six hundred counties with such policies.

The Obama administration's enforcement practices drew criticism from the left and the right. Some immigrant advocacy groups criticized his administration for overseeing the removal of more than three million people during his eight-year tenure, a figure that outpaced the administrations of former Presidents Bill Clinton and George W. Bush. Many Republicans said the administration was soft on enforcement in narrowing its removal efforts to undocumented immigrants who have committed serious crimes.

President Trump decried sanctuary cities throughout his campaign and issued an executive order to block federal funding to such municipalities and to reinstate a controversial program, known as Secure Communities, in which state and local police provide fingerprints of suspects to federal immigration authorities, and hand over individuals presumed to be in the country illegally. He also ordered the expansion of enforcement partnerships among federal, state, and local agencies. Several cities are challenging Trump's order in court.

In March 2018, the Justice Department filed a lawsuit against California alleging that several of the state's laws obstruct federal immigration enforcement.

What Are the Prospects for Immigration Reform?

Experts say the prospect for comprehensive immigration reform is dim given President Trump's positions and general political divisions in Washington. "There is no appetite in the Republican party to try to go down the comprehensive [immigration policy reform] road again," says CFR's Edward Alden. Some lawmakers may attempt to take a piecemeal approach, starting with enforcement measures, but bipartisan support for "cherry picking" policies is unlikely, he says.

However, one area of immigration policy that could see congressional action is the H1B program. Democratic and Republican lawmakers have expressed interest in reforming the program, which critics say has been abused by companies to outsource skilled labor and cut costs. The Trump administration issued an executive order in April 2017 directing federal agencies to suggest changes to the H1B program to ensure that visas are awarded to the most-skilled or highest-paid applicants.

Print Citations

CMS: Felter, Claire, and Danielle Renwick. "The U.S. Immigration Debate." In *The Reference Shelf: The National Debate Topic 2018–2019 Immigration*, edited by Betsy Maury, 12-17. Ipswich, MA: H.W. Wilson, 2018.

MLA: Felter, Claire, and Danielle Renwick. "The U.S. Immigration Debate." *The Reference Shelf: The National Debate Topic 2018–2019 Immigration*. Ed. Betsy Maury. Ipswich: H.W. Wilson, 2018. 12-17. Print.

APA: Felter C., & D. Renwick. (2018). The U.S. immigration debate. In Betsy Maury (Ed.), *The reference shelf: The national debate topic 2018–2019 immigration* (pp. 12-17). Ipswich, MA: H.W. Wilson. (Original work published 2018)

The Facts about Immigration

By John Cassidy
The New Yorker, **March 31, 2017**

During a conference at the Brookings Institution last week, the Princeton economists Anne Case and Angus Deaton presented their latest paper on the rising mortality rates of white working-class Americans, which received, and is still receiving, a huge amount of attention. That's understandable. Even taking account of the critiques of the paper that have been presented, some of which the economics blogger Noah Smith counter-critiqued on Wednesday, the issues raised by Case and Deaton's work are profound.

The subject here, though, is another article that was presented at the Brookings conference, which got nowhere near as much media attention. Co-authored by Gordon Hanson, Chen Liu, and Craig McIntosh—three economists at the University of California, San Diego—it addressed immigration, particularly immigration by low-skilled workers from Mexico and other countries in Latin America.

The basic message of the paper was that the political discussion about building a wall across the U.S.-Mexico border is at least a decade out of date. In the past ten years, the flow of undocumented immigrants entering the U.S. has slowed dramatically. And because many undocumented immigrants are either deported or move home every year, the total number living in the United States is currently falling at rate of about a hundred and sixty thousand a year. Consequently, the competitive pressure being placed on the wages of low-skilled American workers, who do similar jobs to low-skilled immigrant workers, is declining, the paper says. Indeed, many industries that employ a lot of low-skilled immigrant workers—such as agriculture, construction, and food services—are facing a potential shortage of labor.

"The current debate about U.S. immigration policy—with its discussion of walls at the border and mass deportations of undocumented residents—thus has something of an anachronistic feel to it," Hanson, Liu, and McIntosh write. "The dilemma facing the United States is not so much how to arrest massive increases in the supply of foreign labor, but rather how to prepare for a lower-immigration future."

To people who've kept up with the latest immigration trends documented by organizations like the Census Bureau and the Pew Research Center, it's not news that the undocumented population is falling, or that more people from Mexico—the largest source of low-skilled immigrant workers—are now leaving the United States *than are coming in*. Indeed, as far back as the summer of 2015, when Donald

Trump launched his Presidential campaign by accusing Mexico of sending America its criminals and rapists, Bill Clinton pointed out, "Basically between 2010 and 2014, there was no net in-migration from Mexico."

One reason these facts haven't had much impact on the political debate is a widespread presumption that the decline in low-skilled immigrant workers could easily be reversed, especially if the U.S. economy picks up. After 2007, the U.S. construction industry, which had been a major employer of undocumented workers, went into a prolonged slump. If construction picks up—which is already happening in some parts of the country—won't many more undocumented immigrants cross the border in search of work?

One of the most important findings in Hanson, Liu, and McIntosh's new paper is that this is unlikely to happen. The authors explain that demand for unskilled workers is only one of the factors that drive undocumented immigration. Others factors include both the potential supply of immigrants and immigration policy, such as border-security measures. In these last areas, Hanson, Liu, and McIntosh point out, the past decade or so has seen changes that suggest the recent fall in low-skilled immigration will be permanent.

On the supply side, a drop in fertility rates in Latin American countries and an improvement in employment prospects have made young people there less eager to leave their home countries. Since Mexico accounts for more than half the low-skilled foreign-born workers in the United States, developments there are particularly important.

In the nineteen-sixties, Mexican women had almost seven children each, on average. Today, the figure is just over two, not much different than the U.S. fertility rate. Fewer Mexican children being born in 1995 translates to fewer twenty-two-year-olds looking for work today. And with the Mexican economy having expanded over the past couple of decades, the number of jobs available there has risen, too.

To determine the relative importance of labor supply versus labor demand, the authors estimated a statistical model of Mexican emigration, and they found that changes in labor supply could explain up to four-fifths of the recent fall. Since Latin American fertility rates are unlikely to rebound, these results suggest a good part of the decline in undocumented immigration is permanent. "Because U.S. neighbors to the south are today experiencing much slower labor-supply growth, the future immigration of young low-skilled labor looks set to decline rapidly, whether or not more draconian policies to control U.S. immigration are implemented," the paper says.

> It's not news that the undocumented population is falling, or that more people from Mexico—the largest source of low-skilled immigrant workers—are now leaving the United States than are coming in.

It also reminds us that, despite Trump's rhetoric about lax immigration policy, the Bush and Obama Administrations devoted an enormous amount of resources and manpower to beefing up border security, and they also deported large numbers of people. Between 2000 and 2010, the number of federal agents policing the U.S.-Mexico border rose from eight thousand six hundred to more than seventeen thousand. Hundreds of miles of fencing have been erected, and border agents have also been equipped with high-tech equipment, such as surveillance drones and movement sensors.

"In effect," the paper says, "the United States already has a wall in place, with hundreds of miles of new fencing, the rollout of technologically sophisticated border surveillance, a near quintupling of Border Patrol agents since the early 1990s, and the criminalization of illegal border crossings since the late 2000s."

Meanwhile, immigration enforcement inside the United States has become a lot more draconian. In 2001, the U.S. government deported a hundred and sixteen thousand non-criminal aliens, many of whom had been picked up in routine traffic stops or for other minor offenses. Between 2007 and 2015, the government deported almost twice as many non-criminal aliens each year: two hundred and twenty six thousand. Deportation of criminal aliens has also risen sharply: from seventy three thousand in 2001 to an average of a hundred and fifty six thousand a year between 2007 and 2015.

Given all these developments, the makeup of the undocumented population in the U.S. has changed a lot. It is no longer young and itinerant. "By 2015, three quarters (75.1 per cent) of low-skilled immigrant workers had resided in the United States for 11 or more years," the paper says. It also notes that in 1980, the modal Mexican-born resident of the United States was twenty years old. ("Modal" refers to the age that is most common.) Today, the modal age of Mexican-born U.S. residents is about forty years old, and in 2040 it will be almost seventy.

At the end of their analysis, Hanson, Liu, and McIntosh pose an interesting question: "Why build a wall to stop an immigration surge that has largely already occurred?" One possibility they mention is that "voters may be upset by the laxity of past enforcement and willing to reward politicians who are seen as atoning for these transgressions." A second possibility: voters want to "forestall future claims on public resources . . . by increasing deportations today—when many low-skilled immigrant workers are approaching middle age—the United States may avoid demands on social spending in the future."

I suspect that may be apportioning too much foresight to the supporters of the wall. When I e-mailed George Borjas, a Harvard economist who studies immigration, to ask what he thought of the new paper, he suggested that there could also be a precautionary motive for building the wall. "We know that illegal immigration from Mexico responds dramatically to changes in economic conditions," Borjas wrote. "Does anybody know what will happen to the economies of Central America and Mexico in the next 5-10 years? What if there were another economic crisis? Wouldn't there be a valid argument that building a wall today as insurance against future illegal immigration? None of this should be interpreted in terms of whether I support or do not support the wall. But these are questions that somebody who wanted to think through the various possibilities would need to ask and answer."

I put what Borjas had said to Hanson, and he replied: "George is making a perfectly valid point. The question is whether the wall passes the cost-benefit test. With close to 20k border patrol officers already on the ground and 650 miles of border barriers already in place, it seems that the extra deterrence effect of the wall would be low while its cost would be enormous."

Print Citations

CMS: Cassidy, John. "The Facts about Immigration." In *The Reference Shelf: The National Debate Topic 2018–2019 Immigration*, edited by Betsy Maury, 13-21. Ipswich, MA: H.W. Wilson, 2018.

MLA: Cassidy, John. "The Facts about Immigration." *The Reference Shelf: The National Debate Topic 2018–2019 Immigration*. Ed. Betsy Maury. Ipswich: H.W. Wilson, 2018. 13-21. Print.

APA: Cassidy, J. (2018). The facts about immigration. In Betsy Maury (Ed.), *The reference shelf: The national debate topic 2018–2019 immigration* (pp. 13-21). Ipswich, MA: H.W. Wilson. (Original work published 2017)

Bring on the Conservative Debate for Immigration

By Bradley J. Birzer
The American Conservative, **January 12, 2018**

In recent years, probably no matter has split nationalist and populist conservatives from libertarian and anti-statist conservatives more than that of immigration. Yet, very few conservatives are actually taking the time to debate or discuss this issue, so fundamental to understanding the very essence of who we are as an American people. Too many suppositions and assumptions have taken on the air of truth, and, as such, and, if for no other reason, the topic itself demands good discussion and vigorous debate. In particular, the modern American conservative should praise Gerald Russello and *The University Bookman* for its on-going symposium dealing the whole swirling mess. We need much more of this. It's too important to leave to emotion or passion alone.

As Christians around the world celebrated the arrival of the Three Kings—the Magi of the Orient—on Epiphany, the president of the United States called for $33 billion to shore up America's borders with $18 billion for the wall.

Would the Magi have been admitted in 2018? "Excuse me, Balthasar, but I need to see that your papers are in order. Oh, I'm sorry, but your gift of myrrh exceeds our 3.2 ounces of liquid allowed."

Perhaps, President Trump simply chose his timing poorly, but it would be impossible for the Christian to miss the irony.

As a professor of the western canon, the Great Ideas of the West, and the western tradition, I find it nearly impossible to claim that there is a long tradition of excluding those who "aren't us." Even the most cursory examination of the issue reveals that the best of western thinkers have considered political borders a form of selfish insanity and a violation of the dignity of the human person. The free movement of peoples has not only been seen as a natural right throughout much of the western tradition, but it has also been seen as a sacred one.

In the gloriously pagan *Odyssey*, Odysseus survives, again and again, because the highest commandment of Zeus is to welcome the stranger and protect him with all that one has. To this day, one finds remnants of this tradition throughout the Mediterranean as the stranger is greeted with olive oil, bread, and, depending on the predominant religion of the region, wine. As staple crops of the ancient world, these signified not just acceptance but actual joy at the arrival of the stranger. The god of the hearth stood as patron of the sojourner.

The Athenians, during the tumultuous fifth century before Christ, prided themselves on allowing not just the stranger into their communities, but also their very enemies in. After all, what did the Athenians have to hide? Why not expose the ignorant to truth? Let the oppressed see how a free people live.

During the vast, long expanse of the Middle Ages, the Germanic peoples not only thought of themselves as residents of their own little piece of Middle-earth (Midgard), but they also thought of themselves as citizens of what King Alfred the Great labeled Christendom, the *Christiana res publica*, as well as believing themselves sojourners en route to the City of God. What Christian could allow—in good conscience—the accidents of birth such as gender or skin tone in this Veil of Tears to trump the possibilities of eternal salvation in the next? Neither Greek nor Jew, neither male nor female. . . .

Nothing in Christendom better represented the ideals of the free movement of peoples than did the Great Charter of 1215, forced upon King John at Runnymede. Though points 1 and 63 of the Magna Carta demanded freedom of the Church from political interference, points 41 and 42 reveal how fundamental the movement of peoples is to the sanctity of the common law.

> 41. All merchants shall have safe and secure exit from England, and entry to England, with the right to tarry there and to move about as well by land as by water, for buying and selling by the ancient and right customs, quit from all evil tolls, except (in time of war) such merchants as are of the land at war with us. And if such are found in our land at the beginning of the war, they shall be detained, without injury to their bodies or goods, until information be received by us, or by our chief justiciar, how the merchants of our land found in the land at war with us are treated; and if our men are safe there, the others shall be safe in our land.

> 42. It shall be lawful in future for anyone (excepting always those imprisoned or outlawed in accordance with the law of the kingdom, and natives of any country at war with us, and merchants, who shall be treated as if above provided) to leave our kingdom and to return, safe and secure by land and water, except for a short period in time of war, on grounds of public policy-reserving always the allegiance due to us.

If we accept the Magna Carta as one of the most important documents in the history of western civilization, we Americans cannot afford to ignore it, its intent, or its specifics. Common law demanded that a people—and the person—move freely, border or not. Even in time of war, the enemy must be treated with dignity.

Equally important, can we American[s] afford to ignore that the pagans, such as Odysseus, as well as the Christians, such as King Alfred, stood alike for the free movement of peoples and the welcoming of the stranger? To this day, the Roman Catholic Church, following the Hebraic Decalogue, teaches: "The more prosperous nations are obliged, to the extent they are able, to welcome the *foreigner* in search of the security and the means of livelihood which he cannot find in his country of origin. Public authorities should see to it that the natural right is respected that places a guest under the protection of those who receive him." To be sure, the immigrant must fulfill his or her duty as a citizen as well.

As an American conservative, I am not suggesting that we should surrender our own free will to the dictates of the past or even to any one religion, but I do think we would be foolish beyond measure to ignore the advice of our ancestors. And, for what it's worth, the best of our ancestors believed in the free movement of peoples.

When it comes to the specifically American tradition of immigration and the free movements of peoples, the issue becomes more complicated.

Imagine for a moment that the great waves of immigration never came to America. In the colonial period, among those who freely chose to cross the Atlantic, you would have to dismiss the Anglicans to Virginia, the Puritans to New England, the Quakers to Pennsylvania, and the Scotch-Irish. Of the unfree peoples, you would have to take out all of those of African origin. In the 1840s, remove the Germans, the Scandinavians, and the Irish. In the 1880s through the 1910s, remove all Greeks, Poles, Jews, Italians. . . .

Yes, the native American Indian population would be justly celebrating, but, overall, and, from any relatively objective view, there would be no America.

Between 1801 and 1924—with the critical exception of the Chinese and the Japanese—no peoples were barred from entry into the United States. Congress forbade further Chinese immigration in 1882, and a gentleman's agreement ended Japanese immigration in 1905. Otherwise, until 1921 and 1924, any person of any continent, of any religion, of either gender, of any skin color, or any other accident of birth could enter the United States and take up residency the very day of arrival. Only those with known criminal records or those suffering from tuberculosis were turned away.

Unless you are a full-blooded American Indian (less than one percent of the present United States population), you, American reader, would not be here without some ancestor having immigrated—freely or by force—to the United States. And possibly from what one might crassly dismiss as a "sh-hole country."

Thus, our ancestors not only expressed their favor of the freedom of movement among peoples in their writings and laws, but when push came to shove, they also voted with their feet.

Since the tragedies of September 11, 2001, we Americans have surrendered not just our liberties but our very souls to the false notion and false comfort of governmentally-provided security. Tellingly, we have even closed off what was once the freest and longest border in the history of the world, our border with our extremely kind and polite neighbor to the north, Canada.

The free movement of peoples has not only been seen as a natural right throughout much of the western tradition, but it has also been seen as a sacred one.

Again, I am not suggesting we must be slaves to the past, nor am I suggesting that we should dismiss the legitimate security concerns of a sovereign people. But, as an America people, we came into being because of the free movement of peoples. We rebelled against the designs of the 18th-century British, and we mocked the 19th-century Europeans and their passports and border guards.

Now, we seem to have become them.

If we continue to build walls around our country, really, then, just who are we? Only in the last generation or so have so many American conservatives become convinced of the necessity of the vast array of restrictions on those who wish to become a part of the United States. Perhaps they are right, but, regardless, there is much to discuss.

Print Citations

CMS: Birzer, Bradley J. "Bring on the Conservative Debate for Immigration." In *The Reference Shelf: The National Debate Topic 2018–2019 Immigration*, edited by Betsy Maury, 22-25. Ipswich, MA: H.W. Wilson, 2018.

MLA: Birzer, Bradley J. "Bring on the Conservative Debate for Immigration." *The Reference Shelf: The National Debate Topic 2018–2019 Immigration*. Ed. Betsy Maury. Ipswich: H.W. Wilson, 2018. 22-25. Print.

APA: Birzer, B.J. (2018). Bring on the conservative debate for immigration. In Betsy Maury (Ed.), *The reference shelf: The national debate topic 2018–2019 immigration* (pp. 22-25). Ipswich, MA: H.W. Wilson. (Original work published 2018)

Only Mass Deportation Can Save America

By Bret Stephens

The New York Times, June 16, 2017

In the matter of immigration, mark this conservative columnist down as strongly pro-deportation. The United States has too many people who don't work hard, don't believe in God, don't contribute much to society and don't appreciate the greatness of the American system.

They need to return whence they came.

I speak of Americans whose families have been in this country for a few generations. Complacent, entitled and often shockingly ignorant on basic points of American law and history, they are the stagnant pool in which our national prospects risk drowning.

On point after point, America's nonimmigrants are failing our country. Crime? A study by the Cato Institute notes that nonimmigrants are incarcerated at nearly twice the rate of illegal immigrants, and at more than three times the rate of legal ones.

Educational achievement? Just 17 percent of the finalists in the 2016 Intel Science Talent Search—often called the "Junior Nobel Prize" —were the children of United States-born parents. At the Rochester Institute of Technology, just 9.5 percent of graduate students in electrical engineering were nonimmigrants.

Religious piety—especially of the Christian variety? More illegal immigrants identify as Christian (83 percent) than do Americans (70.6 percent), a fact right-wing immigration restrictionists might ponder as they bemoan declines in church attendance.

Business creation? Nonimmigrants start businesses at half the rate of immigrants, and accounted for fewer than half the companies started in Silicon Valley between 1995 and 2005. Overall, the share of nonimmigrant entrepreneurs fell by more than 10 percentage points between 1995 and 2008, according to a Harvard Business Review study.

Nor does the case against nonimmigrants end there. The rate of out-of-wedlock births for United States-born mothers exceeds the rate for foreign-born moms, 42 percent to 33 percent. The rate of delinquency and criminality among nonimmigrant teens considerably exceeds that of their immigrant peers. A recent report by the Sentencing Project also finds evidence that the fewer immigrants there are in a neighborhood, the likelier it is to be unsafe.

And then there's the all-important issue of demographics. The race for the future is ultimately a race for people—healthy, working-age, fertile people—and our nonimmigrants fail us here, too. "The increase in the overall number of U.S. births, from 3.74 million in 1970 to 4.0

> **I have always thought of United States as a country that belongs first to its newcomers—the people who strain hardest to become a part of it because they realize that it's precious.**

million in 2014, is due entirely to births to foreign-born mothers," reports the *Pew Research Center*. Without these immigrant moms, the United States would be faced with the same demographic death spiral that now confronts Japan.

Bottom line: So-called real Americans are screwing up America. Maybe they should leave, so that we can replace them with new and better ones: newcomers who are more appreciative of what the United States has to offer, more ambitious for themselves and their children, and more willing to sacrifice for the future. In other words, just the kind of people we used to be—when "we" had just come off the boat.

O.K., so I'm jesting about deporting "real Americans" en masse. (Who would take them in, anyway?) But then the threat of mass deportations has been no joke with this administration.

On Thursday, the Department of Homeland Security seemed prepared to extend an Obama administration program known as Deferred Action for Childhood Arrivals, or DACA, which allows the children of illegal immigrants—some 800,000 people in all—to continue to study and work in the United States. The decision would have reversed one of Donald Trump's ugly campaign threats to deport these kids, whose only crime was to have been brought to the United States by their parents.

Yet the administration is still committed to deporting their parents, and on Friday the D.H.S. announced that even DACA remains under review—another cruel twist for young immigrants wondering if they'll be sent back to "home" countries they hardly ever knew, and whose language they might barely even speak.

Beyond the inhumanity of toying with people's lives this way, there's also the shortsightedness of it. We do not usually find happiness by driving away those who would love us. Businesses do not often prosper by firing their better employees and discouraging job applications. So how does America become great again by berating and evicting its most energetic, enterprising, law-abiding, job-creating, idea-generating, self-multiplying and God-fearing people?

Because I'm the child of immigrants and grew up abroad, I have always thought of the United States as a country that belongs first to its newcomers—the people who strain hardest to become a part of it because they realize that it's precious; and who do the most to remake it so that our ideas, and our appeal, may stay fresh.

That used to be a cliché, but in the Age of Trump it needs to be explained all over again. We're a country of immigrants—by and for them, too. Americans who don't get it should get out.

Print Citations

CMS: Stephens, Bret. "Only Mass Deportation Can Save America." In *The Reference Shelf: The National Debate Topic 2018–2019 Immigration*, edited by Betsy Maury, 26-28. Ipswich, MA: H.W. Wilson, 2018.

MLA: Stephens, Bret. "Only Mass Deportation Can Save America." *The Reference Shelf: The National Debate Topic 2018–2019 Immigration*. Ed. Betsy Maury. Ipswich: H.W. Wilson, 2018. 26-28. Print.

APA: Stephens, B. (2018). Only mass deportation can save America. In Betsy Maury (Ed.), *The reference shelf: The national debate topic 2018–2019 immigration* (pp. 26-28). Ipswich, MA: H.W. Wilson. (Original work published 2017)

The Case Against Immigration: Why the United States Should Look Out for Itself

By Steven Camarota
Foreign Relations, March 31, 2017

Outlining his position on immigration in August of last year, Donald Trump, then the Republican candidate for U.S. president, made his motivating philosophy clear: "There is only one core issue in the immigration debate, and that issue is the well-being of the American people." Although this nationalistic appeal may strike some readers as conservative, it is very similar to the position taken by U.S. civil rights icon and Democrat Barbara Jordan, who before her death in 1996 headed President Bill Clinton's commission on immigration reform. "It is both a right and a responsibility of a democratic society," she argued, "to manage immigration so that it serves the national interest." Trump's rhetoric has of course been overheated and insensitive at times, but his view on immigration—that it should be designed to benefit the receiving country—is widely held.

In the United States, there is strong evidence that the national interest has not been well served by the country's immigration policy over the last five decades. Even as levels of immigration have approached historic highs, debate on the topic has been subdued, and policymakers and opinion leaders in both parties have tended to overstate the benefits and understate or ignore the costs of immigration. It would make a great deal of sense for the country to reform its immigration policies by more vigorously enforcing existing laws, and by moving away from the current system, which primarily admits immigrants based on family relationships, toward one based on the interests of Americans.

Immigrant Nation

Trump did not create the strong dissatisfaction with immigration felt by his working-class supporters, but he certainly harnessed it. Voters' sense that he would restrict immigration may be the single most important factor that helped him win the long-time Democratic stronghold of the industrial Midwest, and thus the presidency. There are two primary reasons why immigration has become so controversial, and why Trump's message resonated. The first is lax enforcement and the subsequently large population of immigrants living in the country illegally. But although illegal immigration grabs most of the headlines, a second factor makes many Americans uncomfortable with the current policy. It is the sheer number of immigrants, legal or otherwise. The United States currently grants one million immigrants lawful permanent residence (or a "green card") each year, which means that they can stay as long as they wish and become citizens after five years, or three if they are married to a U.S. citizen. Roughly 700,000 long-term visitors, mostly guest workers and foreign students, come annually as well.

Such a large annual influx adds up: In 2015, data from the U.S. Census Bureau indicated that 43.3 million immigrants lived in the country—double the number from 1990. The census data include roughly 10 million illegal immigrants, while roughly a million more go uncounted. In contrast to most countries, the United States grants citizenship to everyone born on its soil, including the children of tourists or illegal immigrants, so the above figures do not include any U.S.-born children of immigrants.

Proponents of immigration to the United States often contend that the country is a "nation of immigrants," and certainly immigration has played an important role in American history. Nevertheless, immigrants currently represent 13.5 percent of the total U.S. population, the highest percentage in over 100 years. The Census Bureau projects that by 2025, the immigrant share of the population will reach 15 percent, surpassing the United States' all-time high of 14.8 percent, reached in 1890. Without a change in policy, that share will continue to increase throughout the twenty-first century. Counting immigrants plus their descendants, the Pew Research Center estimates that since 1965, when the United States liberalized its laws, immigration has added 72 million people to the country—a number larger than the current population of France.

Given these numbers, it is striking that public officials in the United States have focused almost exclusively on the country's 11 to 12 million illegal immigrants, who account for only one quarter of the total immigrant population. Legal immigration has a much larger impact on the United States, yet the country's leaders have seldom asked the big questions. What, for example, is the absorption capacity of the nation's schools and infrastructure? How will the least-skilled Americans fare in labor market competition with immigrants? Or, perhaps most importantly, how many immigrants can the United States assimilate into its culture? Trump has not always approached these questions carefully, or with much sensitivity, but to his credit he has at least raised them.

Times Change

Regarding cultural assimilation, advocates of open immigration policies often argue that there is no problem. During the last great wave of immigration, from roughly 1880 to 1920, Americans feared the newcomers would not blend in, but for the most part they ended up assimilating. Therefore, as this reasoning goes, all immigrants will assimilate.

Unfortunately, however, circumstances that helped Great Wave immigrants assimilate are not present today. First, World War I and then legislation in the early 1920s dramatically reduced new arrivals. By 1970 less than 5 percent of the U.S.

population was foreign-born, down from 14.7 percent in 1910. This reduction helped immigrant communities assimilate, as they were no longer continually refreshed by new arrivals from the old country. But in recent decades, the dramatic growth of immigrant enclaves has likely slowed the pace of assimilation. Second, many of today's immigrants, like those of the past, have modest education levels, but unlike in the past, the modern U.S. economy has fewer good jobs for unskilled workers. Partly for this reason, immigrants do not improve their economic situation over time as much as they did in the past. Third, technology allows immigrants to preserve ties with the homeland in ways that were not possible a century ago. Calling, texting, emailing, FaceTiming, and traveling home are all relatively cheap and easy.

Fourth, the United States' attitude toward newcomers has also changed. In the past, there was more of a consensus about the desirability of assimilation. Supreme Court Justice Louis Brandeis, the son of Jewish immigrants, said in a 1915 speech on "True Americanism" that immigrants needed to do more than just learn English and native manners. Rather, he argued, they "must be brought into complete harmony with our ideals and aspirations." This was a widely held belief. In his book *The Unmaking of Americans*, the journalist John J. Miller has described how at the turn of the twentieth century, organizations such as the North American Civic League for Immigrants put out pamphlets celebrating the United States and helping immigrants understand and embrace the history and culture of their adopted country.

In the United States today, as in many Western countries, this kind of robust emphasis on assimilation has been replaced with multiculturalism, which holds that there is no single American culture, that immigrants and their descendants should retain their identity, and that the country should accommodate the new arrivals' culture rather than the other way around. Bilingual education, legislative districts drawn

> **The Trump administration has suggested moving to a "merit-based" immigration system that would select immigrants who can support themselves.**

along ethnic lines, and foreign language ballots are all efforts to change U.S. society to accommodate immigrants in a way that is very different from the past. Newcomers additionally benefit from affirmative action and diversity initiatives originally designed to help African Americans. Such race- and ethnicity-conscious measures encourage immigrants to see themselves as separate from society and in need of special treatment due to the hostility of ordinary Americans. John Fonte, a scholar at the Hudson Institute, has argued that such policies, which encourage immigrants to retain their language and culture, make patriotic assimilation less likely.

Of course, many Americans still embrace the goal of assimilation. A recent Associated Press survey found that a majority of Americans think that their country should have an essential culture that immigrants adopt. But the kind of assimilation promoted by Brandeis and the North American Civic League no longer has elite backing. As a result, even institutions seemingly designed to help immigrants integrate end up giving them mixed messages. As political psychologist Stanley Renshon points out, many immigrant-based organizations today do help immigrants learn English, but they also work hard to reinforce ties to the old country.

Show Me the Money

A further area of contention in the immigration debate is its economic and fiscal impact. Many immigrant families prosper in the United States, but a large fraction do not, adding significantly to social problems. Nearly one-third of all U.S. children living in poverty today have an immigrant father, and immigrants and their children account for almost one in three U.S. residents without health insurance. Despite some restrictions on new immigrants' ability to use means-tested assistance programs, some 51 percent of immigrant-headed households use the welfare system, compared to 30 percent of native households. Of immigrant households with children, two-thirds access food assistance programs. Cutting immigrants off from these programs would be unwise and politically impossible, but it is fair to question a system that welcomes immigrants who are so poor that they cannot feed their own children.

To be clear, most immigrants come to the United States to work. But because the U.S. legal immigration system prioritizes family relationships over job skills— and because the government has generally tolerated illegal immigration—a large share of immigrants are unskilled. In fact, half of the adult immigrants in the United States have no education beyond high school. Such workers generally earn low wages, which means that they rely on the welfare state even though they are working.

This past fall, an exhaustive study by the National Academies of Sciences, Engineering, and Medicine found that immigrants and their dependents use significantly more in public services than they pay in taxes, and the net drain could be as high as $296 billion per year. The academies also projected the fiscal impact into the future with mixed results—four of their scenarios showed a net fiscal drain after 75 years, and four showed a net fiscal benefit. What is clear, however, is that at present the fiscal effect is large and negative. The study also showed, unsurprisingly, that college-educated immigrants are a net fiscal benefit, while those without a degree are typically a net fiscal drain. Drawing on the academies' finding, the Trump administration has suggested moving to a "merit-based" immigration system that would select immigrants who can support themselves.

Immigration has also affected the U.S. labor market. One of the nation's leading immigration economists, Harvard's George Borjas, recently wrote in the *New York Times* that by increasing the supply of workers, immigration reduces wages for some Americans. For example, only 7 percent of lawyers in the United States are immigrants, but 49 percent of maids are immigrants, as are one-third of construction laborers and grounds workers. The losers from immigration are less-educated Americans, many of them black and Hispanic, who work in these high-immigrant occupations. The country needs to give more consideration to the impact of immigration on the poorest and least-educated Americans.

Another common argument for immigration is that it will solve Western countries' main demographic problem—that of an aging population. Immigrants, so the argument goes, will provide the next generation of workers to pay into welfare-state programs. But to help government finances, immigrants would have to be a net fiscal benefit, which is not the case. Furthermore, the economist Carl Schmertmann showed more than two decades ago that "constant inflows of immigrants, even at relatively young ages, do not necessarily rejuvenate low-fertility populations ... [and] may even contribute to population aging." Analysis by myself and several colleagues supports this conclusion. In short, immigrants grow old like everyone else, and in the United States they tend not to have very large families. In 2015 the median age of an immigrant was 40 years, compared to 36 for the native-born. And the United States' overall fertility rate, including immigrants, is 1.82 children per woman, which only falls to 1.75 once immigrants are excluded. In other words, immigrants increase the fertility rate by just 4 percent. The United States will have to look elsewhere to deal with its aging population.

A final argument in favor of immigration centers on the benefits to immigrants themselves, especially the poorest ones, who see their wages rise dramatically upon moving to the First World. But given the scope of Third World poverty, mass immigration is not the best form of humanitarian relief. More than three billion people in the world live in poverty—earning less than $2.50 a day. Even if legal immigration was tripled to three million people a year, the United States would still only admit about one percent of the world's poor each decade. In contrast, development assistance could help many more people in low-income countries.

The Art of the Deal?

The last time that limiting immigration was on the U.S. legislative agenda, in the mid-1990s, Barbara Jordan's commission suggested limiting family immigration and eliminating the visa lottery, which gives out visas based on chance. Clinton first seemed to endorse the recommendations, but then reversed course after Jordan died and the political winds shifted. The effort to lower the level of immigration was defeated in Congress by the same odd but formidable coalition of businesses, ethnic pressure groups, progressives, and libertarians that has dominated the immigration discourse from then until the Trump era.

With the election of Trump, a political compromise in the United States might be possible. It could involve legalizing some illegal immigrants in return for tightening policies on who gets to come in. Prioritizing skilled immigration while cutting overall numbers would increase the share of immigrants who are well educated and facilitate assimilation. The RAISE Act, sponsored by Senators Tom Cotton (R-Ark.) and David Perdue (R-Ga.), would do just that. Perhaps coupling the RAISE Act with legalization for some share of illegal immigrants could be a way forward.

Yet no matter what policy is adopted, immigration will remain contentious because it involves tradeoffs and competing moral claims. And for the foreseeable future, the number of people who wish to come to the developed countries such as the United States will be much greater than these countries are willing or able to allow.

Print Citations

CMS: Camarota, Steven. "The Case against Immigration: Why the United States Should Look Out for Itself." In *The Reference Shelf: The National Debate Topic 2018–2019 Immigration*, edited by Betsy Maury, 29-34. Ipswich, MA: H.W. Wilson, 2018.

MLA: Camarota, Steven. "The Case against Immigration: Why the United States Should Look Out for Itself." *The Reference Shelf: The National Debate Topic 2018–2019 Immigration*. Ed. Betsy Maury. Ipswich: H.W. Wilson, 2018. 29-34. Print.

APA: Camarota, S. (2018). The case against immigration: Why the United States should look out for itself. In Betsy Maury (Ed.), *The reference shelf: The national debate topic 2018–2019 immigration* (pp. 29-34). Ipswich, MA: H.W. Wilson. (Original work published 2017)

Trump's Assault on Immigrants Will Seriously Damage the Economy

By Herman Schwartz
The Nation, March 15, 2017

President Trump has promised to add millions of "good jobs" to the US economy and to raise the gross domestic product by more than 4 percent annually, at one point asserting: "I think we can do better than that"—as much as 6 percent. "This is the most pro-growth, pro-jobs, pro-family plan put forth in the history of our country," he proclaimed.

At the same time, the president has vowed to deport up to 3 million undocumented immigrants and to curtail future entries, branding immigrants as "gang members," "drug dealers," and "bad hombres." After his January 27 travel ban on people from seven Muslim-majority countries was blocked by the courts, Trump devised a toned-down version applied to six of them—even though his own Department of Homeland Security has concluded that "country of citizenship is unlikely to be a reliable indicator of potential terrorism."

Trump's economic promises verge on the delusional. Most economists think even his 4 percent boast is unrealistic, and any hopes for economic growth will be undercut by his deportation plans. In 2016, GDP grew by only 1.6 percent; since 2009, capital growth has increased by only 1.1 percent. We may get a temporary surge from tax cuts and infrastructure spending, but the Congressional Budget Office estimates in its January 2017 Budget and Economic Outlook report that from 2017 to 2027, GDP will grow at an average annual rate of only 1.9 percent. *New York Times* economics reporter Nelson Schwartz describes Trump's 4 percent target as "audacious at best and fanciful at worst."

Trump's promise to restore good manufacturing jobs to the Rust Belt is also dubious. Because of globalization and automation, few such jobs will return. For example, Trump boasts that he saved 1,000 (actually, fewer than 800) jobs at the Carrier air-conditioning plant in Indiana, but in a few years automation will kill many of those jobs anyway. By 2011, the auto industry was producing just as many cars as before the Great Recession, but with 30 percent fewer workers because of the increased use of robots and computers. As the *Times*'s Eduardo Porter concludes, "No matter what [Trump] does, he cannot bring back the coal jobs of yore or the old labor-intensive manufacturing economy."

Deporting millions of undocumented immigrants will only make things worse. Economic growth requires a large workforce and increasing productivity. But the American population is aging, so we need more young workers. The number of Americans over 60 is expected to increase by more than 22 percent during the current decade, reducing our annual growth by 1.2 percent. And productivity has slowed down markedly in the past 15 years.

Aging has cut our birth rate as well. In 2015, the United States saw its lowest population growth since the Great Depression—and whatever growth we did have was from immigrants. In 2014, immigrant women accounted for about 900,000 US births, more than tripling the 1970 number, while births to US-born women fell by 11 percent. The foreign-born accounted for 23 percent of all babies during that period.

Trump's harsh assault on undocumented immigrants will damage us in many key areas. Much of our recent growth has been in service occupations like retail, hospitality, home care, and health care; the Labor Department expects demand for home health-care aides in particular to rise by 40 percent in the next decade. Over 40 percent of undocumented immigrants are in these occupations.

These immigrants also comprise most of the laborers in agriculture and related industries, like dairy farming. Agriculture Department surveys in 2007 and 2009 found that almost half of these workers were undocumented, and the figure is higher in other sectors. "If you only have legal labor, certain parts of this industry and this region [California's Central Valley] would not exist," says fruit farmer Harold McClarty. Many local businesses in these areas—restaurants, clothing stores, insurance agencies—would close. As one Washington, DC, restaurant owner put it, "Honestly, without immigrants, the restaurant industry wouldn't exist."

To spur growth, Trump plans to spend many billions on roads, sewers, and other infrastructure; housing is also recovering. This will require many construction workers, and there aren't enough now—about 200,000 construction jobs are unfilled today, a rise of 81 percent in just the last two years. This has slowed the revival of the housing market as well as the overall economy. The shortage of construction workers will get worse because of Trump's immigration policies—which, ironically, could even frustrate the construction of his "beautiful wall."

Trump's policies have also dismayed many in the tech sector and in science, medicine, and academia, all of which depend heavily on highly educated and skilled immigrants. For example, 42 percent of doctor's-office visits in rural America are with foreign-born doctors, because immigrants must work in medically underserved areas like small towns, poor cities, and rural regions in order to stay here after their residencies or internships expire. Trump's revised travel ban could immediately degrade patient care: Currently, more than 12,000 doctors in these communities are from two of the countries covered by the ban—almost 9,000 from Iran and 3,500 from Syria.

American universities and students will also suffer from Trump's exclusionary policies. We now have about 1 million foreign students, 5 percent of our total enrollment; Iran alone accounts for more than 12,000. Apart from academic contributions, foreign students pay full tuition and other fees. Loss of this income would probably force a tuition increase for American students, since most universities, especially the public ones, are already financially strapped. A ban on foreign faculty and students will also undermine our educational and research capacities, threatening our leadership in these areas.

Opponents of immigration claim that immigrants take jobs from Americans and drive down wages. There is some truth to this, but not much. American citizens simply don't want many of the jobs now held by immigrants. "No feasible increase in wages or change in conditions would be enough to draw native-born Americans back into the fields," says Jeff Marchini, a fourth-generation radicchio farmer in California, and farmers in Florida and elsewhere agree. This also holds true for our construction-worker shortage. These jobs pay an average of $27 an hour, but American workers don't want them—they are hard, unpleasant, and not steady.

Trump's deep cuts in refugee-acceptance programs also undermine his rosy promises of economic growth. Refugees have helped revitalize cities like Buffalo, New York, which have struggled with obsolete industries and dwindling populations for decades. Nonetheless, Trump insists that he will deport millions of undocumented residents, and in early February, immigration agents began by arresting 678 people in 12 states. Although the DHS insists this was "routine," many of those arrested were minor offenders or even people whose only offense was being undocumented: 26 percent had no criminal record other than their illegal entry, which under US law is a misdemeanor unless repeated. None of them would have been deported under President Obama's "serious crimes" policy.

> "Honestly, without immigrants, the restaurant industry wouldn't exist."—Washington, DC restaurant owner

In fact, immigrants commit fewer crimes than the native-born: Only 820,000 of the 11 million undocumented have any criminal record, and only 690,000 have committed serious crimes. The Obama administration relied heavily on local cooperation to apprehend the latter, but many of these communities are now in sanctuary cities. They will certainly not cooperate, which poses what one Immigration and Customs Enforcement supervisor calls "perhaps [the] biggest challenge" for the agency.

The difference between the Trump program and Obama's is illustrated by Guadalupe García de Rayos, a 35-year-old Phoenix wife and mother of two American-born teenagers. Rayos, who has lived here for 21 years, was convicted of using a fake Social Security number eight years ago—a common offense among the undocumented—in order to become a janitor at an amusement park. Obama's DHS allowed her to stay despite a deportation order, but required her to check in annually with ICE, which she did. When Rayos showed up at ICE's offices in early February, however, she was arrested and promptly deported to Mexico. Her family is now without a wife and mother. And according to DHS Secretary John Kelly's February directives on deportation, *all* undocumented immigrants are deportable.

One group not intended to be affected by the directives so far are the Dreamers, 750,000 young people who were brought here as children and are currently in school or in the military. Under Obama's Deferred Action for Childhood Arrivals (DACA) program, they have temporary but renewable permission to stay and work. That can easily change, however: The new directives state that deportation relief must be determined on a case-by-case rather than class basis. Also, the Dreamers provided the federal government with personal information under a promise of privacy, but Trump's DHS directives abolish privacy rights for all undocumented immigrants.

Among the directives' most frightening provisions is an expansion of the "expedited removal" procedure—quick deportation without a judicial hearing. Under Obama, this procedure was used only for those here less than two weeks and found within 100 miles of the border. Kelly's new orders extend it to people anywhere in the country who have been here for up to two years.

Over 10 million immigrant families have at least one undocumented member, and as a result of these directives, the immigrant community is terrified. In New York, Florida, New Jersey, Arizona, and elsewhere, immigrants are staying off the streets and out of the stores and shopping malls, which is already damaging local economies. Children are being kept home from schools; exploited workers have become even more vulnerable; and law-enforcement officials worry that the immigrant community will no longer cooperate with them.

However, it's unlikely that Trump will be able to deport several million immigrants, at least in the foreseeable future, given the dire shortage of immigration agents, judges, and courts. Kelly does plan to hire thousands of new ICE and Border Patrol agents, but that will take time and many billions of dollars. And congressional Republicans may balk at the latter, especially since Trump hasn't indicated where the money will come from.

Trump's economic and immigration policies are dishonest, stupid, and cruel. His deportation and exclusion orders violate a principle fundamental to every civilized society and honored until now by both Democrats and Republicans: keeping families together. If stone and metal could cry, the Statue of Liberty would be weeping.

Print Citations

CMS: Schwartz, Herman. "Trump's Assault on Immigrants Will Seriously Damage the Economy." In *The Reference Shelf: The National Debate Topic 2018–2019 Immigration*, edited by Betsy Maury, 35-38. Ipswich, MA: H.W. Wilson, 2018.

MLA: Schwartz, Herman. "Trump's Assault on Immigrants Will Seriously Damage the Economy." *The Reference Shelf: The National Debate Topic 2018–2019 Immigration*. Ed. Betsy Maury. Ipswich: H.W. Wilson, 2018. 35-38. Print.

APA: Schwartz, H. (2018). Trump's assault on immigrants will seriously damage the economy. In Betsy Maury (Ed.), *The reference shelf: The national debate topic 2018–2019 immigration* (pp. 35-38). Ipswich, MA: H.W. Wilson. (Original work published 2017)

2
DREAMers and Asylum

Photo by Alfredo Estrella/AFP/Getty Images

Central American migrants taking part in the 'Migrant Via Crucis' caravan which originally planned to reach the US border, look out of a bus window as they arrive at the Casa del Peregrino shelter near the Guadalupe Basilica in Mexico City on April 9, 2018. The caravan, an annual event held since 2010 and which prompted fury from US President Donald Trump, assembled on the border with Guatemala on March 25 but started breaking up on Thursday in southern Mexico after organizers said it had abandoned its goal of reaching the US border and would end its activities with the rally in Mexico City.

Immigration Issues: Dreamers, Workers, and Refugees

The number of immigrants the nation allows to permanently resettle in the country has both expanded and contracted over time. Prior to President Donald Trump, Republicans like George W. Bush and Ronald Reagan railed against illegal immigration as a dire threat to the American economy and workforce, but were generally supportive of legal immigration. Trump, by contrast, seems to have more in common with the broadly anti-immigrant politicians of the 1800s, preferring an isolationist approach aimed at reducing both legal and illegal immigration.

The American DREAMer

The "DREAMers" are unauthorized residents who were brought to the United States as children by undocumented parents. They are called "DREAMers" in reference to the 2006 Republican-crafted DREAM (Development, Relief and Education for Alien Minors) Act, legislation that would have provided a path to citizenship for these individuals but failed to become law due to partisan political manipulation.

The DREAMers arrived in the United States at a median age of 6 and many are now in their 20s and 30s, having lived their entire lives in the United States. Because the DREAMers, having been brought into the country illegally as children, did not consciously choose to violate the law by migrating into the United States, some argue that they should not be penalized for the actions of their parents. Further, because the DREAMers have lived and worked in the United States since childhood, they are, by practice and culture, American, though they lack legal status. Allowing the DREAMers to become citizens changes almost nothing from the current state of things, as these individuals are already part of American society, already work in US jobs, speak English, and are assimilated into US culture. Many, in fact, have little if any experience or knowledge of the country in which they were born and from which their parents brought them when they were children.

A majority of US legislators and a large majority of US citizens favor allowing the DREAMers to stay and become full citizens. In February of 2018, a Quinnipiac poll found 81 percent of Americans favored allowing the DREAMers to stay, as opposed to only 14 percent who opposed their being allowed a path to citizenship. An *ABC News* poll in January of 2018 found 87 percent support, while a *Pew Research* Poll found 74 percent in support of the DREAMers. With such widespread support, both among the populace and across partisan lines in the legislature, it may seem surprising that no Congress since 2006 has been able to pass legislation to provide the path to citizenship so long debated, despite repeated efforts.[1] The failure to pass legislation on the DREAMers is the result of political manipulation, with politicians hoping to use the agreement on the DREAMers to force less popular legislation through Congress. For instance, a DREAMers act in 2010 failed to pass through Congress when a group of Republicans tried to use the issue to force Democrats to vote against repealing the "Don't Ask, Don't Tell" policy that prohibited openly gay individuals from serving in the military.[2]

In 2012, President Barack Obama issued an Executive Order (EO) creating the Deferred Action for Childhood Arrivals (DACA) program, which created temporary protection for DREAMers who agreed to come out of hiding and register with the government. The program was intended as a temporary measure that would protect the DREAMers while Congress debated permanent legislation on the issue. The DACA Program was available to individuals who were under 31 at the time the EO was issued, entered the United States before the age of 16, had resided continually in the United States since at least 2007, had no felony or significant misdemeanor convictions, and were either currently in school, a high school graduate, or enrolled in the armed forces. The Migration Policy Institute has estimated that as many as 1.7 million people qualify as DREAMers, of which 800,000 were approved for the DACA program before the program was cancelled by President Trump.[3]

In 2016, Donald Trump announced that he was cancelling the DACA program.[4] This led to another round of mass protests against the administration, as there is widespread, bipartisan support for the DREAMers. The Trump administration's reasons for cancelling the program became clear when Trump announced he would consider legislation to allow the DREAMers to stay in the country if his political opponents would agree to support some of his other campaign promises, including an $18 billion border wall and a proposal to cut federal funding from sanctuary cities.

The Attack on Legal Immigration

Another program that may be in jeopardy under the Trump administration is the Diversity Lottery Program first established in the 1970s. The diversity program has an interesting history, as it was originally devised as a way to enable more Irish immigrants to come to the United States and was sponsored, primarily, by Irish-American politicians concerned by the large number of Irish immigrants who were overstaying their legal permission to reside in the country when unable to obtain a visa for permanent residence. This was the result of a 1976 immigration reform act that provided 20,000 visas per year for every country. The Irish economy hit a downturn in the 1970s, with thousands of Irish fleeing Ireland in search of work. With many potential immigrants turned away because of the national quotas, a group of Irish-American politicians sponsored a bill that provided 10,000 more "special diversity" visas to individuals from countries "adversely affected" by the existing visa system, like Ireland. However, the diversity lottery did not officially become law until 1986, by which time the Irish economy was rebounding and therefore few Irish immigrants took advantage of the system. Instead, over the years, the diversity visa program was used to provide visas to individuals from countries and ethnicities underrepresented in the United States.[5]

Diversity is a priority for many progressives and liberals who see greater diversity as a strength. To some degree, academic research supports this belief, indicating distinct benefits to diverse educational and professional environments. However, the idea that diversity is a benefit to society is not universally accepted. In a 2017 Pew Research study, for instance, 45 percent of people identifying as conservative believed that diversity made the country a better place, while nearly the same percentage, 42 percent, felt it made no difference and a full 10 percent felt that racial and ethnic diversity made the nation a "worse place." By contrast, 81 percent identifying as liberal felt diversity made the nation a better place, while 15 percent felt it made no difference.[6]

In 2017, an immigrant from Uzbekistan, admitted through the diversity lottery program, drove a vehicle onto a jogging path in New York City, killing 8 people and injuring 11. Police found evidence that the individual had, in the year or so prior to the attack, withdrawn from friends and coworkers and had taken an interest in radical Islamic activism. Trump characterized this incident as a result of the diversity lottery program, which he claimed has let criminals and radicals into the United States and further blamed Democrat Chuck Schumer, who was one of the sponsors of the program in the 1990s.[7] In fact, the diversity lottery program was the result of bipartisan effort and not solely the product of Chuck Schumer or the Democratic Party and an Federal Bureau of Investigation (FBI) investigation indicated that the attacker was radicalized within the United States and not before arriving as an immigrant and therefore suggested that no new immigration policy or "vetting" process could, even in principal, have prevented the individual from becoming radicalized.

The Guest Worker Program

In April of 2017, the Trump administration issued a new EO, known as the "Buy American and Hire American" program, which calls for federal investigators to evaluate another legal immigration program, the H-1B visa program established through the Immigration Act of 1990. The H-1B program is essentially a guest worker program that brings high-skill workers from foreign countries to the United States on a sponsored, temporary basis. Since 2005, the program has been capped at 65,000 visas annually, with an additional 20,000 set aside for foreign nationals with graduate degrees from US academic institutions. Between 2001 and 2015, 1.8 million workers were accepted to participate in the program.[8]

The H-1B program was the result of intensive lobbying by the tech industry, with tech leaders complaining that there were insufficient American workers to fill the demand for engineers and other workers skilled in computer science and other tech fields. Since then, the program has not been highly controversial, though some critics argue that the H-1B program takes jobs away from American workers, while other critics argue that employers take advantage of foreign workers hired through the program, paying them lower wages than a US-born candidate would earn for the same job. In early 2018, the Trump administration announced several changes to the program that, overall, would reduce the number of visas available and make it less advantageous for companies to make use of the program.[9] The development drew criticism from tech companies, like Google and Microsoft, which have been the primary beneficiaries of the program.

An Administration at Odds

The Trump administration's immigration policy proposals are a significant departure from immigration policies in the recent past. Traditionally, modern Republican and Democrat presidents, once taking office, have moderated their policy priorities in an effort to represent the goals and priorities of the entire population, rather than only representing core supporters. This is why policy ideas mentioned during a campaign, when a candidate is marketing him- or herself directly to supporters, differ from the actual form of the policies enacted once a politician takes office.

By contrast, the Trump administration's immigration policies reflect the views and goals of some of his strident supporters rather than the public at large. With between 75 and 85 percent support among the populace for the DACA program, or some other way in which to allow the DREAMers to become citizens, the administration's decision to cancel the DACA program and subsequent threats to begin deporting the DREAMers has stalled legislative action on this issue. Immigration policy remains a bitterly contested issue in 2018 as politicians try to balance legal and illegal immigration, existing conditions and public opinion on comprehensive immigration reform which many Americans believe is due.

Works Used

Bhattacharya, Ananya. "Trump Administration Targets H-1B Visas—Again." *Quartz*. Quartz India. Mar 21, 2018. Web. https://qz.com/1234029/h-1b-visas-trump-administration-suspends-premium-processing-putting-indian-it-on-edge/.

De Haldevang, Max. "Trump's Bureaucracy Is Nearly as White, Male, and Unequal as His Cabinet." *Quartz*. Quartz Magazine. Oct 23, 2017. https://qz.com/1109087/trumps-bureaucracy-is-heavily-white-and-male-like-his-cabinet/.

Dickerson, Caitlin. "What Is DACA? Who Are the Dreamers? Here Are Some Answers." *The New York Times*. The New York Times Co. Jan 23, 2018. https://www.nytimes.com/2018/01/23/us/daca-dreamers-shutdown.html.

Graves, Allison. "Is Trump's Cabinet More White and Male Than Any First Cabinet Since Reagan?" *Politifact*. Politifact. Apr 26, 2017. Web. http://www.politifact.com/truth-o-meter/statements/2017/apr/26/center-american-progress/true-trumps-cabinet-more-white-and-more-male-any-f/.

"Immigration." *Gallup*. Gallup Poll. 2017. http://news.gallup.com/poll/1660/immigration.aspx.

"In First Month, Views of Trump Are Already Strongly Felt, Deeply Polarized." *Pew Research*. Pew Research Center. Feb 16, 2017. http://assets.pewresearch.org/wp-content/uploads/sites/5/2017/02/17094915/02-16-17-Political-release.pdf.

Kessler, Glenn. "The Debate over DACA: A Guide to the Numbers Used by Politicians." *The Washington Post*. The Washington Post Co. Jan 23, 2018. https://www.washingtonpost.com/news/fact-checker/wp/2018/01/23/

the-debate-over-daca-a-guide-to-the-numbers-used-by-politicians/?utm_
term=.687a215d6a80,

Kilgannon, Corey and Joseph Goldstein. "Sayfullo Saipov, the Suspect in the New
York Terror Attack, and His Past." *The New York Times*. The New York Times Co.
Oct 31, 2017. https://www.nytimes.com/2017/10/31/nyregion/sayfullo-saipov-
manhattan-truck-attack.html.

Kirby, Jen. "Trump Blasts 'Diversity Visa Lottery Program,' after NYC Terror Attack." *Vox*. Vox Media. Nov 1 2017. https://www.vox.com/policy-and-poli-
tics/2017/11/1/16590166/trump-tweet-diversity-visa-lottery-program.

Kurtzleben, Danielle. "What the Latest Immigration Polls Do (and Don't)
Say). *NPR*. National Public Radio. Jan 23, 2018. https://www.npr.
org/2018/01/23/580037717/what-the-latest-immigration-polls-do-and-dont-say.

Law, Anna O. "The Irish Roots of the Diversity Visa Lottery." *Politico Magazine*.
Politico. Nov 1, 2017. https://www.politico.com/magazine/story/2017/11/01/
diversity-visa-irish-history-215776.

Matthews, Dylan. "Polls Show Americans Are Closer to Democrats Than Donald
Trump on Immigration." *Vox*. Vox Media. Feb 12, 2018. https://www.vox.com/
policy-and-politics/2018/2/3/16959458/immigration-trump-compromise-pub-
lic-opinion-poll-dreamers-wall.

Newport, Frank. "Democrats Racially Diverse; Republicans Mostly White." *Gallup*.
Gallup Org. Feb 8, 2013. Web. http://news.gallup.com/poll/160373/democrats-
racially-diverse-republicans-mostly-white.aspx.

Ruiz, Neil G. "Key Facts about the U.S. H-1B Visa Program." *Factank*. Pew Research
Center. Apr 27, 2017. Web. http://www.pewresearch.org/fact-tank/2017/04/27/
key-facts-about-the-u-s-h-1b-visa-program/.

Wang, Hansi Lo. "Chinese-American Descendants Uncover Forged Family Histories." *NPR*. National Public Radio. Dec 17, 2013. https://www.npr.org/sections/
codeswitch/2013/12/17/251833652/chinese-american-descendants-uncover-
forged-family-history.

Notes

1. Matthews, "Polls Show Americans Are Closer to Democrats Than Donald
   Trump on Immigration."
2. Kurtzleben, "What the Latest Immigration Polls Do (and Don't) Say."
3. Kessler, "The Debate over DACA: A Guide to the Numbers Used by Politicians."
4. Dickerson, "What Is DACA? Who Are the Dreamers? Here Are Some Answers."
5. Law, "The Irish Roots of the Diversity Visa Lottery."
6. "In First Month, View of Trump Are Already Strongly Felt, Deeply Polarized,"
   Pew Research.
7. Kilgannon and Goldstein, "Sayfullo Saipov, the Suspect in the New York Terror
   Attack, and His Past."
8. Ruiz, "Key Facts about the U.S. H-1B Visa Program."
9. Bhattacharya, "Trump Administration Targets H-1B Visas—Again."

It's Not Illegal Immigration That Worries Republicans Anymore

By Peter Beinart

The Atlantic, **February 18, 2018**

A few weeks ago, the contours of an immigration compromise looked clear: Republicans would let the "Dreamers" stay. Democrats would let Trump build his wall. Both sides would swallow something their bases found distasteful in order to get the thing their bases cared about most.

Since then, Trump has blown up the deal. He announced on Wednesday that he would legalize the "Dreamers," undocumented immigrants brought to the U.S. as children, only if Democrats funded his wall *and* ended the visa lottery and "chain migration." He would support a path to citizenship for undocumented immigrants only if Congress brought the number of legal immigrants down.

There's an irony here, which was pointed out to me by CATO Institute immigration analyst David Bier. Until recently, Republican politicians drew a bright line between illegal immigration, which they claimed to hate, and legal immigration, which they claimed to love. Florida Senator Marco Rubio launched his presidential campaign at the Freedom Tower, Miami's Ellis Island. Texas Senator Ted Cruz, who in 2013 proposed a five-fold increase in the number of H1B visas for highly skilled immigrants, declared in April 2015 that, "There is no stronger advocate for legal immigration in the U.S. Senate than I am." Mitt Romney promised in 2007 that, "We're going to end illegal immigration to protect legal immigration."

Trump has turned that distinction on its head. He's willing to legalize the "Dreamers"—who came to the United States illegally—so long as the number of legal immigrants goes down. He has not only blurred the GOP's long-held moral distinction between legal and illegal immigration. In some ways, he's actually flipped it—taking a harder line on people who enter the U.S. with documentation than those who don't.

What explains this? Trump's great hidden advantage during the 2016 Republican presidential primary was his lack of support from the GOP political and donor class. This allowed him to jettison positions—in support of free trade, in support of the Iraq War, in support of cutting Medicare and Social Security—that enjoyed support among Republican elites but little support among Republican voters. He did the same on immigration, where the "legal good, illegal bad" distinction turned out to be much more popular among the party's leaders than among its grassroots.

> **What really drives Republican views about immigrants, in other words, is less their legal status than their nation of origin, their religion, and their race.**

Cribbing from Ann Coulter's book, *Adios America*, Trump replaced the legal-illegal distinction with one that turned out to have more resonance on the activist right: The distinction between white Christian immigrants and non-white, and non-Christian ones.

The words "illegal immigration" do not appear in Trump's presidential announcement speech. Instead, Trump focused on immigrants' country of origin. "When Mexico sends its people," he declared, "they're not sending their best ... They're sending people that have lots of problems, and they're bringing those problems with us. They're bringing drugs. They're bringing crime. They're rapists ... It's coming from more than Mexico. It's coming from all over South and Latin America, and it's coming probably—probably—from the Middle East."

Trump, who often says bluntly what other Republicans say in code, probably realized that "illegal immigrant" was, for many voters, already a euphemism for Latino or Mexican-immigrants. In their book *White Backlash*, the political scientists Marisa Abrajano and Zoltan Hajnal cite a poll showing that 61 percent of Americans believe that most Latino immigrants are undocumented even though only about a quarter are. "When Americans talk about undocumented immigrants, Latinos or immigrants in general," they note, "the images in their heads are likely to be the same."

What really drove Republican opinion about immigration, Trump realized, was not primarily the fear that the United States was becoming a country of law-breakers. (Republicans, after all, were not outraged about the lack of prosecution of tax cheats.) It was the fear that the United States—which was becoming less white and had just elected a president of Kenyan descent—was becoming a third-world country.

When the Public Religion Research Institute and Brookings Institution asked Americans in 2016 their views of immigration from different parts of the world, it found that Republicans were only three points more likely than Democrats to want to reduce immigration from "predominantly Christian countries" and only seven points more likely to want to reduce immigration from Europe. By contrast, they were 33 points more likely to support reducing immigration from Mexico and Central America and 41 points more likely to support reducing immigration from "predominantly Muslim countries." What really drives Republican views about immigrants, in other words, is less their legal status than their nation of origin, their religion, and their race.

Trump grasped that during the campaign, and in coalition with a bevy of current and former Southern Senators—Jeff Sessions, David Perdue and Tom Cotton—he has used it to turn the GOP into a party devoted to slashing legal immigration. On Thursday, when presented with a bill that traded the legalization of Dreamers for more border security but did not reduce legal immigration, only eight Republican

Senators voted yes. However, 37 voted for a bill that legalized the "Dreamers," added more border security, and substantially reduced legal immigration.

But there's another reason Trump has succeeded in erasing the "legal good, illegal bad" distinction that for years governed GOP immigration debate. He's made Republicans less concerned with legality in general. In 2012, the GOP—which was then-outraged by executive orders that supposedly displayed President Barack Obama's contempt for the constitutional limits of his office—titled the immigration section of its platform, "The Rule of Law: Legal Immigration." The seven paragraph-section used variations of the word "law" 14 times.

That emphasis is harder now. In his ongoing battles with the FBI, Justice Department, judiciary, and Special Counsel Robert Mueller, Trump has convinced many Republicans that the "rule of law" is often a cloak for the partisan biases of the "deep state." As a result, Republicans are now 22 points less likely to hold a positive opinion of the FBI than they were in 2015.

What really matters for many Republicans in Trump's standoff with Mueller and the FBI is not who has the law on their side, since the bureaucracy can twist the law to its own advantage. What really matters is who enjoys the backing of "the people," the authentic America that resides outside the swamp, a construct that definitely does not include the imagined beneficiaries of "chain migration" and the "visa lottery."

In the Trump era, Republicans now justify their immigration views less by reference to law than by reference to tribe. Which, not coincidentally, is how they justify Trump's presidency itself.

Print Citations

CMS: Beinart, Peter. "It's Not Illegal Immigration That Worries Republicans Anymore." In *The Reference Shelf: The National Debate Topic 2018–2019 Immigration*, edited by Betsy Maury, 47-49. Ipswich, MA: H.W. Wilson, 2018.

MLA: Beinart, Peter. "It's Not Illegal Immigration That Worries Republicans Anymore." *The Reference Shelf: The National Debate Topic 2018–2019 Immigration*. Ed. Betsy Maury. Ipswich: H.W. Wilson, 2018. 47-49. Print.

APA: Beinart, P. (2018). It's not illegal immigration that worries Republicans anymore. In Betsy Maury (Ed.), *The reference shelf: The national debate topic 2018–2019 immigration* (pp. 47-49). Ipswich, MA: H.W. Wilson. (Original work published 2018)

The Republican Party Is Turning Against Legal Immigration

The Economist, **August 10, 2017**

Those keen to avoid hearing any more about the 45th president can download a filter that, for a fee, will scrub any mention of him from electronic devices. But for anyone interested in the long-term effects this president will have on America, the problem is the opposite. Donald Trump is so ubiquitous that it is hard to distinguish what really matters from what merely infuriates, and quieter changes can go unnoticed. One such was the unveiling on August 2nd of an immigration bill proposed by two Republican senators, Tom Cotton of Arkansas and David Perdue of Georgia, and praised by the president. Even if the bill never becomes law, it could achieve something profound. Republicans have long denounced illegal immigration while sounding more upbeat about the legal sort. Under Mr Trump, the party is on the point of abandoning its optimism about legal migration, too.

America's system for allowing people into the country to live and work functions fairly well despite, rather than because of, its messy design. About 1m people were granted green cards, which confer permanent residency, last year. Although a detailed breakdown for 2016 is not yet available, in 2015 two-thirds of green cards were handed out to family members of migrants, a share that is unlikely to have changed much. This makes America unusual. Other wealthy English-speaking democracies, including Britain, Australia and Canada, have already moved away from a system granting family members preferential treatment. Then there are the 140,000 green cards issued each year to people sponsored by their employers. Add in the 50,000 green cards issued by lottery to people from countries under-represented in the immigration numbers for the five previous years, sprinkle on refugee admissions, which fluctuate according to how much tumult there is abroad in any given year, and you reach the annual total.

This might sound like a recipe for recruiting low-skilled immigrants, a point often made by the system's critics. In fact, nearly half of immigrants who arrived between 2011 and 2015 had college degrees. How educated immigrants are matters because, although the economic gains for low-skilled migrants of moving to America are great, the benefits to the American economy are not clear. Highly skilled immigrants, by contrast, offer a lot to their adopted country. Education seems to matter much more than where people come from. Two-thirds of Nigerian immigrants have college degrees, for example, and Nigerian-Americans consequently have household incomes that are well above the average.

Under the Cotton-Perdue bill the green card lottery would end and the family preference system would be limited to spouses or dependent children. This makes sense. But the bill also aims to cut by half the number of green cards issued each year, in an effort to restore immigration to "historic norms", which does not.

What counts as a historic norm depends on the figures you choose. Adjusted for population, current levels of immigration are abnormally low. In the 196 years for which data exist, America has issued green cards at an average rate of 4,500 per 1m Americans. Over the past 50 years the rate has been 2,900 per 1m. The proposed bill would reduce immigration as a proportion of the population to levels last seen in 1964, the year before a new federal law led to a rapid, largely unforeseen, increase in the absolute number of immigrants.

Some conservatives see liberal soft-headedness in today's policy, with its bias towards admitting family groups. But at the time, the law of 1965 was defended as a way to let in more migrants from places like Italy or Greece (who had been kept out by discriminatory national quotas imposed in 1924), without risking an influx from much poorer nations. As a co-sponsor of the bill, the New York congressman Emanuel Celler, told colleagues: "Since the people of Africa and Asia have very few relatives here, comparatively few could immigrate from those countries."

Jump forward 52 years, and in addition to reducing the number of green cards, the new bill seeks to reduce the number of refugees America admits each year. The intention is to cut admissions to 50,000 a year, "in line with a 13-year average". If that sounds like a period cherry-picked to give a number that is politically desirable, then that is because it is. Refugee admissions have been below 50,000 in only four of the past 30 years. If the bill's authors had taken a 30-year average, the annual level would have come out at 75,000.

To replace this system, the bill proposes that green cards should be awarded on a points-based system, like those in Australia and Canada, with extra credit according to youth, wealth, ability to speak English, educational attainment, possession of an extraordinary talent and whether the applicant has a high-paying job offer. Evidence from Australia and Canada suggests that government-run points systems do not necessarily do a better job of connecting immigrants with jobs (the optimal system for that is one that

> **The hardest puzzle in immigration policy is not, in fact, picking new arrivals but deciding what to do about the 11m illegal immigrants already in the country, many of whom have children who are citizens.**

gives employers more say). But they are popular with voters, who seem to like the flattering notion that their countries resemble a country club with stringent admission criteria.

When presenting the White House's case, Stephen Miller, an adviser to the president, challenged news outlets to do polling on the proposals, implying that they reflect the public's wishes. Ever keen to help, *The Economist* asked YouGov to do so. The results were not what Mr Miller may have expected. Only 27% of respondents favoured decreasing the level of legal immigration. When asked the question in a less stark way, a slightly higher share either strongly or somewhat supported halving legal immigration, but the combined total of support was still only 37%.

Other details in the proposed bill jarred. A plurality of respondents liked the idea of giving higher priority to potential migrants who already speak English. But they preferred the idea of giving priority to those with a close family member living in the country, suggesting continued support for family preference. Giving shelter to those trying to escape from war was more popular still. For good measure, we also poll-tested the inscription at the base of the Statue of Liberty ("Give me your tired, your poor, your huddled masses yearning to breathe free..."), which is perhaps the antithesis of the White House's approach to immigration. A case can be made that the poem unhelpfully conflates immigration with asylum, and casts the admission of hard-working newcomers as an act of charity, rather than a source of growth over the centuries. Still, it resonates. The vast majority (72%) thought the poem's sentiment applied in the past, a plurality (43%) thought it applied now and a majority (55%) thought it should apply in the future.

When he was elected, there was a faint hope that Mr Trump might be the one politician with both a sufficient command of his base to fix America's broken immigration system. A popular touch would help because the hardest puzzle in immigration policy is not, in fact, picking new arrivals but deciding what to do about the 11m illegal immigrants already in the country, many of whom have children who are citizens. That is far too large a group to deport, even if it were sensible to do so. Perhaps a candidate who promised to build a wall along the Mexican border could be the one to regularise some of the 11m, many of whom have been in America for decades? There is no sign of this Nixon-to-China turn on Mr Trump's part and, given his inclination to conflate illegal immigration and violent crime, it seems highly unlikely. But so did a Trump presidency, once.

Print Citations

CMS: "The Republican Party Is Turning against Legal Immigration." In *The Reference Shelf: The National Debate Topic 2018–2019 Immigration*, edited by Betsy Maury, 50-52. Ipswich, MA: H.W. Wilson, 2018.

MLA: "The Republican Party Is Turning against Legal Immigration." *The Reference Shelf: The National Debate Topic 2018–2019 Immigration*. Ed. Betsy Maury. Ipswich: H.W. Wilson, 2018. 50-52. Print.

APA: The Economist. (2018). The Republican party is turning against legal immigration. In Betsy Maury (Ed.), *The reference shelf: The national debate topic 2018–2019 immigration* (pp. 50-52). Ipswich, MA: H.W. Wilson. (Original work published 2017)

The H1-B Visa Debate, Explained

By Nicole Torres

Harvard Business Review, May 4, 2017

It's hard to overstate the significance—and complexity—of the H-1B visa system in the U.S. It is the country's largest guest worker visa program, and an important channel for high-skilled immigration. It allows companies to hire foreign workers for specialized jobs that can be challenging to fill. It has benefited the tech industry enormously, and other sectors, including health care, science, and finance, have also used it to fill gaps in their workforces.

But in April, just after U.S. Citizen and Immigration Services (USCIS) conducted its annual lottery for selecting H-1B visas (it received 199,000 petitions for the available 85,000 visas), President Trump signed an executive order that will put H-1B and similar programs under new scrutiny. Titled "Buy American and Hire American," it directs federal agencies to review whether existing policies adequately prioritize American products and protect American workers.

The order is the latest development in a long-running debate over how companies use the H-1B program and how it affects American workers. Much of the dispute surrounds whether companies take advantage of the program to hire foreign workers for lower pay, displacing Americans from those jobs. But it's important to understand the underlying elements of this debate: one level rests on the heavy use of H-1B visas by outsourcing firms; another rests on the disagreement over whether the program increases companies' access to scarce skills, or merely helps them minimize costs.

Who Gets H-1Bs?

H-1B visas are granted through an employer-driven system, meaning employers petition the government for visas tied to specific roles. These must qualify as "specialty occupations," which typically require a bachelor's degree (or the equivalent) and are found in fields such as science, engineering, information technology, medicine, and business. Companies have to attest that they will not pay an H-1B worker less than they would an American, and that H-1B workers will not "adversely affect the working conditions" of other workers—but it's often said that this hardly functions as a rule and is not strictly (if at all) enforced. There is also criticism that it opens up various loopholes that firms can exploit. For example, as a Kellogg Insight research summary explains:

> The standards for determining prevailing wages are shaky, and companies can take advantage of loopholes, such as hiring the person through a third-party service. In addition, increasing the supply of workers might drive down everyone's pay over time because employers have more potential employees to choose from and thus do not have to offer high salaries or raises to attract and retain staff.

The program is most often associated with the tech industry, where H-1B workers hold about 12%–13% of jobs, according to a Goldman Sachs report. (For comparison, they hold around 0.6%–0.7% of U.S. jobs overall.) Being able to recruit globally is supposed to help tech powerhouses like Facebook and Amazon find the talent they need.

The companies that bring in the most H-1B workers, however, are not Silicon Valley tech firms but IT services firms, many based in India, that specialize in consulting or outsourcing. These companies, which include Tata Consultancy Services, Cognizant, Infosys, Wipro, Accenture, IBM India, and Deloitte, are contracted by other companies to do IT work. According to an analysis by Ronil Hira, a professor of public policy at Howard University, in 2014 nearly one-third of new H-1B visas went to 13 of these so-called "outsourcers." (Tata received the most visas, with 5,650, while Amazon, the tech company with the highest number, got 877.)

Compared with Silicon Valley firms, IT services companies tend to hire H-1B workers for lower-paying entry-level work. For example, Axios reported that 72.4% of Tata's H-1B visa filings were for jobs paying between $60,000–$70,000 a year. Companies like Amazon, Apple, Facebook, Google, and Microsoft mostly filed for jobs that paid well above $100,000.

This difference in pay gets at one of the main criticisms of the H-1B program: Rather than bringing the world's "best and brightest" talent into the country to work alongside Americans, the system appears to be bringing in cheaper foreign labor that can hurt American workers' employment and income prospects. It's a compelling argument: Numerous American IT workers have been laid off (and then asked to train their H-1B replacements) after their employers chose to outsource IT department work instead of keeping it in-house. These decisions by companies have resulted in a few high-profile lawsuits, such as those brought by workers against Disney and Southern California Edison. And a number of studies have found that H-1B workers can have negative effects on American workers, in terms of displacement and lower earnings.

On the other side of the debate, H-1B supporters argue that the program brings needed skills into the labor market, which helps firms remain innovative, productive, and competitive. A wealth of academic literature has documented how high-skilled immigrants, particularly in STEM, and including those who would enter the U.S. on H-1B visas, boost the economy by increasing innovation, productivity, and sometimes even employment.

It is not exactly easy for many companies to obtain H-1B visas, and members of the tech industry have lobbied Congress to raise the cap on H-1B visas to help meet demand. In 2008 Bill Gates testified before Congress to advocate for more H-1B visas to help compensate for "a deficit of Americans with computer science degrees." (A bill was introduced in 2015 to raise the cap and liberalize other rules around H-1Bs, but died in Congress.) Companies like Tata, Infosys, and Wipro have also lobbied against restrictions on the program, arguing that their services help corporations become more competitive. More broadly, many tech leaders have emphasized the contributions of high-skilled immigrants to the economy—and have spoken out against anti-immigrant actions like President Trump's travel bans.

Is There a Shortage of Technical Skills in the U.S.?

There is mixed evidence about the existence and the extent of a STEM skills shortage. Companies say they struggle to find qualified workers for specialized positions, suggesting there is a shortage of necessary skills. Some experts say that there are plenty of American workers who could fill these jobs, and that if employers were truly desperate for skills, wages for skilled positions would surge (but they haven't).

An analysis led by Hal Salzman, a professor at Rutgers University, found that the U.S. graduates more STEM workers than the tech industry needs and that STEM wages have stayed depressingly flat. They write:

> For every two students that U.S. colleges graduate with STEM degrees, only one is hired into a STEM job. In computer and information science and in engineering, U.S. colleges graduate 50 percent more students than are hired into those fields each year; of the computer science graduates not entering the IT workforce, 32 percent say it is because IT jobs are unavailable, and 53 percent say they found better job opportunities outside of IT occupations.

A literature review by Yi Xue and Richard C. Larson of MIT found that there is and isn't a STEM skills shortage—it depends on where you look. In the academic job market, for example, they conclude there is no noticeable shortage; in fact, there is an oversupply of PhDs competing for tenure-track faculty positions in many fields (e.g., biomedical sciences, physical sciences). But the government sector and private industry have shortages in specific areas. In the private sector, for instance, software developers, petroleum engineers, and data scientists were found to be in high demand.

There is other evidence of a strong demand for workers with tech skills. *The Economist* has reported that the number of unfilled U.S. jobs in computing and information technology could top one million by 2020: "The number of young Americans graduating with qualifications in IT subjects is rising, but nowhere near fast enough to satisfy the burgeoning demand for their skills. Last year, American campuses produced fewer than 56,000 graduates with the sort of qualifications sought by information technology (IT) firms."

When it comes to how much immigrant and native-born U.S. tech workers earn, research by Gordon Hanson of UC San Diego and Matthew Slaughter of

Dartmouth's Tuck School of Business has found that while immigrants usually earn less than native-born workers across most occupations (controlling for factors like age, education, and gender), this difference tends to be smaller in STEM fields. They also found that wages for immigrants in STEM have actually increased: In 1990 native-born STEM workers earned more than immigrants; by 2012, this reversed.

"The workers coming in on H-1Bs are a diverse crowd," Hanson says. "You have superstar computer scientists at Facebook and Amazon and folks doing back-office IT work. But, on average, the earnings of those [foreign] workers, after just a little time in U.S., exceed [Americans'] in comparable jobs."

Hanson cautions, however, that their results do not discount the possibility that the arrival of foreign-born engineers is driving down earnings for U.S.-born engineers. "Standard economic models would say that's happening," he says. "But more engineers is a good thing. There may be some lower earnings opportunities for U.S.-born engineers, but there's more innovation for the country as a whole."

Similarly, an analysis of 2010 H-1B petitions by Jonathan Rothwell and Neil Ruiz, both formerly of Brookings, found that H-1B workers earned more on average ($76,356) than American workers with a bachelor's degree ($67,301), within the same age group and occupation. (It's worth noting that the process of petitioning for an H-1B visa costs companies thousands of dollars, which suggests that they pay a premium for foreign workers' skills.)

> **The program brings needed skills into the labor market, which helps firms remain innovative, productive, and competitive.**

Hanson and Slaughter's paper also noted that although H-1B visas disproportionately go to STEM workers, this is not an inherent feature of the H-1B program. "That most H-1B visas are captured by STEM workers may simply be the consequences of strong relative labor demand for STEM labor by U.S. companies," they write.

Contrarily, Hira, who has been outspoken about abuses of the H-1B visa system, rebuffs the skills shortage theory. "If there was this terrible shortage, I'd think you'd see different behavior and practices," he says. "If there was really a skills shortage, you'd see more diversity in the tech industry—they'd hire underrepresented minorities and women, they'd be training people and investing, they'd be retaining incumbent workers, not laying them off by the thousands, and you wouldn't see rampant age discrimination."

According to Hira, the skills shortage argument is a red herring that has clouded the conversation about how H-1Bs are used. "The top occupation of H-1B workers is computer systems analyst. These are back-end IT workers. I don't see how anybody could argue there's a shortage of those folks," he says. "Hiring an H-1B should, but doesn't, require an employer to demonstrate any shortage, so the shortage argument is moot. If there is a severe shortage, then it would be easy for employers to show one. Yet they've opposed any such requirement."

How Much of the Debate Is about Outsourcing?

One of the most consequential criticisms of the H-1B program is its heavy use by IT outsourcing firms such as Infosys, Tata Consultancy Services, and Wipro. Outsourcing has been a trend in information management for years, as companies have increasingly hired contractors (at lower cost) to do tasks such as software programming and data entry, processing, and storage.

Here's a simplified way to explain how this plays out: Say you're a big company with your own IT department. To reduce overhead, or to cut costs, or to increase efficiency, you decide to contract out (outsource) some or all of your IT work. So you hire an IT services firm to do that work on a temporary, as-needed basis. That firm sends workers, many of whom are on H-1B visas, to do those tasks. Sometimes, these contract workers supplement your IT staff; other times, you lay off your IT staff and the contractors effectively replace them.

Because these IT firms receive so many H-1B visas, there are fewer for other companies. "No matter what your view on outsourcing is, this was not the original intent of the program," says William Kerr, an economist at Harvard Business School who has studied the effects of high-skilled immigration in the U.S. "One of the implications of this is it reduces the number of visas available for their original purposes."

"The outsourcing companies bring lower-level workers than the American tech companies," Kerr says. "That work has $60,000 salaries, which is not minimum wage by any means, but it's lower paid than a typical computer scientist at a large U.S. tech employer."

IT companies in India and the U.S. have lobbied against making the H-1B program more restrictive, arguing that they help American companies become more competitive by handling their IT operations. They've also said that the visa programs allow them to keep jobs in the U.S., so reducing the number of visas they're allowed may result in them shifting work back to India. (However, Bloomberg recently reported that Infosys plans to create thousands of new jobs for Americans over the next two years.)

What Could Change?

Any big changes to the H-1B program would have to be passed by Congress. At least four proposals to reform it have recently surfaced, and USCIS has suspended expedited processing of H-1B applications.

Wider reforms would change the way many companies, especially tech and IT firms, recruit and hire highly skilled talent. Further restricting the number of visas could cost the U.S. a competitive edge in the global war for tech talent.

"This might sound self-serving, coming from someone who works in academia, but one thing that has helped maintain our technological leadership is innovation and technical research, and immigration has helped us do that," Hanson says. "Immigration is an important part of why the U.S. is able to maintain its elite status."

Trump's "Buy American and Hire American" order aims to address some of the concerns surrounding the H-1B visa system. The larger effects on high-skilled immigration—and on the economy—remain to be seen.

Print Citations

CMS: Torres, Nicole. "The H-1B Visa Debate, Explained." In *The Reference Shelf: The National Debate Topic 2018–2019 Immigration*, edited by Betsy Maury, 53-58. Ipswich, MA: H.W. Wilson, 2018.

MLA: Torres, Nicole. "The H-1B Visa Debate, Explained." *The Reference Shelf: The National Debate Topic 2018–2019 Immigration*. Ed. Betsy Maury. Ipswich: H.W. Wilson, 2018. 53-58. Print.

APA: Torres, N. (2018). The H-1B visa debate, explained. In Betsy Maury (Ed.), *The reference shelf: The national debate topic 2018–2019 immigration* (pp. 53-58). Ipswich, MA: H.W. Wilson. (Original work published 2017)

Feds Prosecuting Illegal Immigrants for Enticing Relatives to U.S.

By Stephen Dinan
The Washington Times, **March 12, 2018**

An illegal immigrant from Guatemala was sentenced to seven months in jail late last month for paying human smugglers to bring his 16-year-old brother-in-law into the U.S., in what officials say is one of the first cases to punish a relative for enticing a family member to make the dangerous trek north.

Miguel Pacheco-Lopez admitted he paid $6,100 to "coyotes," as the smugglers are called, to bring his wife's brother into the U.S. last year. He expected the teen— identified in court documents by the initials S.M. —to pay the majority of the money back at 8 percent interest.

The prosecution was part of a groundbreaking strategy to try to slow the stream of unaccompanied alien children by going after the people they are trying to join in the U.S.

"This criminal jeopardized his own family members by paying human smugglers," said James C. Spero, special agent in charge at the Tampa office of homeland security investigations. "He endangered a child's life with a dangerous and unlawful journey into the United States, and now he will be held accountable."

Pursuing people who are paying to have their family members smuggled to the U.S. has always been among the trickiest parts of the immigration debate.

Immigrant rights activists say they are often trying to help relatives escape terrible conditions back home and should be viewed as part of a humanitarian mission.

But analysts who have pushed for stiffer policies toward illegal immigration cheered the conviction and sentencing.

"It's long overdue, and it's something that they have to do to deter people from paying smugglers," said Jessica Vaughan, policy studies director at the Center for Immigration Studies. "It's dangerous for the kids, not to mention that it enriches a criminal enterprise."

She said the courts have tied the administration's hands on many other areas of enforcement, such as the ability to detain and quickly deport illegal immigrant children, so some other deterrent was needed.

President Trump teased the policy in his initial immigration executive orders. As homeland security secretary, John F. Kelly elaborated on the plan in a Feb. 20, 2017, implementation memo. He said the parents were putting their children through unimaginable hardship on the journey north.

Beatings, killings and rape are reportedly common—so much so that some teen girls preparing to make the journey would take birth control to avoid becoming pregnant from rape along the way.

"Regardless of the desires for family reunification, or conditions in other countries, the smuggling or trafficking of alien children is intolerable," Mr. Kelly wrote in the memo.

He ordered his agencies to consider deporting or even criminally charging those who paid the children's way.

Bryan Johnson, an immigration lawyer who penned a letter to Mr. Kelly last year asking him to drop the policy, said he had heard of no other conviction like Pacheco-Lopez

"DHS is using this one conviction in hopes that it deters future unaccompanied minors from entering USA. Same philosophy as under Obama but with more extreme tactics," Mr. Johnson told the *Washington Times*. "And, just as in Obama administration, this deterrence-at-all-costs policy may have temporary effects, but in long term it will do little to nothing to stop unaccompanied minors from coming so long as the conditions there—extreme violence and poverty—persist."

> **Pursuing people who are paying to have their family members smuggled to the U.S. has always been among the trickiest parts of the immigration debate.**

A spokeswoman for U.S. Immigration and Customs Enforcement declined to provide more details about the case, but Pacheco-Lopez turned out to be the thread that unraveled a much bigger illegal immigration operation.

Court documents show that when agents went to first talk to Pacheco-Lopez, the address they were given in Jacksonville turned out to have at least a half-dozen other illegal immigrants living there and working at a Japanese steakhouse along with Pacheco-Lopez.

The owners of Fujiyama Steakhouse and Sushi Lounge, a husband and wife from China, were paying illegal immigrants low wages but letting them live in the crowded house. They were convicted and sentenced to probation.

The case illustrated some of the other difficulties presented by the surge of illegal immigrants.

Pacheco-Lopez's native language is K'iche', which is Mayan. Authorities had to find qualified K'iche' interpreters. Those interpreters didn't speak English well, so they translated Pacheco-Lopez's words into Spanish. ICE officers who were fluent in English and Spanish did the final translation into English.

Agents and prosecutors said they weren't surprised that just one person has been convicted of paying for smuggling.

One immigration agent said federal officers have a tough time getting prosecutors to take the cases. The agent said it can be difficult to prove the trail of cash and that prosecutors may be reluctant to take on cases in which the illegal immigrants may seem sympathetic.

The agent said the Florida case might have been easier to make because Pacheco-Lopez was charging his brother interest, suggesting a business transaction more than a family unification effort.

Parents' and other family members' involvement in smuggling has been a sore spot for authorities for years.

In one groundbreaking 2013 opinion, U.S. District Judge Andrew S. Hanen blasted the Obama administration for complicity in human smuggling. He said that by delivering illegal immigrant children to their parents—usually also in the U.S. illegally—the government was effectively "completing the criminal mission" of the smugglers.

He was reviewing a case in which an illegal immigrant mother living in Virginia paid for her daughter to be smuggled into the country. The woman attempting the smuggling was caught after using one of her daughters' birth certificates for the illegal immigrant girl.

But Homeland Security delivered the girl to her mother anyway. Judge Hanen said he was stunned that Homeland Security didn't arrest or even try to deport the mother.

"The DHS, instead of enforcing our border security laws, actually assisted the criminal conspiracy in achieving its illegal goals," he wrote.

Judge Hanen went on to become the first to invalidate the 2014 Deferred Action for the Parents of Americans policy that Mr. Obama tried to create. DAPA would have expanded the 2012 DACA deportation amnesty to include parents of U.S. citizens, which would have covered millions of illegal immigrants.

Print Citations

CMS: Dinan, Stephen. "Feds Prosecuting Illegal Immigrants for Enticing Relatives to U.S." In *The Reference Shelf: The National Debate Topic 2018–2019 Immigration*, edited by Betsy Maury, 59-61. Ipswich, MA: H.W. Wilson, 2018.

MLA: Dinan, Stephen. "Feds Prosecuting Illegal Immigrants for Enticing Relatives to U.S." *The Reference Shelf: The National Debate Topic 2018–2019 Immigration*. Ed. Betsy Maury. Ipswich: H.W. Wilson, 2018. 59-61. Print.

APA: Dinan, S. (2018). Feds prosecuting illegal immigrants for enticing relatives to U.S. In Betsy Maury (Ed.), *The reference shelf: The national debate topic 2018–2019 immigration* (pp. 59-61). Ipswich, MA: H.W. Wilson. (Original work published 2018)

"Dreamers" Could Give US Economy—and Even American Workers—a Boost

By Amy Hsin
The Conversation, January 19, 2018

Earlier this month, hopes were high that a bipartisan deal could be reached to resolve the fate of the "Dreamers," the millions of undocumented youth who were brought to the U.S. as children.

Those hopes all but vanished on Jan. 11 as President Donald Trump aligned himself with hard-line anti-immigration advocates within the GOP and struck down bipartisan attempts to reach a resolution.

As we enter the final hours before a potential government shutdown, many Democrats are insisting that any short-term funding agreement must include a resolution for Dreamers.

One of the arguments advanced by those who oppose giving them citizenship is that doing so would hurt native-born workers and be a drain on the U.S. economy. My own research shows the exact opposite is true.

Lives in Limbo

All in all, about 3.6 million immigrants living in the U.S. entered the country as children. Without options for legal residency, their lives hang in the balance.

To address this problem, the Obama administration created the Deferred Action for Childhood Arrivals program in 2012. DACA gave almost 800,000 of them temporary legal work permits and reprieve from deportation. Although his successor terminated the program in September, this month a federal court halted that process, allowing current recipients the ability to renew their status.

Any cause for celebration, however, was short-lived as the Department of Justice immediately responded by asking the Supreme Court to overturn the ruling. The Supreme Court has not yet announced a decision. In the meantime, the future of DACA recipients remains uncertain.

Today, the best hope for a permanent fix for the Dreamers rests on bipartisan efforts to enact the 2017 DREAM Act—for Development, Relief and Education for Alien Minors—which would extend pathways to citizenship to undocumented youth who entered the United States as children, graduated from high school and have no criminal record. A version of the act was first introduced in 2001.

The debate surrounding the DREAM Act is often framed around two seemingly irreconcilable views.

On one side, immigration activists advocate for legalization based on pleas to our common humanity. These Dreamers, after all, were raised and educated in the United States. They are American in every sense but legally.

On the other, critics contend that legalization will come at a cost to U.S.-born workers, and their well-being should be prioritized.

Impact of Dreamer Citizenship on Wages

My research with economists Ryan Edwards and Francesco Ortega estimated the economic impact of the 2017 DREAM Act if it were to become law. About 2.1 million of the undocumented youths would likely be eligible to become citizens based on its age and educational requirements.

Our research showed that immigrants given permanent legal work permits under the DREAM Act would not compete with low-skilled U.S.-born workers because only those with at least a high school degree are eligible for legalization. The act also encourages college attendance by making it one of the conditions for attaining legal residency.

We also found that the act would have no significant effect on the wages of U.S.-born workers regardless of education level because Dreamers make up such a small fraction of the labor force. U.S.-born college graduates and high school dropouts would experience no change in wages. Those with some college may experience small declines of at most 0.2 percent a year, while high school graduates would actually experience wage increases of a similar magnitude.

> Our research shows a policy that affirms our common humanity also increases economic growth without hurting U.S.-born workers.

For the legalized immigrants, however, the benefits would be substantial. For example, legalized immigrants with some college education would see wages increase by about 15 percent, driven by expansions in employment opportunities due to legalization and by the educational gains that the DREAM Act encourages.

Broader Economic Benefits

The DREAM Act also promotes overall economic growth by increasing the productivity of legalized workers and expanding the tax base.

Lacking legal work options, Dreamers tend to be overqualified for the jobs they hold. My ongoing work with sociologist Holly Reed shows that the undocumented youth who make it to college are more motivated and academically prepared compared with their U.S.-born peers. This is at least in part because they had to overcome greater odds to attend college.

We find that they are also more likely than their native-born peers to graduate college with a degree. Yet despite being highly motivated and accomplished, undocumented college graduates are employed in jobs that are not commensurate with their education level, according to sociologist Esther Cho. With legal work options, they will be able to find jobs that match their skills and qualifications, making them more productive.

Legalization also improves the mental health of immigrants by removing the social stigma of being labeled a criminal and the looming threat of arrest and deportation.

From an economic standpoint, healthier and happier workers also make for a more productive workforce.

Overall, we estimate that the increases in productivity under the DREAM Act would raise the United States GDP by US$15.2 billion and significantly increase tax revenue.

Everyone Can Win

The U.S. continues to grapple with how to incorporate the general population of nearly 11 million undocumented immigrants living in the country.

The inability of the Trump administration and lawmakers from both parties to find common ground is emblematic of just how deeply divided Americans are between those who want to send most of them home and others who favor a path toward citizenship for many if not most of them.

While there appears to be no resolution in sight for the general population of 11 million undocumented immigrants living in the United States, common bipartisan ground can be found on the issue of Dreamers. A recent survey found that 86 percent of Americans support granting them amnesty.

The DREAM Act offers an opportunity to enact a permanent resolution for a group widely supported by the public. What is more, our research shows a policy that affirms our common humanity also increases economic growth without hurting U.S.-born workers.

This is a win-win for everyone, whether you care about social justice or worry about U.S. workers.

Print Citations

CMS: Hsin, Amy. "'Dreamers' Could Give US Economy—and Even American Workers—a Boost." In *The Reference Shelf: The National Debate Topic 2018–2019 Immigration*, edited by Betsy Maury, 62-64. Ipswich, MA: H.W. Wilson, 2018.

MLA: Hsin, Amy. "'Dreamers' Could Give US Economy—and Even American Workers—a Boost." *The Reference Shelf: The National Debate Topic 2018–2019 Immigration*. Ed. Betsy Maury. Ipswich: H.W. Wilson, 2018. 62-64. Print.

APA: Hsin, A. (2018). "Dreamers" could give US economy—and even American workers—a boost. In Betsy Maury (Ed.), *The reference shelf: The national debate topic 2018–2019 immigration* (pp. 62-64). Ipswich, MA: H.W. Wilson. (Original work published 2018)

To Curb Illegal Immigration, DHS Separating Families at the Border

By John Burnett
NPR, February 27, 2018

The Department of Homeland Security has undertaken its most extreme measure yet to discourage asylum seekers from coming to the U.S.—family separation.

A 39-year-old mother is named as Ms. L in a lawsuit brought against the U.S. Department of Homeland Security by the American Civil Liberties Union. Ms. L traveled with her 7-year-old daughter, named as S.S., from the Democratic Republic of Congo to Mexico. They surrendered to immigration agents at the San Ysidro Port of Entry near San Diego in December and asked for asylum. They said they were fleeing violence in DRC.

The mother is being held in the Otay Mesa Detention Center in San Diego, Calif. by Immigration and Customs Enforcement; her daughter is 2,000 miles away at a youth shelter in Chicago run by the U.S. Office of Refugee Resettlement. They are only able to speak by phone.

"When the daughter was taken, she (Ms. L) could hear her daughter in the next room, screaming, 'Mommy, don't let them take me!'" said Lee Gelernt, deputy director of the ACLU Immigrants' Rights Project.

The lawsuit claims that immigration agents violated the Congolese mother's constitutional right to due process when they took her daughter away. It asks the government, if it is going to detain them during the asylum process, at least allow them to be together.

"The child has become the pawn in a public policy move by the administration trying to deter other asylum seekers," said Gelernt.

Under Obama, DHS detained some unauthorized families in camps in South Texas rather than release them in the U.S. while their cases are heard. But the Trump administration has gone further, arresting immigrant parents in the U.S. who paid smugglers to bring their children across the border. It also wants to expand detention space for immigrants.

Asked why the mother and child were separated, Katie Waldman, a public affairs officer with Homeland Security emailed NPR: "As a matter of policy, we don't comment on pending litigation."

The practice of separating undocumented families to discourage them from coming to the U.S. is not a formal, stated policy of the Trump administration. But immigrant activists say it has been quietly growing in frequency along the southern border.

"The increase in family separation is something that's being documented by organizations around the country. We began to hear a noticeable increase in this practice in the summer," said Katharina Obser, senior policy advisor with the Women's Refugee Commission. Her organization and other immigrant advocates released a report in December denouncing ICE's use of family separation. And earlier this

> **The Department of Homeland Security has undertaken its most extreme measure yet to discourage asylum seekers from coming to the U.S.— family separation.**

month, 75 Democratic members of Congress sent a letter to Homeland Security Secretary Kirstjen Nielsen blasting family separation as wrong and unlawful.

Lutheran Immigration and Refugee Service has documented 53 incidents of family separation in the last nine months, mostly Central Americans. Other immigrant support groups say there are many more cases.

Asylum seekers from Central America say they're fleeing rampant gang violence. But the administration believes most of them are gaming the system.

"It's terrible what these smugglers do to these individuals," Matt Albence, an executive associate director with ICE told NPR's *All Things Considered* in December. "We need to realize that stopping this flow and preventing these crossings is the best thing that we can do right now."

He added, "It's a huge operational problem. We have hundreds of thousands of these cases clogging up the immigration court docket. A vast majority of these individuals that get to this country and served with a notice to appear in front of an immigration judge don't show up."

Immigration lawyers say the tactic is effective—mothers may drop their cases and go home in order to be reunited with their children.

But is that a reasonable way to curtail illegal immigration?

"Separations from their parents, especially in moments of extreme distress and displacement, has very negative impact on child well being, mental health, and development," said Dr. Lisa Fortuna, director of Child and Adolescent Psychiatry at Boston Medical Center. As an expert on the impact of trauma on immigrant families, she submitted an amicus brief in the ACLU lawsuit.

"And I don't think that we want to be a society that does that to children," Fortuna said.

Print Citations

CMS: Burnett, John. "To Curb Immigration, DHS Separating Families at the Border." In *The Reference Shelf: The National Debate Topic 2018–2019 Immigration*, edited by Betsy Maury, 65-67. Ipswich, MA: H.W. Wilson, 2018.

MLA: Burnett, John. "To Curb Immigration, DHS Separating Families at the Border." *The Reference Shelf: The National Debate Topic 2018–2019 Immigration*. Ed. Betsy Maury. Ipswich: H.W. Wilson, 2018. 65-67. Print.

APA: Burnett, J. (2018). To curb immigration, DHS separating families at the border. In Betsy Maury (Ed.), *The reference shelf: The national debate topic 2018–2019 immigration* (pp. 65-67). Ipswich, MA: H.W. Wilson. (Original work published 2018)

3
The Census

New York Attorney General Eric Schneiderman speaks at a press conference to announce a multi-state lawsuit to block the Trump administration from adding a question about citizenship to the 2020 Census form, at the headquarters of District Council 37, New York City's largest public employee union, April 3, 2018 in New York City. Also pictured, L to R, U.S. Rep. Nydia Velazquez (D-NY), U.S. Rep. Jerrold Nadler, Steve Choi, executive director of the New York Immigration Coalition, U.S. Rep. Grace Meng (D-NY) , U.S. Rep. Carolyn Maloney (D-NY), Oregon Attorney General Ellen Rosenblum. Critics of President Donald Trump's administration's decision to reinstate the citizenship question contend that that it will frighten people in immigrant communities from responding to the census. The Trump administration has stated a citizenship question on the census will help enforce voting rights.

The Politics of Demography: The Census Bureau and Immigration

The news is filled with statistics. Stock prices are ticked off in financial columns, unemployment rates, crime rates, divorce rates, and graduation rates fuel the calls to arms of activists and pundits, and opinion polls track the daily progress of the government. Each day, news consumers are presented with a dizzying variety of mathematical measures representing the abstracted enumeration of their past, present, and potential futures. Beneath all of this is the US Census Bureau, a branch of the government responsible for collecting demographic data on the US population and making that data available to researchers, politicians, and the public alike.

Every ten years, the Census Bureau provides a statistical snapshot that guides the next decade of policy, governmental priority, and activism. These official statistics affect the daily lives of Americans. They influence the tax structure, they determine where federal and state money will be spent, and they provide heft to the many social movements in every generation.

Collecting and analyzing data is a scientific process and based, in part, on adherence to rules and methods designed to increase accuracy and to enhance the usefulness of the data derived from each study. However, this does not mean that the data resulting from such activities is a quantitative reflection of reality. As William Alonso and Paul Starr write in their 1986 book *The Politics of Numbers*, "Official statistics do not merely hold a mirror to reality. They reflect presupposition and theories about the nature of society. They are products of social, political, and economic interests that are often in conflict with one another."[1] What the authors mean is that the census is a political process and the US Census Bureau a political organ, subject to the same contests for power that underlie all political evolution. Each time a new decennial census arrives, politicians and political activists debate changes to the census that might increase the accuracy the information derived but might also have wide reaching impacts on the lives of some American citizens. Approaching the 2020 decennial study, immigration has become a central issue as experts and politicians debate whether the Census Bureau should ask Americans about their citizenship status.

By law, all information collected by census takers is confidential and cannot be shared with other branches of government in such a way as to identify individuals from the data they provide. Laws protecting the confidentiality of census data are intended to establish trust such that individuals in the public will give accurate information, even on issues concerning criminal activities or involving private information. Employees of the census bureau are also legally prohibited from using the data derived from the census to further any specific political cause or goal of a single party, administration, or movement. However, the history of the census makes it clear that the information collected and how it is used has always been highly political and this fact of history makes it difficult for some Americans to trust the census system.

The Political History of the Census

According to the United States Constitution, the Census Bureau is only officially responsible for executing a simple population count every ten years. The first census count was held in 1790, at which time census data was collected by US Federal Marshals. The first census gathered information on six categories of US persons, free white males over 16, free white males under 16, free white females, all other free persons, and slaves.

Whether or not to count slaves was the first major census controversy and, in 1787, there was a fierce debate on the issue in Congress. This was because the population of each state determined the level of representation that the state would be afforded in Congress. Southern states wanted slaves to be counted, because it would mean more representation for the South, while northern representatives argued that this would be unfair to the northern populations. The result was the now infamous "three-fifths compromise," in which each slave was counted as three-fifths of a person for the purposes of determining representation. This compromise, and the debate surrounding it, was part of a larger philosophical debate about whether slaves should be considered property or persons.[2]

It was in the 1850s that the Census Bureau began collecting "social statistics" on the population, including data on taxes, school attendance, graduation rates, crime, and wages and it was also during this census, the seventh decennial census, that census takers began asking about nation of birth and thus developing statistics that could be used, in conjunction with data from immigration authorities, to evaluate immigration and migration patterns.[3] When census takers began asking questions about country of origin, specific data was taken on western European immigrants, with far less attention paid to the specifics of immigrant populations from other parts of the world.

Twenty years later, in the 1870s census, the bureau added, for the first time, the racial categories of "Indian" and "Chinese" to the census and the decision to add these new categories reflects the political controversies of the era. The anti-Chinese movement that emerged in the 1840s led to calls for a legal response, preventing Chinese immigration, ostensibly to protect jobs though the underlying motivation was more realistically racial prejudice and income inequality. Data on the number of Chinese citizens and immigrants collected in the 1870 census became a political tool used by pundits calling for legal remedies and this resulted in the 1882 Chinese Exclusion Act that prohibited all Chinese immigration.

In the 1920s, the United States adopted a new framework for immigration in which the number of visas available to people from each country was based on the proportion of people from that country living in the nation as of the time of the 1890 census. The goal of the system was to preserve the balance of races and ethnicities living in the United States; this was based entirely on demographic data from the decennial census. One of the primary goals of the quota system was to prevent the immigration of Jewish people and nonwhite people. For this reason, the 1890 census was chosen as the basis for the quotas, rather than using the 1900, 1910, or 1920 census data, which was also available. There were fewer non-white people living in the United States in 1890 and so basing the quotas on this census guaranteed that few visas would be made available to Jewish people from eastern or southern Europe or to nonwhite people from any other country. The quota system lasted until the 1960s and demonstrates another time in history when census data was used in an overtly political manner to preserve the dominance of America's white, Christian population.

When the quota system ended in 1965, there was an influx of immigrants from Asia, Africa, and the Americas. Gradually the US Census Bureau adjusted by adding new categories for national origin and racial identification, such as the addition of "Hispanic" in the 1970 census. This change, a major milestone in the census bureau's measurements of racial minorities was inspired in part by lobbying through the Chicano civil rights movement. This is an important development leading to the modern debate about whether or not the census should include citizenship data. Until the 1950s, census takers did ask about citizenship status, but this question was abandoned in an effort to encourage more accurate information from respondents.[4] On March 27, 2018, the US Department of Commerce revealed that the 2020 decennial census would contain a question about citizenship, a decision designed to gather more data on the nation's immigrant population. Critics argue that the citizenship question will discourage honesty and so skew the information collected.

Citizenship and the Census

Immediately after the announcement that the 2020 census could contain a citizenship question, CNN reported that 19 state attorneys general had already announced their intention to fight the inclusion of the question on the census. Kristen Clarke, President and Executive director of the Lawyers' Committee for Civil Rights Under Law told CNN, "This is an arbitrary and untested decision that all but guarantees that the Census will not produce a full and accurate count of the population as the constitution requires."[5]

Supporters of the decision argue that data on citizenship status is already collected for the yearly American Community Survey (ACS) a Census Bureau program established in 2005 to gather more detailed data within larger American communities. The Department of Commerce's official position is that, like the ACS, more detailed data on ethnicity and origin is needed to increase the accuracy of the census.[6] Critics are not convinced, and many worry that the change will be used to create new political districts in such a way as to benefit Republican candidates. This kind of political manipulation is common in history and the Republican Party has frequently used redistricting and voter-ID laws as methods of limiting the impact of minority voters, who do not typically favor conservative candidates. Another possibility is that undocumented migrants simply won't complete the census, thereby resulting in undercounting and this could mean reduced federal support for the 20 metropolitan areas where the majority of the nation's undocumented migrant population resides.[7]

The rules for the collection and use of census data are provided in Title 13 of the U.S. Code, which became law on August 31, 1954. According to Title 13 provisions, private information is never published and it is against the law to disclose or publish information that can be used to identify an individual from the data collected. Data collected by the Census Bureau also cannot legally be used by any government agency or court. Each employee of the Census Bureau must swear an oath to maintain the confidentiality of their data and violations of Title 13 can hold penalties including federal imprisonment of up to five years and fines of up to $250,000.[8] Therefore, in theory, data collected by the Census Bureau is confidential and those participating would have nothing to fear in revealing their citizenship status. However, this does not mean that the nation's undocumented residents can and will trust that Title 13 will be honored.

A 2007 study by sociologists Margo Anderson and statistician William Seltzer revealed details of a controversial chapter in census history with relevance to the modern census debate. The researchers, studying years of US Department of Commerce documents found that the US Census Bureau collected the names and addresses of Japanese people living in the United States and turned these names over to the US Secret Service during World War II. The Secret Service then used this data to detain and intern over 100,000 Japanese immigrants and citizens for the duration of the war. Supporters of Japanese internment argued that Japanese individuals still had hidden allegiance to Japan and so might serve as spies and saboteurs while the United States was fighting Japan in the Pacific Theater of the war. However, history clearly shows that the internment of Japanese people was the result of racism more than political consideration. Consider, for instance, that German and Italian immigrants and descendants were not targeted for surveillance or interned despite the fact that German citizens had been discovered involved in plots to sabotage the United States from within.[9]

The revelation that census data was used, illegally and inappropriately, in secret governmental surveillance programs is one of many controversial developments in the twentieth and twenty-first centuries that have eroded public faith and trust in the government. In 2017, for instance, *Pew Research* reported that only 18 percent of Americans believe they could trust the government to do what was right all (3 percent) or most of the time (15 percent). In 1958, by contrast, nearly three quarters of Americans trusted their government all or most of the time. While demographic data on citizenship might provide a useful source of information for researchers, demographers, and politicians, the distrust of the government—especially by immigrants and minority Americans—creates the potential that the addition of a citizenship question will influence how the data is collected and will potentially skew the information derived from the study.

Works Used

Alonso, William and Paul Starr. *The Politics of Numbers*. New York: Russel Sage Foundation, 1986.

Applestein, Donald. "The Three-Fifths Compromise: Rationalizing the Irrational." *Constitution Center*. The National Constitution Center. Feb 12, 2013. Web. Retrieved from https://constitutioncenter.org/blog/the-three-fifths-compromise-rationalizing-the-irrational/.

Blakemore, Erin. "How the U.S. Census Defines Race." *Smithsonian Mag*. Smart News. Smithsonian Institution. Nov 9, 2015. Web. https://www.smithsonian-mag.com/smart-news/how-us-census-defines-race-america-180957189/.

Brusk, Steve and Gregory Wallace. "Commerce Department Says Citizenship Question Will Be Reinstated in 2020 Census." *CNN Politics*. CNN. Mar 27, 2018. Web. https://www.cnn.com/2018/03/26/politics/census-citizenship-question/index.html.

Hartmann, Margaret. "Trump's Census Change Could Give the GOP an Advantage for Years to Come." *New York Magazine*. Daily Intelligencer. Mar 27, 2018. Web. http://nymag.com/daily/intelligencer/2018/03/trumps-census-change-could-boost-the-gop-for-years-to-come.html.

"History." *Census.gov*. United States Census Bureau. 2018. Web. https://www.census.gov/history/.

Minkel, J.R. "Confirmed: The U.S. Census Bureau Gave Up Names of Japanese-Americans in WW II." *Scientific American*. Smithsonian Institution. Mar 30, 2007. Web. https://www.scientificamerican.com/article/confirmed-the-us-census-b/.

"Public Trust in Government: 1958-2017." *Pew Research*. Pew Research Center. May 3, 2017. Web. http://www.people-press.org/2017/05/03/public-trust-in-government-1958-2017/.

"Title 13, U.S. Code." *Census Bureau*. U.S. Census Bureau. Web. https://www.census.gov/history/www/reference/privacy_confidentiality/title_13_us_code.html.

"Trump Is Intelligent, but Not Fit or Level Headed," *Quinnipiac University*. Jan 10, 2018. Web. https://poll.qu.edu/images/polling/us/us01102018_uss771.pdf/.

"Why We're Reinstating Census Citizenship Question." *USA Today*. Mar 27, 2018. Web. https://www.usatoday.com/story/opinion/2018/03/27/census-question-editorials-debates/33340397/.

Notes

1. Alonso and Starr, *The Politics of Numbers*, 1.
2. Applestein, "The Three-Fifths Compromise: Rationalizing the Irrational."
3. "History," *Census Bureau*.
4. Blakemore, "How the U.S. Census Defines Race."
5. Brusk and Wallace, "Commerce Department Says Citizenship Question Will Be Reinstated in 2020 Census."
6. "Why We're Reinstating Census Citizenship Question," *USA Today*.

7. Hartmann, "Trump's Census Change Could Give the GOP an Advantage for Years to Come."
8. "Title 13, U.S. Code," *Census Bureau*.
9. Minkel, "Confirmed: The U.S. Census Bureau Gave Up Names of Japanese-Americans in WW II."

The Controversial Question DOJ Wants to Add to the U.S. Census

By Priscilla Alvarez
The Atlantic, January 10, 2018

A recent request by the Department of Justice to add a question on citizenship to the 2020 census could threaten participation, and as a consequence, affect the allocation of federal money and distribution of congressional seats.

In December, the Department of Justice sent a letter to the Census Bureau asking that it reinstate a question on citizenship to the 2020 census. "This data is critical to the Department's enforcement of Section 2 of the Voting Rights Act and its important protections against racial discrimination in voting," the department said in a letter. "To fully enforce those requirements, the Department needs a reliable calculation of the citizen voting-age population in localities where voting rights violations are alleged or suspected." The request immediately met pushback from census experts, civil-rights advocates, and a handful of Democratic senators, who say that the argument is unfounded and that the timing of the request is irresponsible.

The census is used for allocating nearly $700 billion a year in federal money, electoral votes, as well as for the apportionment of House districts—that is, deciding how many representatives a state sends to Congress each year. The Census Act requires that all questions asked on the census fulfill a purpose. "If the Census Bureau or the administration can establish that there is a legal requirement, a requirement in law for citizenship data for the smallest levels of geography, then that would be justification for asking every household about the citizenship status of household members but no such law exists right now," said Terri Ann Lowenthal, an independent consultant and leading expert on census issues. The bureau is then required to submit a final list of questions, which are tested beforehand, for the decennial census two years before its roll out. The bureau needs to send the questions for the 2020 census to Congress by April, leaving the bureau little opportunity to test a new question before submitting it to Congress.

Congressional apportionment is based on overall population, not citizens, specifically, therefore an inaccurate count would directly affect how seats in the U.S. House are distributed. That means that if fewer undocumented immigrants or minorities are willing to participate in the census, it could affect the political balance in Congress, since those populations tend to be concentrated in cities, where Democrats draw most of their support. According to a study by Election Data Services

Inc., based on population estimates by the Census Bureau, up to 16 states could either lose or gain a congressional seat as a result of the decennial census. Minnesota, for example, is at risk of losing a seat in the House and is relying on an accurate census count to keep it.

Some Republicans and anti-immigration groups see the undocumented population as conferring an unfair advantage on Democrats.

"If 50 percent of the illegal alien population resides in California and we're not differentiating them in the census and we're basing apportionment in the census on those figures, then some states are losing representation while others are over-represented," said Chris Chmielenski, the director of content and activism at NumbersUSA, which supports reduced immigration. Republican Representative Steve King of Iowa, an ardent opponent of immigration in the House, expressed support for the DOJ's request, arguing that it would benefit his state: "In districts like Maxine Waters, who only needs about 40,000 votes to get reelected in her district and it takes me over 120,000 in mine because hers is loaded with illegals and mine only has a few."

The Justice Department says that asking the entire U.S. population about their citizenship status is necessary for the enforcement of the Voting Rights Act, which prohibits racial discrimination at the polls. The last time the entire U.S. population was asked about citizenship status was in 1950, 15 years before the law's passage. Since then, the question has been included in the American Community Survey, which is sent out every year to a sample of the population; census experts say that's enough to enforce the Voting Rights Act.

"I think the argument ridiculous. The Justice Department has never needed or asked for that question on the short form of the census before and the enforcement of the Voting Rights Act does not need it," said Vanita Gupta, the president and CEO of the Leadership Conference on Civil and Human Rights who ran DOJ's Civil Rights Division under Obama, referring to the form that is sent to every household. Census experts and civil-rights advocates argue that there's no justification for asking everyone in the United States about their citizenship status and that doing so could have a crippling effect on participation.

The Census Bureau said in a statement that it's "evaluating the request from the U.S. Department of Justice and will process it in the same way we have historically dealt with such requests." It continued: "The final list of questions must be submitted to Congress by March 31, 2018. Secretary Ross will then make a decision. Our top priority is a complete and accurate 2020 census."

Questions on the census, the first of which took place in 1790, have changed over the years depending on what was most relevant to the time period. In the mid-19th century, for example, the census began asking respondents where they were born to track internal migration. "Why questions go off and on the census often has to do with competing interests," said Margo Anderson, a professor of history and urban studies at the University of Wisconsin-Milwaukee and author of *The American Census: A Social History*. She added that after the passage of the Immigration and Nationality Act of 1965, which dramatically changed U.S. immigration policy by ending a quota system based on national origin, the census reinstated a question on citizenship but only to a sample of respondents.

Statisticians over the years had been learning new ways to collect data, particularly in sample sizes, allowing the bureau to pose questions to a segment of the population and therefore lessen the burden on people while still gathering useful data. There was no longer a need then to ask everyone about their citizenship, which is considered an identifier and not a characteristic that would be used for statistical analysis; it could instead be asked to only some respondents. The "long-form" census, which

> **Based on population estimates by the Census Bureau, up to 16 states could either lose or gain a congressional seat as a result of the decennial census.**

included more questions and was only sent out to some respondents every 10 years, included a question on citizenship. Those answers quickly became dated, so the bureau introduced the American Community Survey, which would ask questions included in the "long-form" but do so every year. That continues to be the case today, fueling arguments against the DOJ's request to reinstate it in the general census.

Civil-rights and immigrant advocates worry that changes to the census will stunt the progress made in recent years to increase participation among minorities. Arturo Vargas, a member of the National Advisory Committee on Racial, Ethnic, and Other Populations, and the executive director of NALEO Educational Fund, a Latino advocacy group, noted that historically, the biggest challenge for the Census Bureau has been overcoming people's distrust.

"People are scared of how the federal government is enforcing immigration laws," Vargas said. "If a citizenship question is added to the decennial census, then this fear people have is going to result in less people wanting to respond to the census, which will produce a very inaccurate census and will actually increase the Census Bureau's cost and budget to conduct the census." In cases where the Census Bureau doesn't receive a response, it has to send enumerators to the address to interview those who haven't responded—an expensive process.

Respondents' recent reactions have led the bureau to believe this may be an issue in the 2020 census. Last year, field representatives found that respondents "intentionally provided incomplete or incorrect information about household members" and "seemed visibly nervous." In one Spanish interview, the respondent said, "The possibility that the Census could give my information to internal security and immigration could come and arrest me for not having documents terrifies me."

In fact, by law, the Census Bureau cannot provide personal information of any kind to a government agency. But that doesn't keep people from worrying about it, particularly those who may be undocumented or have mixed-status families. In the past, people unable to distinguish between immigration officers and government workers have been afraid of raids as officials went door-to-door asking for information, said Eric Rodriguez, the vice president of UnidosUS's Office of Research, Advocacy, and Legislation.

The federal government has tried to remedy these concerns. In 2000, U.S. Immigration and Naturalization issued a moratorium on highly visible enforcement so as not to interfere with the census. "It is crucial that undocumented as well as documented aliens understand that they are expected to respond to census-takers and questionnaires, and that there is no nexus between the census and INS enforcement activities," Michael A. Pearson, an executive assistant commissioner at the INS, wrote in a memo at the time.

Concerns shared about how some communities might react to the census therefore are not new, but they are worsened by this administration's crackdown on immigration.

This puts Latino advocacy groups in a bind: They need to encourage people to participate and raise awareness about the census, but they're doing so under an administration that has consistently used harsh rhetoric against immigrants and rolled out policies aimed at casting a wider net on those eligible for deportation.

Rodriguez said that what the government does in the coming years will have an effect on how respondents behave. "Quite honestly, it's just making sure that the government doesn't do things to create less trust in the census itself and doesn't do things to undermine the integrity of the Census Bureau in the process and that does have to do with information sharing agreements between agencies, what Homeland Security might in fact be doing over the next few years around deportations and enforcement and usage of government information," Rodriguez said. "All of those things could in fact substantively call into question what the government is doing and so, there's work that has to be done to in fact make sure that the government is obviously abiding to the law but not doing things that are detrimental to communities for whom we need a great and effective count in 2020."

Rodriguez likened the situation to the Deferred Action for Childhood Arrivals program, which Trump ended last year: Advocates encouraged people to sign up to the program, which shields immigrants brought to the U.S. as minors from deportation, but years later, those recipients are in limbo, as a result of the program's termination. "We have to go on the information that you have at the time, and for many, coming out of the shadows is an important opportunity," he said.

The prospect of asking millions of people what their citizenship status is enough to stir concern among observers and alienate minorities already worried about the information provided on the questionnaire.

Print Citations

CMS: Alvarez, Priscilla. "The Controversial Question DOJ Wants to Add to the U.S. Census." In *The Reference Shelf: The National Debate Topic 2018–2019 Immigration*, edited by Betsy Maury, 77-81. Ipswich, MA: H.W. Wilson, 2018.

MLA: Alvarez, Priscilla. "The Controversial Question DOJ Wants to Add to the U.S. Census." *The Reference Shelf: The National Debate Topic 2018–2019 Immigration*. Ed. Betsy Maury. Ipswich: H.W. Wilson, 2018. 77-81. Print.

APA: Alvarez, P. (2018). The controversial question DOJ wants to add to the U.S. census. In Betsy Maury (Ed.), *The reference shelf: The national debate topic 2018–2019 immigration* (pp. 77-81). Ipswich, MA: H.W. Wilson. (Original work published 2018)

The Census Has Always Been Political: Especially When It Comes to Race, Ethnicity, and National Origin

By Shom Mazumder
The Washington Post, **March 30, 2018**

Should the 2020 Census revive an old question about citizenship status—or is doing so too glaringly political? That's been debated hotly this week by pundits, state attorneys general, and more. Many worry that such a question will suppress minority responses—leading to an undercount of the population in "blue" states, with serious consequences for apportioning members of Congress and allocating federal funding for social programs.

But for better and for worse, the census has been political for a long time.

The U.S. Constitution mandates that the federal government run a census every decade to enumerate the country's residents. Though the census is primarily designed to count the population, the Supreme Court has recognized the government's ability to ask questions far beyond this scope.

That's where politics comes in.

Census Politics about Race Could Be Overt or Subtle—With Serious Consequences

Let's start with an overtly political question asked after the Civil War. To check on the progress of Reconstruction in the former Confederate South, the U.S. government included a question in 1870 asking whether a male citizen age 21 or above had had his "right to vote ... denied or abridged on other grounds than rebellion or other crime." The goal was to ensure that former slaves were being accepted as free citizens.

As the political will for Reconstruction quickly subsided, so too did the will to use this information for monitoring the progress of the 14th and 15th Amendments. The 1870 Census was the first and only one to ask about voting restrictions.

But that wasn't the end of the census's politicization of racial and ethnic identity and citizenship, which simply became more subtle. Jennifer Hochschild and Brenna Powell's research has shown how the census shapes and is shaped by our understanding of race, ethnicity and social identity.

Starting in 1850, the census began asking individuals about their country of birth—a move toward using the census to create racial and ethnic categories. Before 1930, the census experimented with a variety of options in which individuals could characterize themselves racially and ethnically, including identifying as "Hindoos" or as a member of the "Mexican race." All that shifted over time.

Take the case of Mexican Americans. For much of history, the U.S. census treated Mexicans as white. But in 1930, the Census Bureau began including a new option under race that was explicitly labeled "Mexican" —thereby separating Mexicans from whiteness. This was loudly protested by Mexican Americans and the Mexican diplomatic mission.

As the census director in 1936, William Lane Austin, commented, "The classification by race or color of individuals, or even entire populations, is not only very difficult, but is a very delicate matter to the United States Government." Recognizing the fraught intricacies of racial classification and its relationship to racial hierarchy, future censuses took the separate classification of Mexican off the table for several decades.

Such categories could have extremely serious consequences. For instance, during World War II, the Census Bureau gave the Secret Service the names and residences of people classified as Japanese or of Japanese descent, so they could be rounded up into camps.

The Politics of Asking about Citizenship

Asking about citizenship in tandem with national origin has been debated before. During the major immigration wave between 1850 and 1930, the United States had another heated debate about the pluses and minuses of the influx of "foreign" ethnicities, like the Irish, Italians and Slavs. Beginning in 1850 and lasting until 1950, in response to congressional and public demand for tracking the entrance of "desirable" races, the census asked where each individual was born, as well as his or her naturalization status.

The government used these censuses to track how well immigrants had assimilated, largely by comparing English literacy rates, employment status, and whether immigrants continued to live in enclaves. The Dillingham Commission—a House commission specifically appointed to investigate U.S. immigration in 1911—specifically drew on this data in concluding that Congress should restrict immigration. From this recommendation, Congress wrote and passed the 1924 Emergency Quota Acts, which severely restricted "undesirable" immigration from Southern and Eastern European countries, based on statistics computed from the results of the census.

Asking about Race and Ethnicity Always Has Political Consequences

Beginning in 2000, the census began allowing individuals to mark more than one race, in response to increasing rates of immigration and intermarriage. Civil rights groups such as the NAACP opposed the change, fearing that this would weaken

> **Though the census is primarily designed to count the population, the Supreme Court has recognized the government's ability to ask questions far beyond this scope.**

enforcement of voting rights and segregation policies, which were based on single-race population counts.

From these debates we get the prediction that the United States will be "majority minority" as of 2044—but based, of course, on previous generations' definitions, which will continue to change.

Not everyone agrees that measuring multiculturalism by enabling individuals to check as many boxes as they feel applies is sufficient. Some, including the American Anthropological Association (AAA), have repeatedly and unsuccessfully lobbied to eliminate the term "race" entirely. The idea is that not enumerating racial differences would help push American society into a post-racial world—that the definition is itself the division.

This is part of a broader argument advanced by the AAA that race itself is a social construct—a categorization without inherent meaning.

So What's at Stake Now?

There may be something to the AAA's argument. Work by political scientists Evan Lieberman and Prerna Singh shows that simply enumerating new groups in a census can create conflict. Looking at data across countries, and particularly examining India, they find that countries that enumerate new groups are more likely to have ethnic violence.

What's more, the questions asked on surveys can influence who responds and how they respond. For instance, an internal research report by the Census Bureau noted that, when asked about citizenship and national origin, respondents in a pilot survey "provided incomplete or incorrect information about household members ... tried to break off the interview ... and seemed visibly nervous."

Of course, that's the issue currently up for debate: Would merely asking about citizenship status reduce the number of people who fill out their census forms, thus artificially lowering the count of ethnic groups with large numbers of undocumented immigrants, and reducing the power of blue states? We shall see.

Print Citations

CMS: Mazumder, Shom. "The Census Has Always Been Political: Especially When It Comes to Race, Ethnicity, and National Origin." In *The Reference Shelf: The National Debate Topic 2018–2019 Immigration*, edited by Betsy Maury, 82-85. Ipswich, MA: H.W. Wilson, 2018.

MLA: Mazumder, Shom. "The Census Has Always Been Political: Especially When It Comes to Race, Ethnicity, and National Origin." *The Reference Shelf: The National Debate Topic 2018–2019 Immigration*. Ed. Betsy Maury. Ipswich: H.W. Wilson, 2018. 82-85. Print.

APA: Mazumder, S. (2018). The census has always been political: Especially when it comes to race, ethnicity, and national origin. In Betsy Maury (Ed.), *The reference shelf: The national debate topic 2018–2019 immigration* (pp. 82-85). Ipswich, MA: H.W. Wilson. (Original work published 2018)

Illegal Immigration Gives Cities Political Power

By James W. Lucas
National Review, March 30, 2018

The Commerce Department has announced that a question will be added to the 2020 Census asking about respondents' citizenship status. Democrats have responded with fury, and twelve states, led by California, will be suing to stop the change. While their argument is that the question will discourage illegal immigrants from participating in the survey, there is another, related reason why the urban elites who now dominate the Democratic party are afraid of this simple question.

With this question, the 2020 Census will better quantify the extent to which immigration, including illegal immigration, gives Democrats disproportionate political power—despite the fact that immigrants themselves are not allowed to vote. This happens because seats in the House, and consequently Electoral College votes as well, are given out based on the total number of people residing in a state.

California illustrates the problem. While the Census Bureau stopped asking about citizenship on the main Census form in 1960, it has continued to ask about it in other surveys. One of these, the American Community Survey, shows that the non-citizen proportion of the population in the states varies widely, ranging from 14 percent in California to less than 1 percent in West Virginia. Based on these estimates, California, the first sanctuary state, has five or six more members of the House than it would if House seats were based on citizen population alone.

No wonder California fears and opposes the citizenship question. What could happen if Americans in other states start asking why California should get more members of Congress and electoral votes by defying the nation's immigration laws?

Immigration has a profound effect on politics at the intra-state level as well. As between states, non-citizen immigrant populations are unevenly dispersed within states. They generally concentrate in urban areas, where they distort the apportionment of state legislatures and congressional seats even more than nationally. In my new book *Fifty States, Not Six*, I show how New York City has at least ten more seats in the 150-member assembly (the lower house of the New York State legislature) than it would if apportionment were based on the citizen population. In Illinois, Cook County (Chicago) has at least one extra seat in the U.S. House of Representatives based on counting its large non-citizen population. This pattern is found across the nation.

So, who benefits from these extra seats in the House of Representatives and state legislatures? It is not the non-citizen immigrants, who at least in theory are not allowed to vote. Instead, the votes for these extra seats go to the citizen residents of these urban areas. In *Fifty States, Not Six* I calculated that, owing to the presence of his non-citizen neighbors, a resident of New York City had 15 percent more voting power than did a New York State resident from outside the city.

California's non-citizen residents give California voters (mostly Democrats) about 11 percent more voting power than Americans in states with smaller immigrant populations have. So when Democrats like California senator Dianne Feinstein claim that the Census question will "disenfranchise millions of California voters," she is, of course, ignoring the comparative disenfranchisement of hundreds of millions of Americans in non-sanctuary states that respect the immigration laws.

This is not the first time citizens have had unequal voting power. At the beginning, the Constitution provided that slaves were counted as three-fifths of a person in apportioning the House of Representatives. Slave states wanted slaves to be counted fully, even though slaves of course could not vote; these states argued that the votes of slave owners represented the interests of slaves. A similar argument was deployed against women's suffrage: Husbands

> **The votes for these extra seats go to the citizen residents of these urban areas.**

and fathers would represent the interest of their womenfolk at the ballot box. How long will it be before elite urban Democrats start justifying their extra voting power by arguing that their leftist policies represent the interests of their poor non-citizen neighbors?

When Democrats were raging against the Electoral College for putting Donald Trump in the White House, one of the institution's darkest marks was its use to implement the three-fifths rule. But basing apportionment on gross population is deeply rooted in the three-fifths rule as well.

The comprehensive information the Census will now provide will make it feasible to apportion on the basis of the citizen population rather than the gross population. Unfortunately, a constitutional amendment may be needed to correct this imbalance on the federal level. (Such an amendment is proposed in *Fifty States, Not Six*.) On the other hand, states arguably could apportion their legislatures based on citizen rather than gross population, and with the 2020 Census they will now have the data to do that.

In addition to the simple issue of fairness, such a move could resolve a serious political problem plaguing many of our states. Within many states, politically competitive rural and suburban areas are dominated by overwhelmingly Democratic urban areas. These tensions exist between inland and coastal California, and in states across the country including Oregon, Washington, Illinois, Pennsylvania, New York, and Florida. This has raised campaigns to split up states and created enormous political frustrations. Glenn Reynolds has proposed various constitutionally difficult ways of establishing a less unequal political balance within these states, short of secession. However, simply apportioning state legislatures on the basis of citizen rather than gross population might give suburban and rural areas enough sway to address their concerns.

One of the most fundamental questions for any representative democracy is how the representatives are selected. In our era of historically high immigration, the introduction of the citizenship questions on the Census should begin a much-needed debate about whether our country will be governed equally by all of its citizens.

Print Citations

CMS: Lucas, James W. "Illegal Immigration Gives Cities Political Power." In *The Reference Shelf: The National Debate Topic 2018–2019 Immigration*, edited by Betsy Maury, 86-88. Ipswich, MA: H.W. Wilson, 2018.

MLA: Lucas, James W. "Illegal Immigration Gives Cities Political Power." *The Reference Shelf: The The National Debate Topic 2018–2019 Immigration*. Ed. Betsy Maury. Ipswich: H.W. Wilson, 2018. 86-88. Print.

APA: Lucas, J.W. (2018). Illegal immigration gives cities political power. In Betsy Maury (Ed.), *The reference shelf: The national debate topic 2018–2019 immigration* (pp. 86-88). Ipswich, MA: H.W. Wilson. (Original work published 2018)

The 2020 Census Citizenship Question Is Spelling Trouble in Texas

By E.A. Crunden
ThinkProgress, April 3, 2018

Last week, the Commerce Department announced that a citizenship question would be added to the upcoming decennial Census for the first time in 70 years. The implications are stark for the entire country, but results could be dire for one state in particular: Texas.

The Census is a constitutionally mandated project, one that meets a number of crucial national needs. But years of funding shortages, stalled efforts to upgrade its technology, and general leadership issues within the Census Bureau have thrown the 2020 project for a loop. Now, with a citizenship question on the line, it could burden the program—and individual states—even further.

Texas was already facing an undercount in the 2020 Census, but experts and advocates say the citizenship question will likely exacerbate the problem. That means the second-largest state in the country could soon find itself facing a major dilemma with ramifications for millions of people.

According to Election Data Services, Texas stands to gain as many as three new congressional seats following the 2020 Census. The state also relies on billions of dollars to fund programs like Medicare, to say nothing of infrastructure upgrades and other necessities. An accurate Census count will ensure that funding continues—but at the moment, experts say, that assurance is far from certain.

"Texas has at least three challenges facing it as it seeks a fair and accurate count for the 2020 Census," Phil Sparks, who heads the non-partisan Census Project, told *ThinkProgress*. "And it's a matter of money and politics."

A sweeping look at the Census in Texas by the *Texas Tribune* last week indicated that Texans are already hard to count: low-income residents, college students, and inhabitants in remote areas are only a few of the populations that pose a logistical challenge to enumerators. Sparks also pointed to the state's rural population, saying that internet is essential for the Census to be fully effective, something that residents in the countryside don't always have.

Another issue plaguing the count is internal displacement. Hurricane Harvey destroyed a large part of the Texas coast last fall, leaving the sprawling, densely populated city of Houston struggling to recover. Sparks noted that, much like New

Orleans post-Hurricane Katrina in the last Census, counting Houston and the wider Gulf Coast region will be much more difficult this time around.

But these problems pale in comparison to the citizenship question, an addition that could be a nightmare for Texas.

"Texas stands to gain new congressional districts in the upcoming Census, but if we fail to account for every person in the state, it'll be difficult to get true representation in Congress we deserve," Mario Carillo, director of America's Voice Texas, an organization working on immigration reform, told *ThinkProgress*.

Carillo noted, "Latinos and immigrants in Texas have been historically difficult to count, and to include a question on citizenship, during a time when immigrants are living under one of the most anti-immigrant policies in the country, will scare people from wanting to be counted. If an immigrant is fearful of being deported for answering a question on their legal status, we will again find that Texas will be undercounted, and underrepresented."

Texas is a "majority minority" state where people of color outnumber white residents, something that correlates directly with its large immigrant population. Eleven percent of all U.S. immigrants live in Texas. They account for approximately 17 percent of the state, according to the American Immigration Council, and one in six Texas residents is an immigrant.

The state also has the second-highest population of undocumented immigrants in the country after California—around 1.7 million—and more than 1 million Texans have a family member who is undocumented. Latinx Texans, meanwhile, make up nearly 40 percent of the population.

Under President Trump, hardline anti-immigration rhetoric has sparked fears across the country, but for Texas residents, those concerns are nothing new. Deportations during the Obama administration still haunt immigrant communities there. Last year, Gov. Greg Abbott (R) also introduced SB4, a law targeting so-called sanctuary cities; under that law, officials who fail to comply with federal immigration policies are subject to staggering fines, time in prison, or even removal from public office.

A number of Latinx organizers told *ThinkProgress* that the mistreatment of those communities is intentional, with many pointing to the recent Census question as a prime example.

"This administration wants communities of color and immigrants under-counted, under-represented and and under-resourced," Cristina Tzintzun, founder and executive director of Jolt, a Texas organization working to make the state's Latinx community a political force, told *ThinkProgress*. "They know that immigrant communities distrust

> **For every 1 percent of the Texas population undercounted, the state could lose $291 million in federal funding.**

and fear the federal government, and that because of this fear and mistrust millions of people would likely not participate in the Census and not be counted."

The Census is meant to be non-partisan, but controversy over the citizenship question is rapidly making the endeavor a political fault line. A number of conservative figures, including Texas Attorney General Ken Paxton, requested the question prior to its implementation. Following confirmation that the question would be added, Sen. Ted Cruz (R) lauded the move, calling it a "commonsense addition."

By contrast, Cruz's 2018 midterm challenger, Democrat Beto O'Rourke—who is from the border city of El Paso—has taken a stark opposition stance.

"Adding a Census question on citizenship is specifically intended to undercount communities with large immigrant populations," O'Rourke said through a spokesperson, in a statement to *ThinkProgress* and other outlets. "For El Paso, for Houston, for every community across our defining border state, that means a loss of millions in resources for health care, public education, infrastructure and transportation, disaster relief and preparedness, and the distribution of billions in federal funds critical to projects in Texas."

Vincent Harding, the party chair for the Democratic party in Travis County, home to Austin, was more blunt in his response, telling *ThinkProgress* that adding the citizenship question was an "un-American" move designed to hurt immigrants that "contribute to our workforce, buy goods in our neighborhoods, and pay taxes."

An inaccurate Census count could hurt Republicans as well as Democrats, costing either party expanded representation in Washington. The Census Bureau's own panel of experts has notably rebuked the decision to add a question about citizenship, but the Trump administration is standing by its decision. A Commerce Department spokesperson told *ThinkProgress* the move gave all U.S. residents the opportunity to provide an answer, allowing for a more complete picture of the country.

Many advocates rallying against the question say supporters should consider the financial cost to all Texans. The state currently receives $43 billion based on Census counts. According to the Center for Public Policy Priorities in Austin, for every 1 percent of the Texas population undercounted, the state could lose $291 million in federal funding. Texas already has the highest rate of uninsured residents in the country, in addition to a staggeringly high maternal mortality rate. Opponents of the citizenship question say a reduction in federal funding won't help fix those problems—instead, it could create more issues in a state where high quality of life is far from a guarantee.

In the Rio Grande Valley, home to some of the most vulnerable communities in the state, officials are considering drastic measures to counter the administration's decision. In a Lower Rio Grande Valley Development Council meeting last week, Brownsville Mayor Tony Martinez seemed to weigh filing suit against the Trump administration to prevent the question from being included in the Census, part of an effort to protect border residents from being undercounted.

Other regions of the country have also begun fighting back: In March, shortly after the citizenship question was officially announced, California filed its own lawsuit, arguing that its inclusion in the 2020 Census was "illegal." New York also announced on March 27 that it would lead its own multi-state suit.

Progressive Texans aren't counting on such actions from their conservative state government. Facing a stark choice, some advocates say they will push their communities to strike a balance.

"[I]t's more important than ever that every person in Texas, regardless of their immigration status, be counted in the upcoming Census," Carillo said. "If the question is added, those of us who work in the community will have to work harder to ensure immigrants that filling out the Census will be beneficial to them, and potentially encourage them to leave the question on citizenship blank."

Print Citations

CMS: Crunden, E.A. "The 2020 Census Citizenship Question Is Spelling Trouble in Texas." In *The Reference Shelf: The National Debate Topic 2018–2019 Immigration*, edited by Betsy Maury, 89-92. Ipswich, MA: H.W. Wilson, 2018.

MLA: Crunden, E.A. "The 2020 Census Citizenship Question Is Spelling Trouble in Texas." *The Reference Shelf: The National Debate Topic 2018–2019 Immigration*. Ed. Betsy Maury. Ipswich: H.W. Wilson, 2018. 89-92. Print.

APA: Crunden, E.A. (2018). The 2020 census citizenship question is spelling trouble in Texas. In Betsy Maury (Ed.), *The Reference Shelf: The national debate topic 2018–2019 immigration* (pp. 89-92). Ipswich, MA: H.W. Wilson. (Original work published 2018)

Why a Census Question about Citizenship Should Worry You, Whether You're a Citizen or Not

By Michael Blake
The Conversation, April 3, 2018

Commerce Secretary Wilbur Ross announced last week that the 2020 census will include a question about citizenship. Ross argued that such a question is required for a "complete and accurate" count of Americans. Others in the Department of Justice have argued that the knowledge produced would be useful in ensuring against voter fraud.

Much recent commentary has focused on the ways in which Ross' proposal might shift power from states with many undocumented residents to those with comparatively few—and, therefore, from Democratic states to Republican ones.

As a political philosopher who studies how abstract moral notions such as justice apply to political institutions, I am more concerned with the fact that undercounting the undocumented might introduce bias into our public policy. This bias might lead to injustice—toward citizens and noncitizens alike.

Injustice Toward Citizens

There is a long tradition in political philosophy that understands injustice as unequal treatment without justification. A state is unjust, on this account, when it treats different people in different ways—unless that particular difference in treatment can be shown to reflect some morally important difference between those people. In other words, if you and I are both subject to the law, I have the right to have my interests and desires treated as equal in importance to yours—unless we can find some morally important reason for us to be treated differently. The legal notion of equality before the law reflects this ideal.

It is for this reason that undercounting the undocumented could lead to injustice. The census will be the basis for the allocation of a great deal of funding—over US$600 billion, in areas including health, public health, nutrition and law enforcement. If the census were to count only citizens, rather than all residents, the budget allocations will not accurately reflect the actual number of people who will make demands upon public institutions.

To take a simple example: The police have a legal duty to respond to crimes committed by undocumented residents, as well as toward crimes committed against them. If a state with far more undocumented residents receives the same amount of money as one with very few undocumented residents, it will end up serving more people with fewer resources.

To understand how significant this difference could be, consider these numbers: There are approximately 22 million noncitizens in the United States—which amounts to 7 percent of the population. These residents are not distributed equally between states. California, for example, has more than 2.5 million undocumented residents, whereas states such as North Dakota, West Virginia and Maine have fewer than 5,000.

The citizens of states with a great many noncitizens may be placed at a significant disadvantage, in comparison with the citizens of states with few noncitizen residents.

If there is no good moral reason to justify this inequality—and in my view there is none—then we have a reason to regard this inequality as unjust.

Rights of the Undocumented

Furthermore, undercounting the undocumented might also entail injustice toward the undocumented themselves.

One immediate reply here, of course, is to say that the question of injustice toward the undocumented does not arise. Since they have no right to legal residency, there cannot be an issue about fairness toward their interests.

From my perspective, the proper response to that objection is to notice that there are some things states must do even for those who are present without right. Think, again, of police protection. The police are bound by law and morality to protect the bodily and property interests even of those present illegally.

It is true that a person who is a resident in the United States without right is liable to deportation. But that liability does not give the local police the right to refuse to act on that person's behalf. Someone can be rightly subject to deportation, but still be entitled to have their basic human rights defended prior to deportation.

The Supreme Court's recent decision, in *Evenwel v. Abbott*, reflects these moral facts. This case involved a challenge to the Texan policy of creating districts that reflected total population, rather than the population of legal voters. A unanimous court declared that Texas was permitted to apportion voting districts by population—including the undocumented.

There are some interests, said the court, that are held by everyone resident in a place, "regardless of whether they qualify as voters."

Impact on the Climate of Fear

The proposed question about citizenship, finally, is liable to exacerbate an existing inequality in the administration of justice. It is likely to make the current climate of fear in immigrant communities worse. The police are charged with protecting the rights of the undocumented, but they are also frequently called upon to deport them.

This dual role has made the relationship between the undocumented and the police more ad-

> **If the census were to count only citizens, rather than all residents, the budget allocations will not accurately reflect the actual number of people who will make demands upon public institutions.**

versarial than effective policing would recommend. As Houston Police Chief Art Acevedo has noted, when people are afraid about interacting with the police, they are less likely to come forward as victims and as witnesses. The police, he argues, ought to "focus on crime, not be ICE agents."

What is true for the policeman may also be true for the census-taker. Questions about citizenship may lead to a sense that even the census-taker—whose job is simply to get an accurate count of those resident[s] within the United States—is helping the federal government with deportation. Sunshine Hillygus, who advises the federal government on the census, notes that this question is likely to fuel suspicion on the part of the undocumented that the census will become a political tool to be used against them—with negative implications for both data accuracy and for the long-run reputation of the Census Bureau as a nonpartisan agency.

It is not clear, at this point, that a question about citizenship will actually end up being a part of the 2020 census. Several states have filed a lawsuit, seeking to block Ross' proposed question. Whether or not that lawsuit succeeds, the fact that this question is being considered should give all of us some moral concern—regardless of our perspectives on migration, and regardless of whether we are citizens ourselves.

Print Citations

CMS: Blake, Michael. "Why a Census Question about Citizenship Should Worry You, Whether You're a Citizen or Not." In *The Reference Shelf: The National Debate Topic 2018–2019 Immigration*, edited by Betsy Maury, 93-95. Ipswich, MA: H.W. Wilson, 2018.

MLA: Blake, Michael. "Why a Census Question about Citizenship Should Worry You, Whether You're a Citizen or Not." *The Reference Shelf: The National Debate Topic 2018–2019 Immigration.* Ed. Betsy Maury. Ipswich: H.W. Wilson, 2018. 93-95. Print.

APA: Blake, M. (2018). Why a census question about citizenship should worry you, whether you're a citizen or not. In Betsy Maury (Ed.), *The reference shelf: The national debate topic 2018–2019 immigration* (pp. 93-95). Ipswich, MA: H.W. Wilson. (Original work published 2018)

4
Border Wall

US President Donald Trump inspects border wall prototypes in San Diego, California on March 13, 2018.

The Wall Before the Storm

Building a wall between two societies, to stop members of one society from entering the other, is perhaps the most basic, primitive strategy for protecting one's borders. Border walls have appeared throughout history and have been used in many different societies to prevent unauthorized movement and to protect against military encroachment. The most famous walls in history—like the Great Wall of China or the potentially mythological walls of Jericho—were not as effective as their architects and advocates hoped, with both Jericho and China having been invaded and conquered after the construction of their historic palisades. There are also the famed political barriers, constructed less for military security and more for societal insulation. The most famous of these is the Berlin Wall, which was erected to prevent pollution within the authoritarian regime of East Berlin but is most famous for the moment in which the wall was symbolically torn down, representing the victory of unity over isolationism and of freedom over state control.[1]

President Donald Trump has called for a wall along the US-Mexico border, for the purpose of preventing unauthorized migration into the United States. International examples indicate that, in the most basic, short-term sense, if handled correctly, the border wall could reduce illegal migration across the border. However, the project has drawn passionate criticism from environmentalists, human rights advocates, and economists. The consensus is that the border wall is economically burdensome, impractical given the wealth of other options and current migration patterns, harmful to both businesses and communities, and likely to become an environmental catastrophe.

The Border Fence Odyssey: From Bush to Trump

The first federal attempt to construct a barrier along the US-Mexican border came with the George W. Bush administration's Secure Fence Act of 2006. Altogether, this effort resulted in the construction of 670 miles of fencing, at a cost to taxpayers of $2.4 billion, covering one-third of the border. The project was more expensive and difficult than projected and is not considered a major success, though evidence suggests that the fence contributed to an overall reduction in illegal crossings. US Customs and Border Protection apprehended 1,071,972 illegal border crosses in 2006, as compared to 200,000 the following year. However, sociologists have found that the reduction in crossings was also due to increased security (due to the fence construction) and to the US recession, which discouraged immigration because there were fewer employment opportunities for those who crossed the border.[2]

The Bush administration was well aware that the fence alone would not address unauthorized migration and thus the fence was part of a far more comprehensive immigration reform effort that also included a temporary worker program that would have brought millions of Mexican migrants into the United States for seasonal work. Bush's immigration reform policy was an attempt to balance viewpoints surrounding the issue, and thus is best described as a political compromise between moderates on both sides of the issue. The compromise failed because, at the time, the hard-line conservative faction of the Republican Party was dominant in the legislature and so the guest worker program was scrapped and the fence was the only part of the immigration reform package that came to fruition.[3]

The hard-line conservative approach to immigration is, and has always been, simple and absolute. Individuals and politicians who favor this approach often call for solutions such as mass deportation, detention, and imprisonment of undocumented migrants. What is appealing about these approaches is their simplicity, as a person doesn't need to understand or address complex geopolitics or humanitarian/ethical issues to embrace the idea that putting up a wall keeps people out, or that people who break laws should face penalties. Furthermore, such ideas are easy to implement because they require only a very narrow focus. Compared to the strict conservative approach, most of the other potential strategies and solutions for dealing with unauthorized migration/immigration are complex as politicians, law enforcement agencies, and researchers struggle to address not just the superficial factors, but the deeper causes, motivations, and geopolitical factors that contribute to migration patterns. Solutions in this vein are far more difficult to market because they require balancing priorities.

In June 2015, when announcing his candidacy for president, Donald Trump said:

> I will build a great wall—and nobody builds walls better than me, believe me—and I'll build them very inexpensively. I will build a great, great wall on our southern border, and I will make Mexico pay for that wall. Mark my words.[4]

In 2018, it was revealed that the wall, as currently envisaged, will cover one-half of the Mexican border, will utilize fences already in place, and will take 10 years to complete at an estimated cost of $18 billion for the first phase of the project. There have been no official claims from the White House regarding the ultimate cost and timeline, but experts in the field have suggested that, like most large-scale infrastructure projects, the cost will be higher than initially believed and the project will take longer than estimated. By January of 2018, prototypes of possible walls had been created, at a cost to taxpayers of $20 million, including $2 million in expenditures in San Diego, where extra police were needed to protect the border wall prototypes from American citizens who objected to the potential wall's construction.[5]

Will the Wall Control Drugs?

One of the claims about the wall is that it will stop drug trafficking. However, experts in the field have repeatedly noted that most drugs arrive in the United States through legal points of passage and not as a result of unauthorized border crossings. Further, the drug trade is fueled, primarily, by consumer demand and thus American citizens actively participate in the process of bringing drugs illegally into the

United States. Smugglers have used boats, drones, tunnels, and even catapults to bring drugs into the country, but bringing drugs along with migrants is not a significant factor. Rosalie Pacula, co-director of the RAND Drug Policy Research Center told *Politifact*, "Traffickers have been very innovative in finding strategies to circumvent existing walls and border control thus far, and more of the same strategy (i.e., more of a wall) doesn't offer much promise as a successful strategy."[6]

In a February 2018 article, *New York Times* journalist Josh Katz asked 30 experts, including police officials, politicians, and sociologists, how they would spend $100 billion to combat the drug crisis. A full 47 percent of the solutions chosen by participants were based on providing treatment to addicted individuals, while another 27 percent involved efforts to reduce the demand for drugs. None of the 30 experts mentioned the border wall or border security as a potential solution to the problem and only 4 percent mentioned efforts like local police or prescription monitoring that might be used to address the supply of drugs.[7] In essence, the vast weight of opinion from experts in drug abuse and prevention suggests that border security is not a fruitful area to explore when looking for solutions.

Will the Wall Prevent Illegal Immigration?

On the issue of whether or not the wall might serve its primary purpose, to combat illegal immigration, Trump has repeatedly referred to Israel's border walls as examples of how the border wall might succeed in this regard. *Politifact* conducted an investigation to discover whether Israel's experiments with border walls and fences had been effective and found that the fences and walls had reduced illegal immigration significantly. However, the reduction in immigration was also the result of many other factors, including a vast increase in border security and continued, permanent investment in maintaining the nation's barriers. Further, Israel has passed additional laws making it less beneficial for immigrants to live and work in the country and the effect of these laws on the reduction in immigration is also an important factor.[8]

It is also important to note that Israel's border control efforts have not significantly solved the nation's international issues. For instance, nearly two-thirds of Israeli citizens favor a "two-state" solution to the nation's long-term conflict with the stateless Palestinians unofficially interned outside the nation's borders for decades. However, Prime Minister Benjamin Netanyahu and the hard-line Israeli conservatives have not pursued this strategy and instead have opted for the far simpler strategy of increasing border security.[9] Netanyahu, meanwhile, has consistently lost support in the polls despite the success in reducing immigration rates and this is largely because the reduction has not resulted in increased safety, a reduction in radical attacks, or marked improvements in the Israeli economy. As an example for US policy, the Israeli experiments in building border walls indicate potential success in reducing numbers (thus addressing the supply side of the problem) but also that such solutions are not effective at helping to create longer-term solutions.

What Will the Wall Do to the Environment?

President Trump's policy proposals indicate that he considers the environment a minor concern, despite the fact that environmental protection ranks in the top five concerns for Americans overall. In an effort to speed up construction of the border wall, in January of 2018 Trump waived 18 separate environmental laws, including the Endangered Species Act, the Clean Water Act, and the Environment Policy Act. Several environmental groups have already brought suit as of April 2018, though the results of these legal actions is as yet unknown.[10]

Some of the most passionate critics of the border wall proposal, however, are concerned about the natural environment and the impact that the wall might have. The most comprehensive study on the effect of border fences already in place indicated that 45 species and three subspecies have already been put at serious risk by existing border fences, which bisect natural territories and reduce resources for animal populations. Among the species biologists say will be negatively affected by the wall are the ocelot, jaguarondi, mountain lion, Mexican wolf, bobcat, collared peccary, the nine-banded armadillo, the Texas horned lizard, and the southern yellow bat. Many of these species are already endangered or threatened and the presence of barriers blocking access to important seasonal resources is likely to have serious impact on the small populations that remain. The proposed route for the fence also runs directly through wildlife refuges, which brought objections from ecological protection groups.[11]

Scientists also warn that the border wall project will increase the impact of climate change in the region, will lead to inevitable and possibly catastrophic pollution in key waterways, and will divert rainwater essential to both human and nonhuman life. While there may be pros and cons to consider with regard to the border wall idea, when it comes to environmental integrity, protection, and preservation, there are no positive effects even possible from the construction of the wall. Though the extent of environmental damage is speculative as of April 2018, there will be serious environmental impact and this impact will not be positive.

Opinions on the Wall

Trump is a president who is often at odds with the weight of public opinion and this is particularly evident in the administration's immigration stance. One example of this has been public support to find a solution to keep undocumented DREAMers in the United States, a view not embraced by the president. The margin of support for the border wall is far narrower, though some polls indicate that a significant majority of Republicans support the wall in principal. For instance, a January 2018 CBS News Poll found that 61 percent opposed the wall, including 24 percent of Republicans, 88 percent of Democrats, and 61 percent of independents.[12]

There is no law holding that a sitting president must always adhere to public will when deciding how to craft policy. However, some critics have argued that, with the enormous taxpayer cost, potentially disastrous environmental consequences, and lack of support from experts in the field, a project like the border wall should not be completed without at least narrow majority support from the American people.

Works Used

Barclay, Eliza and Sarah Frostenson. "The Ecological Disaster That Is Trump's Border Wall: A Visual Guide." *Vox*. Vox Media. Oct 29 2017. Web. https://www.vox.com/energy-and-environment/2017/4/10/14471304/trump-border-wall-animals.

"Build a Wall, and Make Mexico Pay for It." *Politifact*. Politifact. Jan 16, 2017. Web. http://www.politifact.com/truth-o-meter/promises/trumpometer/promise/1397/build-wall-and-make-mexico-pay-it/.

De Pinto, Jennifer. "Where Americans Stand on Immigration." *CBS News*. CBS. Aug 9, 2017. Web. https://www.cbsnews.com/news/where-americans-stand-on-immigration/.

De Pinto, Jennifer, Backus, Fred, Khanna, Kabir, and Anthony Salvanto. "Most Americans Support DACA, but Oppose Border Wall–CBS News Poll." *CBS News*. CBS. Jan 20, 2018. Web. https://www.cbsnews.com/news/most-americans-support-daca-but-oppose-border-wall-cbs-news-poll/.

"Fact Sheet: The Secure Fence Act of 2006." *Georgewbush-Whitehouse*. Oct 26, 2006. Web. https://georgewbush-whitehouse.archives.gov/news/releases/2006/10/20061026-1.html.

"Here's What We Know about Trump's Mexico Wall." *Bloomberg*. Bloomerg Politics. Dec 11, 2017. Web. https://www.bloomberg.com/graphics/2017-trump-mexico-wall/will-a-wall-be-effective/.

Katz, Josh. "How a Police Chief, a Governor and a Sociologist Would Spend $100 Billion to Solve the Opioid Crisis." *The New York Times*. The New York Times Co. Feb 14, 2018. Web. https://www.nytimes.com/interactive/2018/02/14/upshot/opioid-crisis-solutions.html.

Miroff, Nick and Erica Werner. "First Phase of Trump's Border Wall Gets $18 Billion Price Tag, in New Request for Lawmakers." *The Washington Post*. The Washington Post Co. Jan 5, 2018. Web. https://www.washingtonpost.com/.

Popovich, Nadja, Albeck-Ripka, Livia, and Kendra Pierre-Louis. "67 Environmental Rules on the Way Out Under Trump." *The New York Times*. The New York Times Co. Jan 31, 2018. Web. https://www.nytimes.com/interactive/2017/10/05/climate/trump-environment-rules-reversed.html.

Sterman, Adiv. "Two-Thirds of Israelis Support Peace with Palestinians that Ensures Security, Polls Find." *Times of Israel*. Dec 31, 2012. Web. https://www.timesofisrael.com/two-thirds-of-israelis-support-peace-with-palestinians-that-ensures-security-polls-find/.

Thomsen, Jacqueline. "Trump Waives Dozens of Environmental Rules to Speed Construction of Border Wall." *The Hill*. The Hill. Jan 22, 2018. Web. http://thehill.com/latino/370202-trump-admin-waives-dozens-of-environmental-rules-to-speed-up-construction-of-border.

Valverde, Miriam. "Border Fence in Israel Cut Illegal Immigration by 99 Percent, GOP Senator Says." *Politifact*. Politifact. Feb 13, 2017. Web. http://www.politifact.com/truth-o-meter/statements/2017/feb/13/ron-johnson/border-fence-israel-cut-illegal-immigration-99-per/.

Valverde, Miriam. "Will a Border Wall Stop Drugs from Coming into the United

States?" *Politifact*. Politifact. Oct 26, 2017. Web. http://www.politifact.com/
truth-o-meter/article/2017/oct/26/will-border-wall-stop-drugs-coming-united-
states/.

Yurkevich, Vanessa and Alexander Rosen. "Not Just Trump's Idea: A Short History
on Famous Walls and the Environment." *CNN Politics*. CNN. Feb 13, 2018.
Web. https://www.cnn.com/2018/02/13/politics/history-of-walls/index.html.

Notes

1. Yurkevich and Rosen, "Not Just Trump's Idea: A Short History on Famous
   Walls and the Environment."
2. "Here's What We Know about Trump's Mexico Wall," *Bloomberg*.
3. "Fact Sheet: The Secure Fence Act of 2006," *Georgewbush-Whitehouse*.
4. "Build a Wall, and Make Mexico Pay for It," *Politifact*.
5. Miroff and Werner, "First Phase of Trump Border Wall Gets $18 Billion Price
   Tag, in New Request to Lawmakers."
6. Valverde, "Will a Border Wall Stop Drugs from Coming into the United States?"
7. Katz, "How a Police Chief, a Governor and a Sociologist Would Spend $100
   Billion to Solve the Opioid Crisis."
8. Valverde, "Border Fence in Israel Cut Illegal Immigration by 99 Percent, GOP
   Senator Says."
9. Sterman, "Two-Thirds of Israelis Support Peace with Palestinians That Ensures Security, Polls Find."
10. Thomsen, "Trump Waives Dozens of Environmental Rules to Speed Up Con-
    struction of Border Wall."
11. Barclay and Frostenson, "The Ecological Disaster That Is Trump's Border
    Wall: A Visual Guide."
12. 13 De Pinto, Backus, Khanna, and Salvanto, "Most Americans Support
    DACA, but Oppose Border Wall—CBS News Poll."

The High Cost and Diminishing Returns of a Border Wall

American Immigration Council, January 25, 2017

For generations, politicians have talked about constructing a border wall. The fact is that building a fortified and impenetrable wall between the United States and Mexico might make for pithy sound bites, but in reality it is unnecessary, complicated, ineffective, expensive, and would create a host of additional problems.

Extensive physical barriers already exist along the U.S.-Mexico border.

- The U.S.-Mexico border is 1,954 miles long. Border security involves managing the flow of people and goods across the border and preventing the illegal entry of people and goods. The existing border security infrastructure includes physical barriers, aerial surveillance, and technology. More than 21,000 Border Patrol agents—as well as other Department of Homeland Security (DHS) and Department of Justice (DOJ) personnel—staff ports of entry, Border Patrol stations, forward operating bases, and checkpoints.

- Current physical barriers along the U.S.-Mexico border include those intended to prevent illegal border crossings by foot (pedestrian fencing) and impede vehicles from smuggling persons or contraband (vehicle fencing). Secondary and tertiary layers of fencing further impede illegal crossings.

- As of early 2017, approximately 650 miles of border fence already exists: 350 miles of primary pedestrian fencing, 300 miles of vehicle fencing, 36 miles of secondary fencing behind the primary fencing, and 14 miles of tertiary pedestrian fencing behind the secondary fence.

- The existing barriers include tall metal or concrete posts, solid corrugated steel walls, metal fencing, and combinations of these designs.

- In addition to physical barriers, surveillance tools, towers, cameras, motion detectors, thermal imaging sensors, stadium lighting, ground sensors, and drones are part of the vast existing infrastructure aimed at stopping the unauthorized entry of people, drugs, arms, and other illicit items.

Congress acknowledged that additional physical barriers are not necessary.

- The Secure Fence Act of 2006 (Pub.L. 109-367), a law that passed with bipartisan support in both the House and Senate, required the construction of about 850 miles of double-layer fencing along five segments of the border.

- A few years after passage, Congress recognized that 850 miles of additional border fencing was not feasible or necessary. In 2008, the Consolidated Appropriations Act of 2008 amended the 2006 law to reduce the required mileage of reinforced fencing to "not less than 700 miles of the southwest border where fencing would be most practical and effective . . . ." In addition, DHS is not required to install fencing "in a particular location along the international border of the United States if the Secretary determines that the use or placement of such resources is not the most appropriate means to achieve and maintain operational control over the international border at such location."

- Even Senator Chuck Grassley (R-IA), a long-time opponent of immigration reform, said in early January 2017, "We've already appropriated money for walls. We've got walls right now."

The wall is expensive.

- The Government Accountability Office found that single-layer pedestrian fencing could cost approximately $6.5 million per mile. In addition, millions would have to be spent on roads and maintenance.

- The easiest parts of the border fence have been built, according to Marc Rosenblum, formerly of the Migration Policy Institute and the current DHS Deputy Secretary of the Office of Immigration Statistics. The estimated cost of the remaining border wall segments are between $15 and $25 billion, with each mile of fencing costing $16 million.

- According to the Fiscal Year (FY) 2017 DHS budget, $274 million was spent on border fence maintenance. Based on that expense, one can extrapolate that if fencing is built on the final two-thirds of the Southern border, the maintenance costs will triple to more than $750 million annually.

- In FY 2006, appropriations for building and maintaining border infrastructure was $298 million, and then jumped to $1.5 billion in FY 2007 to pay for the fencing mandated in the Secure Fence Act. FY 2016 appropriations were $447 million.

The federal border agencies have not asked for a wall.

- Outgoing Commissioner of U.S. Customs and Border Protection (CBP) Gil Kerlikowske said in January 2017, "I think that anyone who's been familiar with the southwest border and the terrain ... kind of recognizes that building a wall along the entire southwest border is probably not going to work," adding that he does not "think it is feasible" or the "smartest way to use taxpayer money on infrastructure."

- The head of the National Border Patrol Council, a union representing 16,000 Border Patrol agents which endorsed President Trump during his campaign, said, "We do not need a wall along the entire 2,000 miles of border." He went on to say, "If I were to quantify an actual number, I would say that we need about 30 percent. Thirty percent of our border has to have an actual fence [or] wall." The existing 650 miles make up more than 30 percent of the 2,000 mile border.

- According to an internal U.S. government study obtained by Reuters in April 2016, CBP believes that more technology is needed along the border to create a "virtual wall." The agency requested better radios and more aerial drones, but only 23 more miles of fences.

There are complications to building a wall.

- **Natural barriers.** The Rio Grande River runs along 1,254 miles of the border between Mexico and the United States and does not flow in a straight line—instead twisting, turning, and flooding regularly. Under the International Boundary and Water Commission, created in 1889 between the U.S. and Mexico, border barriers may not disrupt the flow of the Rio Grande. As a result, the current border fencing in Texas is located miles away from the border on private land owner's property. In addition, the mountain range at Otay Mesa in California makes it extremely impractical to construct a wall or fencing.

- **Private land ownership.** After the passage of the Secure Fence Act, the government attempted to seize private property for purposes of constructing border barriers through eminent domain. These efforts led to protracted legal battles that in some cases lasted seven years. The federal government had to provide monetary compensation to the landowners and agreed to construct several access points along the fence on that property. Some of the existing gaps in the fence are in affluent areas where residents fought construction. It would likely cost the federal government considerable amounts of money to purchase land and build in those areas.

> Building a fortified and impenetrable wall between the United States and Mexico might make for pithy sound bites, but in reality it is unnecessary, complicated, ineffective, expensive, and would create a host of additional problems.

- **Native American land.** The Tohono O'odam Nation runs along 75 miles of the southwest border, and members of the tribe have already stated they will not allow a border wall to be built on their reservation. A wall would effectively cut the reservation in half and make movement across the border, but within the reservation, difficult. It would separate families and make it difficult for tribe members to care for burial sites located in Mexico. Additionally, federal law requires the federal government to consult with tribal governments before constructing on the land. Without the tribe's support, the federal government could resort to condemning the land and removing it from the trust of the Tohono O'odam Nation.

The wall would create a host of additional problems.

- **Border deaths.** History has shown that when barriers are erected along the border, people attempt to cross at more remote and dangerous locations. According to U.S. Border Patrol statistics, the southwest border witnesses approximately one death per day. Over the past 18 years, nearly 7,000 people have died of hypothermia, drowning, heat exhaustion, or dehydration.

- **Harm to wildlife.** The border region is home to many species and some of the most endangered species, including the Sonoran Pronghorn, the Mexican gray wolf, and the jaguar. If their natural habitat is divided by a large barrier, animals are left with a smaller habitat and may venture outside their usual ranges, causing potential harm to the animals and people.

- **Damage to the environment.** A wall could impede the natural flow of floodwaters, resulting in damage and erosion, as it did in 2008.

Print Citations

CMS: "The High Cost and Diminishing Returns of a Border Wall." In *The Reference Shelf: The National Debate Topic 2018–2019 Immigration*, edited by Betsy Maury, 105-108. Ipswich, MA: H.W. Wilson, 2018.

MLA: "The High Cost and Diminishing Returns of a Border Wall." *The Reference Shelf: The National Debate Topic 2018–2019 Immigration*. Ed. Betsy Maury. Ipswich: H.W. Wilson, 2018. 105-108. Print.

APA: American Immigration Council. (2018). The high cost and diminishing returns of a border wall. In Betsy Maury (Ed.), *The reference shelf: The national debate topic 2018–2019 immigration* (pp. 105-108). Ipswich, MA: H.W. Wilson. (Original work published 2017)

The Wall: The Real Costs of a Barrier Between the United States and Mexico

By Vanda Felbab-Brown
The Brookings Institution, August 2017

The cheerful paintings of flowers on the tall metal posts on the Tijuana side of the border fence between the U.S. and Mexico belie the sadness of the Mexican families who have gathered there to exchange whispers, tears, and jokes with relatives on the San Diego side.

Many have been separated from their family members for years. Some were deported to Mexico after having lived in the United States for decades without authorization, leaving behind children, spouses, siblings, and parents. Others never left Mexico, but have made their way to the fence to see relatives in the United States. With its prison–like ambience and Orwellian name—Friendship Park—this site is one of the very few places where families separated by immigration rules can have even fleeting contact with their loved ones, from 10 a.m. to 2 p.m. on Saturdays and Sundays. Elsewhere, the tall metal barrier is heavily patrolled.

So is to be the wall that President Donald Trump promises to build along the border. But no matter how tall and thick a wall will be, illicit flows will cross.

Undocumented workers and drugs will still find their way across any barrier the administration ends up building. And such a wall will be irrelevant to those people who become undocumented immigrants by overstaying their visas—who for many years have outnumbered those who become undocumented immigrants by crossing the U.S.–Mexico border.

Nor will the physical wall enhance U.S. security.

The border, and more broadly how the United States defines its relations with Mexico, directly affects the 12 million people who live within 100 miles of the border. In multiple and very significant ways that have not been acknowledged or understood it will also affect communities all across the United States as well as Mexico.

What the Wall's Price Tag Would Be

The wall comes with many costs, some obvious though hard to estimate, some unforeseen. The most obvious is the large financial outlay required to build it, in whatever form it eventually takes. Although during the election campaign candidate

Trump claimed that the wall would cost only $12 billion, a Department of Homeland Security (DHS) internal report in February put the cost at $21.6 billion, but that may be a major underestimate.

The estimates vary so widely because of the lack of clarity about what the wall will actually consist of beyond the first meager Homeland Security specifications that it be either a solid concrete wall or a see–through structure, "physically imposing in height," ideally 30 feet high but no less than 18 feet, sunk at least six feet into the ground to prevent tunneling under it; that it should not be scalable with even sophisticated climbing aids; and that it should withstand prolonged attacks with impact tools, cutting tools, and torches. But that description doesn't begin to cover questions about the details of its physical structure. Then there are the legal fees required to seize land on which to build the wall. The Trump administration can use eminent domain to acquire the land but will still have to negotiate compensation and often face lawsuits. More than 90 such lawsuits in southern Texas alone are still open from the 2008 effort to build a fence there.

The Trump administration cannot simply seize remittances to Mexico to pay for the wall; doing so may increase flows of undocumented workers to the United States. Remittances provide many Mexicans with amenities they could never afford otherwise. But for Mexicans living in poverty—some 46.2 percent in 2015 according to the Mexican social research agency CONEVAL—the remittances are a veritable lifeline which can represent as much as 80 percent of their income. These families count on that money for the basics of life—food, clothing, health care, and education for their children.

I met the matron of one of those families in a lush but desperately poor mountain village in Guerrero. Rosa, a forceful woman who was initially suspicious, decided to confide in me. Her son had crossed into the United States eight years ago, she said. The remittances he sent allowed Rosa's grandchildren to get medical treatment at the nearest clinic, some thirty miles away. Like Rosa, many people in the village had male relatives working illegally in the United States in order to help their families make ends meet. Sierra de Atoyac may be paradise for a birdwatcher (which I am), but Guerrero is one of Mexico's poorest, most neglected, and crime and violence–ridden states. "Here you have few chances," Rosa explained to me. "If you're smart, like my son, you make it across the border to the U.S. If you're not so smart, you join the *narcos*. If you're stupid, but lucky, you join the [municipal] police. Otherwise, you're stuck here farming or logging and starving."

Any attempt to seize the remittances from such families would be devastating. Fluctuating between $20 billion and $25 billion annually during the past decade, remittances from the United States have amounted to about 3 percent of Mexico's GDP, representing the third–largest source of foreign revenue after oil and tourism. The remittances enable human and economic development throughout the country, and this in turn reduces the incentives for further migration to the United States—precisely what Trump is aiming to do.

Why the Wall Won't Stop Smuggling

Why the DHS believes that a 30–foot tall wall cannot be scaled and a tunnel cannot be built deeper than six feet below ground is not clear.

Drug smugglers have been using tunnels to get drugs into the United States ever since Mexico's most famous drug trafficker, Joaquín "El Chapo" Guzmán of the Sinaloa Cartel, pioneered the method in 1989. And the sophistication of these tunnels has only grown over time. In April 2016, U.S. law enforcement officials discovered a drug tunnel that ran more than half a mile from Tijuana to San Diego and was equipped with ventilation vents, rails, and electricity. It is the longest such tunnel to be found so far, but one of 13 of great length and technological expertise discovered since 2006. Altogether, between 1990 and 2016, 224 tunnels have been unearthed at the U.S.–Mexico border.

Other smuggling methods increasingly include the use of drones and catapults as well as joint drainage systems between border towns that have wide tunnels or tubes through which people can crawl and drugs can be pulled. But even if the land border were to become much more secure, that would only intensify the trend toward smuggling goods as well as people via boats that sail far to the north, where they land on the California coast.

Another thing to consider is that a barrier in the form of a wall is increasingly irrelevant to the drug trade as it is now practiced because most of the drugs smuggled into the U.S. from Mexico no longer arrive on the backs of those who cross illegally. Instead, according to the U.S. Drug Enforcement Administration, most of the smuggled marijuana as well as cocaine, heroin, and methamphetamines comes through the 52 legal ports of entry on the border. These ports have to process literally millions of people, cars, trucks, and trains every week. Traffickers hide their illicit cargo in secret, state–of–the art compartments designed for cars, or under legal goods in trailer trucks. And they have learned many techniques for fooling the border patrol. Mike, a grizzled U.S. border official whom I interviewed in El Paso in 2013, shrugged: "The *narcos* sometimes tip us off, letting us find a car full of drugs while they send six other cars elsewhere. Such write–offs are part of their business expense. Other times the tipoffs are false. We search cars and cars, snarl up the traffic for hours on, and find nothing."

Beyond the Sinaloa Cartel, 44 other significant criminal groups operate today in Mexico. The infighting within and among them has made Mexico one of the world's most violent countries. In 2016 alone this violence claimed between 21,000 and 23,000 lives. Between 2007 and 2017, a staggering 177,000 people were murdered in Mexico, a number that could actually be much higher, as many bodies are buried in mass graves that are hidden and never found. Those Mexican border cities that are principal entry points of drugs into the Unites States have been particularly badly affected by the violence.

Take Ciudad Juárez, for example. Directly across the border from peaceful El Paso. Ciudad Juárez was likely the world's most violent city when I was there in 2011 and it epitomizes what can happen during these drug wars. In 2011 the Sinaloa Cartel was battling the local Juárez Cartel, trying to take over the city's smuggling routes to the United States, and causing a veritable bloodbath. Walking around the contested *colonías* at the time was like touring a cemetery: Residents would point out places where people were killed the day before, three days before, five weeks ago.

Juan, a skinny 19–year–old whom I met there that year, told me that he was trying to get out of a local gang (the name of which he wouldn't reveal). He had started working for the gang as a *halcone* (a lookout) when he was 15, he said. But now as the drug war raged in the city and the local gangs were pulled into the infighting between the big cartels, his friends in the gang were being asked to do much more than he wanted to do—to kill. Without any training, they were given assault weapons. Having no shooting skills, they just sprayed bullets in the vicinity of their assigned targets, hoping that at least some of the people they killed would be the ones they were supposed to kill, because if they didn't succeed, they themselves might be murdered by those who had contracted them to do the job.

I met Juan through Valeria, whose NGO was trying to help gang members like Juan get on the straight and narrow. But it was tough going for her and her staff to make the case. As Juan had explained to me, a member who refused to do the bidding of the gangs could be killed for his failure to cooperate.

"And America does nothing to stop the weapons coming here!" Valeria exclaimed to me.

While President Trump accuses Mexico of exporting violent crime and drugs to the United States, many Mexican officials as well as people like Valeria, who are on the ground in the fight against the drug wars, complain of a tide of violence and corruption that flows in the opposite direction. Some 70 percent of the firearms seized in Mexico between 2009 and 2014 originated in the United States. Although amounting to over 73,000 guns, these seizures still likely represented only a fraction of the weapons smuggled from the United States. Moreover, billions of dollars per year are made in the illegal retail drug market in the United States and smuggled back to Mexico, where the cartels depend on this money for their basic operations. Sometimes, sophisticated money–laundering schemes, such as trade–based deals, are used; but large parts of the proceeds are smuggled as bulk cash hidden in secret compartments and among goods in the cars and trains daily crossing the border south to Mexico.

And of course it is the U.S. demand for drugs that fuels Mexican drug smuggling in the first place. Take, for example, the current heroin epidemic in the United States. It originated in the over–prescription of medical opiates to treat pain. The subsequent efforts to reduce the over–prescription of painkillers led those Americans who became dependent on them to resort to illegal heroin. That in turn stimulated a vast expansion of poppy cultivation in Mexico, particularly in Guerrero. In 2015, Mexico's opium poppy cultivation reached perhaps 28,000 hectares, enough to distill about 70 tons of heroin (which is even more than the 24–50 tons estimated to be necessary to meet the U.S. demand).

Mexico's large drug cartels, including El Chapo's Sinaloa Cartel, which is estimated to supply between 40 and 60 percent of the cocaine and heroin sold on the streets in the United States, are the dominant wholesale suppliers of illegal drugs in the United States. For the retail trade, however, they usually recruit business partners among U.S. crime gangs. And thanks to the deterrence capacity of U.S. law enforcement, insofar as Mexican drug–trafficking groups do have in–country operations in the U.S., such as in wholesale supply, they have behaved strikingly peacefully and have not resorted to the vicious aggression and infighting that characterizes their business in Mexico. So the U.S. has been spared the drug–traffic–related explosions of violence that have ravaged so many of the drug–producing or smuggling areas of Mexico.

Both the George W. Bush administration and the Obama administration recognized the joint responsibility for drug trafficking between the United States and Mexico, an attitude that allowed for unprecedented collaborative efforts to fight crime and secure borders. This collaboration allowed U.S. law enforcement and intelligence agents to operate in Mexico and help their Mexican counterparts in intelligence development, training, vetting, establishment of police procedures and protocols, and interdiction operations. The collaboration also led to Mexico being far more willing than it ever had been before to patrol both its northern border with the United States and its southern border with Central America, as part of the effort to help apprehend undocumented workers trying to cross into the United States.

The Trump administration's hostility to Mexico could jeopardize this progress. In retaliation for building the wall, for any efforts the U.S. might make to force Mexico to pay for the wall, or for the collapse of NAFTA, the Mexican government could, for example, give up on its efforts to secure its southern border or stop sharing counterterrorism intelligence with the United States. Yet Mexico's cooperation is far more important for U.S. security than any wall.

What the Wall Would Mean for Crime in the U.S.

Although President Trump has railed against the "carnage" of crime in the United States, the crime statistics, with few exceptions, tell a very different story.

In 2014, 14,249 people were murdered, the lowest homicide rate since 1991 when there were 24,703, and part of a pattern of steady decline in violent crime over that entire period. In 2015, however, murders in the U.S. did shoot up to 15,696. This increase was largely driven by three cities—Baltimore, Chicago, and Washington, D.C. Baltimore and Chicago have decreasing populations, and all three have higher poverty and unemployment than the national average, high income and racial inequality, and troubled relations between residents and police—conditions conducive to a rise in violent crime. In 2016, homicides fell in Washington and Baltimore, but continued rising in Chicago.

There is no evidence, however, that undocumented residents accounted for either the rise in crime or even for a substantial number of the crimes, in Chicago or elsewhere. The vast majority of violent crimes, including murders, are committed by native–born Americans. Multiple criminological studies show that foreign–born individuals commit much lower levels of crime than do the native–born. In California, for example, where there is a large immigrant population, including of undocumented migrants, U.S.–born men were incarcerated at a rate 2.5 times higher than foreign–born men.

Unfortunately, the Trump administration is promoting a policing approach that insists on prioritizing hunting down undocumented workers, including by using regular police forces, and this kind of misguided law enforcement policy is spreading: In Texas, which has an estimated 1.5 million undocumented immigrants, Republican Governor Greg Abbott recently signed a law to punish sanctuary cities. Among the punishments are draconian measures (such as removal from office, fines, and up to one–year imprisonment) to be enacted against local police officials who do not embrace immigration enforcement. Abbott signed the law despite the fact that police chiefs from all five of Texas's largest cities—Houston, San Antonio, Dallas, Austin, and Fort Worth—published a statement condemning it: "This legislation is bad for Texas and will make our communities more dangerous for all," they wrote in their *Dallas Morning News* op–ed. They argued that immigration enforcement is a federal, not a state responsibility, and that the new law would widen a gap between police and immigrant communities, discouraging cooperation with police on serious crimes, and resulting in widespread underreporting of crimes perpetrated against immigrants. There is powerful and consistent evidence that if people begin to question the fairness, equity, and legitimacy of law enforcement and government institutions, then they stop reporting crime, and homicides increase.

> If in retaliation for the Trump administration's vitriolic, anti–Mexican language and policies, Mexico decided not to live up to its side of the water bargain, U.S. farmers and others along the Rio Grande would be under severe threat of losing their livelihoods.

Police chiefs in other parts of the country, from Los Angeles to Denver, have expressed similar concerns and also their dismay at having to devote their already overstrained resources to hunting down undocumented workers.

The Trump administration has broadened the Obama–era criteria for "expedited removal." Under Obama any immigrant arrested within 100 miles of the border who had been in the country for less than 14 days—i.e., before he or she could establish roots in the United States—could be deported without due process. The result: In fiscal year 2016, 85 percent of all removals (forced) and returns (voluntary) were of noncitizens who met those criteria. Almost all (more than 90 percent) of the remaining 15 percent had been convicted of serious crimes.

Now, however, any undocumented person anywhere in the country who has been here for as long as two years can be removed. And although it claims it will focus on deporting immigrants who commit serious crimes, the Trump administration is gearing up for mass deportations of many of the 11.1 million undocumented residents in the U.S., by far the largest number of whom come from Mexico (6.2 million), Guatemala, El Salvador, Honduras, Ecuador, and Colombia. To that end, it is vastly expanding the definition of what constitutes deportable crime, including fraud in any official matter, such as abuse of "any program related to the receipt of public benefits" or even using a fake Social Security number to pay U.S. taxes. The Trump administration is also reviving the highly controversial 287(g) program under which local law enforcement officials can be deputized to perform immigration duties and can inquire about a jaywalking.

Many of the people being targeted have for decades lived lawful, safe, and productive lives here. About 60 percent of the undocumented have lived in the United States for at least a decade. A third of undocumented immigrants aged 15 and older have at least one child who is a U.S. citizen by birth. The ripping apart of such families has tragic consequences for those involved, as I have seen first–hand.

Antonio, whom I interviewed in Tijuana in 2013, had lived for many years in Las Vegas, where he worked in construction and his wife cleaned hotels. Having had no encounters with U.S. law enforcement, he risked going back to Mexico to visit his ailing mother in Sinaloa. But he got nabbed trying to sneak back into the U.S. After a legal ordeal, which included being handcuffed and shackled and a degrading stay in a U.S. detention facility, he was dumped in Tijuana, where I met him shortly after his arrival there. He dreaded being forever separated from his wife and their two little boys, who had been born seven and five years before. But Sinaloa is a poor, tough place to live, strongly under the sway of the *narcos*, and Antonio did not want his loved ones to sacrifice themselves in order to rejoin him. As Antonio choked back tears talking about how much he missed his family, I asked him whether they might travel to San Diego to speak with him across the bars of Friendship Park. But Antonio wasn't sure how long he could stay in Tijuana. He was afraid he would be arrested again, this time in Mexico, because in order to please U.S. law enforcement officials by appearing diligent in combating crime, Tijuana's police force had gotten into the habit of arresting, for the most minor of infractions, Mexicans and Central Americans deported from the United States. Sweeping homeless poor migrants and deportees off the streets made Tijuana's city center appear peaceful, bustling, and clean again, after years of a cartel bloodbath. Mexican businesses were pleased by the orderly look of the city center, the U.S. was gratified by Mexico's cooperation, and tourists were returning, with U.S. college students again partying and getting drunk in Tijuana's *cantinas* and clubs. If harmless victims of U.S. deportation policies like Antonio had to pay the price for these benefits, so be it.

How the Wall Would Hurt the U.S. Economy

If immigrants are not responsible for any significant amount of crime in the United States and in fact are considerably less likely than native–born citizens to commit crime, then what about the other justification for President Trump's vilification of immigrants, legal and illegal, and his determination to wall them out: Do immigrants steal U.S. jobs and suppress U.S. wages?

There is little evidence to support such claims. According to a comprehensive National Academies of Sciences, Engineering, and Medicine analysis, immigration does not significantly impact the overall employment levels of most native–born workers. The impact of immigrant labor on the wages of native–born workers is also low. Immigrant labor does have some negative effects on the employment and wages of native–born high school dropouts, however, and also on prior immigrants, because all three groups compete for low–skilled jobs and the newest immigrants are often willing to work for less than their competition. To a large extent, however, undocumented workers often work the unpleasant, back–breaking jobs that native–born workers are not willing to do. Sectors with large numbers of undocumented workers include agriculture, construction, manufacturing, hospitality services, and seafood processing. The fish–cutting industry, for example, is unable to recruit a sufficient number of legal workers and therefore is overwhelmingly dependent on an undocumented workforce. Skinning, deboning, and cutting fish is a smelly, slimy, grimy, chilly, monotonous, and exacting job. Many workers rapidly develop carpal tunnel syndrome. It can be a dangerous job, with machinery for cutting off fish heads and deboning knives everywhere frequently leading to amputated fingers. The risk of infections from cuts and the bloody water used to wash fish is also substantial. Over the past ten years, multiple exposés have revealed that both in the United States and abroad, workers in the fishing and seafood processing industries, often undocumented in other countries also, are subjected to forced labor conditions, and sometimes treated like slaves.

While paying more than jobs she could obtain in Honduras, the fish cutting job was hard for 38–year–old Marta Escoto, profiled by Robin Shulman in a 2007 article in *The Washington Post*. But she put up with it for the sake of her two young children, one of them a four–year–old daughter who couldn't walk and suffered from a gastrointestinal illness that prevented her from absorbing enough nutrition. Yet the fear of raids to which the Massachusetts fish–cutting industry was subjected a decade ago, in an earlier wave of anti–immigrant fervor, drove her to seek a job as a seamstress in a Massachusetts factory producing uniforms for U.S. soldiers. But misfortune struck there, too. Like the seafood processing plants, the New Bedford factory was raided by U.S. immigration officers; and although Marta had no criminal record, she was arrested and rapidly flown to a detention facility in Texas while her children were left alone in a day care center. Unlike many other immigrants swept up in those raids, Marta was ultimately lucky: She had a sister living in Massachusetts who could retrieve her children. And as a result of large political outcry in Massachusetts following those raids, with Senators John F. Kerry and Edward M. Kennedy strongly speaking out against them, Marta was released and could reunite with her two small children. But she remained without documents authorizing her to work and stay in the United States and would again be subject to deportation in the future.

Immigrant workers are actually having a net positive effect on the economy. Because of a native–born population that is both declining in numbers and increasing in age, the U.S. needs its immigrant workers. The portion of foreign–born now accounts for about 16 percent of the labor force, with immigrants and their children accounting for the vast majority of current and future workforce growth in the United States, If the number of immigrants to the United States was reduced—by deportation or barriers to further immigration—so that foreign–born represented only about 10 percent of the population, the number of working–age Americans in the coming decades would remain essentially static at the current number of 175 million. If, however, the proportion of foreign–born remains at the current level, then the number of working–age residents in the U.S. will increase by about 30 million in the next 50 years. We need these workers not just to fill jobs but to increase productivity, which has diminished sharply. We also need them because the number of the elderly drawing expensive benefits like Medicare and Social Security—the costs of which are paid for by workers' taxes—is growing substantially. Nearly 44 million people aged 65 or older currently draw Social Security; in 2050 that number is estimated to rise to 86 million. Even undocumented workers support Social Security: Since at least 1.8 million were working with fake Social Security cards in 2010 in order to get employment but were mostly unable to draw the benefits, they contributed $13 billion that year into the retirement trust fund, and took out only $1 billion.

If immigrants are not stealing U.S. jobs and suppressing wages to any significant extent, is NAFTA doing so? Sal Moceri, a 61–year–old Ford worker in Michigan, fervently believes so. He has not lost his job himself, but he saw his co–workers and neighbors lose jobs and sees new workers accepting lower wages for which he would not settle. Although he calls himself a "lifelong Democrat," he voted for Trump in 2016 because of Trump's promise to renegotiate or end NAFTA. In a *CNNMoney* interview with Heather Long, he blamed NAFTA for the job losses and decreases in wages around him, disbelieving the claims of economists that automation, not NAFTA, is the source of the job losses in U.S. manufacturing. He loves automation and hates NAFTA.

But contrary to Trump's claim and Moceri's passionate belief, NAFTA has not siphoned off a large number of U.S. jobs. It did force some U.S. workers to find other kinds of work, but the net number of jobs that was lost is relatively small, with estimates varying between 116,400 and 851,700, out of 146,135,000 jobs in the U.S. economy. Countering these losses is the fact that the bilateral trade fostered by NAFTA has had far–reaching positive effects on the economy.

The trade agreement eliminated tariffs on half of the industrial goods exported to Mexico from the United States (tariffs which before NAFTA averaged 10 percent), and eliminated other Mexican protectionist measures as well, allowing, for example, the export of corn from the United States to Mexico.

NAFTA has enabled the development of joint production lines between the United States and Mexico and allows the U.S. to more cheaply import components used for manufacturing in the United States. Without this kind of co–operation, many jobs would be lost, including jobs provided by cars imported from Mexico. In 2016, for example, the United States imported 1.6 million cars from Mexico—but about 40 percent of the value of their components was produced in the United States. Leaving NAFTA could jeopardize 31,000 jobs in the automotive industry in the United States alone. But now that it is threatened with the collapse or renegotiation of NAFTA, Mexico has already begun actively exploring new trade partnerships with Europe and China.

The big picture: Mexico is the third largest U.S. trade partner after China and Canada, and the third–largest supplier of U.S. imports. Some 79 percent of Mexico's total exports in 2013 went to the United States. Yes, the United States had a $64.3 billion deficit with Mexico in 2016, but trade with Mexico is a two–way street. The United States *exports* more to Mexico than to any other country except Canada, its other NAFTA partner. Moreover, the half trillion dollars in goods and services traded between Mexico and the United States each year since NAFTA was enacted over 23 years ago has resulted in millions of jobs for workers in both countries. According to a Woodrow Wilson Center study, nearly five million U.S. jobs now depend on trade with Mexico.

Trade, investment, joint production, and travel across the U.S.–Mexico border remain a way of life for border communities, including those in the United States. Disrupting them will create substantial economic costs for both countries. And a significantly weakened Mexican economy will also exacerbate Mexico's severe criminal violence and encourage violence–driven immigration to the United States.

What the Wall Would Do to Communities and the Environment

If erected, Trump's wall will not be the first significant barrier to be built on the border. That distinction goes to the 700–mile fence the U.S. began to put up—over protests from those on both sides of the border—some years ago.

These people include 26 federally–recognized Native American Nations in the U.S. and eight Indigenous Peoples in Mexico. The border on which the wall is to be built cuts through their tribal homelands and separates tribal members from their relatives and their sacred sites, while also sundering them from the natural environment which is crucial not just to their livelihoods but to their cultural and religious identity. In recognition of this problem, the U.S. Congress passed an act in 1983 allowing free travel across the borders within their homelands to one of the Native American Nations tribes. But when the fence was built, by waiving statutes like the National Historic Preservation Act of 1966, the Native American Graves Protection and Repatriation Act of 1990, and the American Indian Religious Freedom Act of 1994, Congress compromised that freedom of travel and made it hard for indigenous people to visit their family members and sacred sites.

Trump's wall will, of course, exacerbate the damage to these Native American communities, causing great pain and anger among the inhabitants. "If someone came into your house and built a wall in your living room, tell me, how would you feel about that?" asked Verlon Jose, vice chairman of the Tohono O'odham Nation, in an interview by *The New York Times*' Fernanda Santos in February 2017. Stretching out his arms to embrace the saguaro desert around him, he said, "This is our home." Many in his tribe want to resist the construction of the wall. Others fear that if the border barrier is weaker on the tribal land, drug smuggling will be funneled there as happened before with the fence, harming and ensnarling the community.

As Native American communities, conservation biologists, and the U.S. Fish and Wildlife Service all have highlighted, the wall will also have significant environmental costs in areas that host some of the greatest biodiversity in North America. Deriving its name from the isolated mountain ranges whose 10,000–foot peaks thrust into the skies, the "Sky Islands" region spanning southeastern Arizona, southwestern New Mexico, and northwestern Mexico, for example, features a staggering array of flora and fauna. Its precious, but fragile, biodiversity is due to the unusual convergence of four major ecoregions: the southern terminus of the temperate Rocky Mountains; the eastern extent of the low–elevation Sonoran Desert; the northern edge of the subtropical Sierra Madre Occidental; and the western terminus of the higher–elevation Chihuahuan Desert. Among the endangered species that will be affected by the wall are the jaguar, Sonoran pronghorn, Chiricahua leopard frog, lesser long–nose bat, Cactus ferruginous pygmy–owl, Mexican gray wolf, black–tailed prairie dog, jaguarondi, ocelot, and American bison. Other negatively–affected species will include desert tortoise, black bear, desert mule deer, and a variety of snakes. Even species that can fly, such as Rufous hummingbirds and Swainson and Gray hawks could be harmed, and vital insect pollinators that migrate across the border could be burnt up by the lights necessary to illuminate the wall.

Altogether, more than 100 species of animals that occur along the U.S.–Mexico border, in the Sky Islands area as well as in the Big Bend National Park in Texas and in the Rio Grande Valley, are endangered or threatened. But just as the DHS waived numerous cultural protection statutes to build the fence, it also overrode many crucial environmental laws—including the Endangered Species Act of 1973, the Migratory Bird Treaty Act of 1918, the National Environmental Policy Act of 1970, the Coastal Zone Management Act of 1972, and the Clean Water Act of 1972. The Trump administration wants to bulldoze through any remaining environmental considerations.

The administration's approach threatens years of binational environmental border cooperation that has protected not only many wild species, but also agriculture on both sides of the border. Take the boll weevil, a beetle that flies between Mexico and the United States and devastates cotton crops. In the late 1890s, the boll weevil nearly wiped out the U.S. cotton industry. Since then, the United States and Mexico have spent decades trying to eradicate the pest and almost succeeded. But the wall may so sour U.S.–Mexico environmental and security cooperation that Mexico may simply give up on eradication efforts. This will cause little damage to those in Mexico, since there is little cotton cultivation along that part of the Mexican border, but it will result in significant damage to U.S. farmers.

A poisoned U.S.–Mexican relationship could also prevent the renegotiation of water sharing agreements that are critical to the environment as well as to water and food security, and to farming. For example, the 1970 Boundary Treaty between the United States and Mexico specifies that officials from both the U.S. and Mexico must agree if either side wants to build any structure that could affect the flow of the Rio Grande or its flood waters, water that is vital to livestock and agriculture along the border. The fence was built despite Mexico's objections to it, and because its steel slats become clogged with debris during the rainy season, it has caused floods affecting cities and previously protected areas on both sides of the border, resulting in millions of dollars in damages.

It wasn't just Mexico that didn't want that fence. U.S. farmers and businessmen along the Texas border in the Rio Grande valley opposed it, too, since it blocks their access to the river water and also augments the severity of floods. Now the wall is to be brought to flood plain areas in Texas where water issues precisely like these had prevented the construction of the fence before.

Meanwhile, manufacturing, agriculture, hydraulic fracking, energy production, and ecosystems on both sides of the border depend on equitable and effective water sharing from the Rio Grande and the Colorado River, with both sides vulnerable to water scarcities. Over the decades there have been many challenges to the joint agreements governing water usage, and both Mexico and the U.S. have at times considered themselves the aggrieved parties. But in general, U.S.–Mexico cooperation over both the Rio Grande and Colorado rivers has been exceptional by international standards and has been hugely beneficial to both partners to the various treaties. That kind of co–operation is now at risk.

If in retaliation for the Trump administration's vitriolic, anti–Mexican language and policies, Mexico decided not live up to its side of the water bargain, U.S. farmers and others along the Rio Grande would be under severe threat of losing their livelihoods. One of them is Dale Murden in Monte Alto, who on his 20,000–acre farm cultivates sugarcane, grapefruit, cotton, citrus, and grain. Named in January 2017 the Citrus King of Texas, the former Texas Farm Bureau state director has dedicated his life to agriculture in southern Texas, relying on a Latino workforce. Yet he has memories of devastating water shortages in 2011 and 2013, when because of a severe drought Mexico could not send its allocation of the Rio Conches to the United States and 30 percent of his land became unproductive, with many crops dying. At that time he hoped that the U.S. State Department could persuade Mexico to release some water, even as Mexican farmers were also facing immense water shortages and devastation. U.S. diplomacy did work, no doubt helped by the rain that replenished Mexico's tributaries of the Rio Grande. Without the rain, Mexico would not have been able to pay back its accumulated water debt. But without collaborative U.S.–Mexico diplomacy and an atmosphere of a closer–than–ever U.S.–Mexico cooperation, Mexico still could have failed to deliver the water despite the rain. That positive spirit of cooperation also produced one of the world's most enlightened, environmentally–sensitive, and water–use–savvy version of a water treaty, the so–called Minute 319 of the 1944 Colorado River U.S.–Mexico water agreement. Unique in its recognition of the Colorado River delta as a water user, the update committed the United States to sending a so–called "pulse flow" to that ecosystem, thus helping to restore those unique wetlands. The United States also agreed to pay $18 million for water conservation in Mexico. In turn, Mexico delivered 124,000 acre–feet of Mexican water to Lake Mead. It was a win–win–win: for U.S. farmers, Mexican farmers, and ecosystems. But those were the good days of the U.S.–Mexico relationship, before the Trump administration. A new update to the treaty is under negotiation—once again a vital agreement and a lifeline for some 40 million people on both sides of the border that could fall prey to the Trump administration's approach to Mexico.

Yet this is a moment when maintaining cooperation is crucial because climate–change–increased evaporation rates, invasive plant infestation, and greater demands for water around the border and deep into U.S. and Mexican territories will only put further pressure on water use and increase the likelihood of severe scarcity.

Rather than a line of separation, the border should be conceived of as a membrane, connecting the tissues of communities on both sides, enabling mutually beneficial trade, manufacturing, ecosystem improvements, and security, while enhancing inter–cultural exchanges.

In 1971, When First Lady Pat Nixon attended the inauguration of Friendship Park—that tragic place that allows separated families only the most limited amount of contact—she said, "I hope there won't be a fence here too long." She supported two–way positive exchanges between the United States and Mexico, not barriers. In fact, for her visit, she had the fence in Friendship Park torn down. Unfortunately, it's still there, bigger, taller, and harder than when she visited, and with the wall about to get much worse yet.

Print Citations

CMS: Felbab-Brown, Vanda. "The Wall: The Real Costs of a Barrier between the United States and Mexico." In *The Reference Shelf: The National Debate Topic 2018–2019 Immigration*, edited by Betsy Maury, 109-121. Ipswich, MA: H.W. Wilson, 2018.

MLA: Felbab-Brown, Vanda. "The Wall: The Real Costs of a Barrier between the United States and Mexico." *The Reference Shelf: The National Debate Topic 2018–2019 Immigration*. Ed. Betsy Maury. Ipswich: H.W. Wilson, 2018. 109-121. Print.

APA: Felbab-Brown, V. (2018). The wall: The real costs of a barrier between the United States and Mexico. In Betsy Maury (Ed.), *The reference shelf: The national debate topic 2018–2019 immigration* (pp. 109-121). Ipswich, MA: H.W. Wilson. (Original work published 2017)

What Geology Has to Say About Building a 1,000-Mile Border Wall

By Maya Wei-Haas
Smithsonian.com, **February 7, 2017**

Last month, President Donald Trump took steps to make good on a campaign promise to turn the United States' existing border fence into a "big, beautiful" wall. On January 25, the White House issued an Executive Order announcing the creation of a "secure, contiguous, and impassable physical barrier … to prevent illegal immigration, drug and human trafficking, and acts of terrorism." Now the U.S. Customs and Border Protection—the office tasked with enforcing border regulations—is scrambling to make that order a concrete reality.

Today's fence consists of roughly 650 miles of disparate segments, made out of a combination of steel posts and rails, metal sheeting, chain link, concrete vehicle barriers and wire mesh. To replace that fence with what has been described as a 20- to 50-foot concrete structure that will traverse 1,000 of the some 2,000 miles of the U.S.'s border with Mexico will be no easy feat. Besides dealing with a proposed Mexican lawsuit and navigating the private ownership of much of Texas' lands, there is another concern few have addressed in detail: geology.

Compared to building a marble palace or high-steepled church, erecting a wall may seem relatively straightforward. It isn't. (Just ask the Chinese, whose Great Wall took 2,000 years to build and failed to keep out invaders.) Though most wall designs are fairly simple, builders must adapt to a wide range of terrains, explains Gary Clendenin, a senior hydrogeologist at ICF. The southern U.S. border alone contains desert, wetlands, grasslands, rivers, mountains and forests—all of which create vastly different problems for builders.

"The length of this thing presents challenges that just aren't typically undertaken in a construction project," says Clendenin.

Can these hurdles be overcome? *Smithsonian.com* asked two scientists, a geophysicist and a hydrogeologist, which geologic factors the wall's builders should take into account first if they are to execute this ambitious project.

Surveying the Situation

The Tower of Pisa was never meant to lean. Built between 1173 and 1370, the off-kilter structure was positioned atop roughly 30 feet of fine river sediments underlain by a layer of ancient marine clay. But as builders assembled the tons of marble, the river sediments didn't compact evenly. So by 1178, when they had finished work on the third story, the tower had already acquired its characteristic tilt.

The Italian government has since spent millions of dollars to make sure this beloved landmark doesn't topple over. Such structural failures serve as a reminder that, while our ancestors did manage to successfully erect many impressive feats, "they don't necessarily stay upright," in the words of field geophysicist Mika McKinnon. To circumvent such problems today, modern builders have added a crucial step to the construction process: surveying. Though time-consuming, this step is critical to ensure that the resulting structure can remain standing on *terra firma* for years to come.

Before a single brick is laid, teams of scientists assemble on scene to investigate a litany of details, from bedrock depth to soil chemistry. In the case of the border wall, they would have to traverse the entire length of the proposed path, working in segments to evaluate the region, collect data, develop plans. (This necessity makes the process of erecting walls—especially ones spanning thousands of miles—more challenging than building, say, a 95-story skyscraper.)

"Quite frankly, that would take years to do," says Clendenin, who specializes in linear projects like railways and roads. McKinnon agrees. One project she worked on, a three-mile stretch of pipeline, is now on year five of field surveys.

Yet Trump's order appears to allow a mere six months for all surveying and planning efforts. Within its long list of required steps, his executive order states:

> Produce a comprehensive study of the security of the southern border, to be completed within 180 days of this order, that shall include the current state of southern border security, all geophysical and topographical aspects of the southern border, the availability of Federal and State resources necessary to achieve complete operational control of the southern border, and a strategy to obtain and maintain complete operational control of the southern border.

When contacted by *Smithsonian.com*, the Customs and Border Protection agency declined to comment on the current timeline for the wall, saying in an email that "it would be speculative to address the questions that you're asking at this point." But according to scientists *Smithsonian.com* spoke to, it isn't going up anytime soon.

Getting to Bedrock

The prehistoric city of Petra stands as a prime example of ancient geologic foresight. Around the 4th century BC, Petra's inhabitants carved the basis for this once-bustling trading city directly into the rugged pink and tan sandstone cliffs between the Red Sea and the Dead sea. Though winds and rain threatened to erode the structure top down, its firm rooting in bedrock—the solid rock that lies beneath the earth's loose layers—has kept this structure standing tall for thousands of years.

Such grounding in bedrock is a key feature when building a megastructure, says McKinnon. For something as extensive as a 1,000-mile wall that stands upwards of

20 feet tall, builders will need to anchor the whole thing beneath the surface to the underlying rock if they want it to stay upright.

The problem is, getting to bedrock can be a doozy. Great swaths of the border feature a hefty layer of loose sediments—dirt, soils, sand—laying atop the bedrock. In some regions the bedrock is hundreds if not thousands of feet down. "Some places the bedrock will be too deep—you'll never be able to reach the bedrock in an affordable fashion," says McKinnon.

"That's okay if you want to [build] a tiny house because you just have it floating on its foundation," she adds.

But if you're building a megastructure, "you have a problem," she says.

That's not to say that building on sand is impossible. But to safely erect such structures, geophysicists today conduct extensive seismic surveys to image what lies beneath. To create these pictures, they install rows of spike-like geophones, which are 3D microphones that detect minute vibrations of the ground, converting them into an electric signal. Then they make a large noise, often by triggering an explosion or using a heavy weight to thump the ground. The geophones record the scattering and reflection of vibrations to image underground structures, and tease out problems that may lay under the surface.

McKinnon experienced one of these problems firsthand, during the construction of a hydroelectric dam that was meant to be built across a valley that spanned about a mile. The team did all the proper surveys of the region, and discovered that beneath their riverbed lay a second channel buried in dirt. "If we hadn't found it and we tried to build our dam across, then the water would have just eroded that old channel underneath and we would have had a river under our dam," she says.

There are two options for overcoming such problems with sediment: compact the sediment and add a deeper foundation. For a wall roughly 20 feet tall, the foundation should extend six to eight feet beneath the surface, Clendenin says. All of these steps are expensive and time-consuming. But skimp on any of them, and "you get your Leaning-Tower-of-Pisa situation," says McKinnon.

Of course, many modern regions don't have the economic resources to do such surveys and construction of deep foundations. The cities of Campania, Italy, are built atop loose sediments that are prone to sliding—a situation worsened by local clearcutting of the vegetation and unregulated construction that commonly lacks adequate foundations. These factors leave them vulnerable to the whims of their region's geology: In 1998, when a mudslide rippled through the city, the houses crumpled under the weight and movement of the sludge, leaving at least 95 dead.

Dirt Drama

"Something there is that doesn't love a wall / That sends the frozen-ground-swell under it," begins Robert Frost's poem "Mending Wall." Frost may not have been a geological surveyor, but he got one thing right: When it comes to building walls, soil swelling is a major headache. That's why, after surveyors finish assessing the kind of rock and earth they'll be building over, they start studying the dirt.

Sediments, particularly in clay-rich materials, can take on water, swelling like a sponge in a bowl of water. The resulting cycles of swelling and shrinking during wet and

The southern border alone contains desert, wetlands, grasslands, rivers, mountains and forests—all of which create vastly different problems for builders.

dry periods can crack the very foundation of structures. And these types of soils are common in many states where the border wall will be built, including Texas and parts of New Mexico. In fact, about half of American homes are built on soils that expand significantly, and nearly half of those suffer damage yearly because of the soil, according to the American Society of Civil Engineers.

Dirt can also eat up the wall's support system. Soils that are naturally acidic or have high chloride levels can rapidly degrade iron-rich metals, says McKinnon. These soils could "corrode any, say, nice big metal rebar that you're putting in there to stabilize your foundation," she says. Other soils have a high amount of sulfates, a compound found in the common mineral gypsum that breaks down both metals and concrete. Sulfate-rich soils are common in what's known as the Trans-Pecos soils along the border in the southwestern arm of Texas.

"You're going to encounter hundreds, if not thousands, of different types of soils along [such a lengthy] linear pathway," says Clendenin. (In fact, there are over 1,300 kinds of soil in Texas alone.) And many of those soils aren't going to be the right type to build on top of. At that point, would-be wall-builders have two options: Spend more time and money excavating the existing soils and replacing them with better dirt—or avoid the region altogether.

One thing they can't always avoid, though, are regions at risk of earthquakes and floods. Rivers run along a sizeable portion of the U.S.-Mexico border, which can create a very real danger of flood. Building adjacent to rivers can also present unexpected legal issues: A 1970 treaty necessitates that the fence be set back from the Rio Grande river, which delineates the Texas-Mexico border. Because of this, the current fence crosscuts Texas landowner's property and has gaps to allow landowners to pass.

Earthquakes are also relatively common in the western U.S. Depending on the build, some of these tremblors could cause cracks or breaks in the wall, says McKinnon. One example is the magnitude 7.2 quake that struck in 2010 near the California-Mexico Border, according to Austin Elliott, a postdoctoral student at the University of Oxford whose research is focused on the history of earthquakes. "If there had been a wall at El Centinela [a mountain in northern Mexico] it would have been offset," Elliott writes on Twitter.

Even if all the proper surveys are completed and the boxes checked, success isn't guaranteed. "There are just so many things that have to be done before you even shovel out the first scoop of dirt," says Clendenin.

Despite all of our modern surveying tools and careful planning, the earth will still surprise you, adds McKinnon. "This part that you thought was boring and simple and easy to predict is actually totally complicated," she says. "Look at any major excavation for a subway system, any major bridge construction, any large tower complex; all of them had intense surveys beforehand, extensive design phases, and still had to modify while building."

After the announcement of Trump's Executive Order, McKinnon took to Twitter to leave a foreboding reminder of the consequences of underestimating the Earth. "Earth doesn't forgive sloppy," she wrote. She added in an interview: "Ignore geology at your peril."

Print Citations

CMS: Wei-Haas, Maya. "What Geology Has to Say about Building a 1,000-Mile Border Wall." In *The Reference Shelf: The National Debate Topic 2018–2019 Immigration*, edited by Betsy Maury, 122-126. Ipswich, MA: H.W. Wilson, 2018.

MLA: Wei-Haas, Maya. "What Geology Has to Say about Building a 1,000-Mile Border Wall." *The Reference Shelf: The National Debate Topic 2018–2019 Immigration*. Ed. Betsy Maury. Ipswich: H.W. Wilson, 2018. 122-126. Print.

APA: Wei-Haas, M. (2018). What geology has to say about building a 1,000-mile border wall. In Betsy Maury (Ed.), *The reference shelf: The national debate topic 2018–2019 immigration* (pp. 122-126). Ipswich, MA: H.W. Wilson. (Original work published 2017)

Trump Privately Presses for U.S. Military to Pay for Border Wall

By Josh Dawsey Mike DeBonis
Chicago Tribune via *The Washington Post*, March 27, 2018

President Donald Trump, who repeatedly insisted during the 2016 campaign that Mexico would pay for a wall along the southern border, is privately pushing the U.S. military to fund construction of his signature project.

Trump has told advisers that he was spurned in a large spending bill last week when lawmakers appropriated only $1.6 billion for the border wall. He has suggested to Defense Secretary Jim Mattis and congressional leaders that the Pentagon could fund the sprawling project, citing a "national security" risk.

After floating the notion to several advisers last week, Trump told House Speaker Paul Ryan, R-Wis., that the military should pay for the wall, according to three people familiar with the meeting last Wednesday in the White House residence. Ryan offered little reaction to the idea, these people said, but senior Capitol Hill officials later said it was an unlikely prospect.

Trump's pursuit of defense dollars to finance the U.S.-Mexico border wall underscores his determination to fulfill a campaign promise and build the barrier despite resistance in the Republican-led Congress. The administration's last-minute negotiations with lawmakers to secure billions more for the wall failed, and Trump grudgingly signed the spending bill Friday after a short-lived veto threat.

Four days later, Trump continued to express regret over signing the $1.3 trillion package, which funded the government and averted a shutdown, saying it was a mistake and he should have followed his instincts.

In another interaction with senior aides last week, Trump noted that the Defense Department was getting so much money as part of the spending bill that the Pentagon could surely afford the border wall, two White House officials said. The Pentagon received about $700 billion in the spending package, which Trump repeatedly lauded as "historic."

Meanwhile, the $1.6 billion in the bill for some fencing and levees on the border not only fell far short of the $25 billion that Trump was seeking, but it came with tight restrictions on how the money could be spent.

The individuals and officials spoke on the condition of anonymity to talk freely about private discussions.

White House press secretary Sarah Huckabee Sanders deflected a question Tuesday about money dedicated to the military being used to fund construction of the wall. "I can't get into the specifics of that at this point, but I

Defense hawks in the Republican ranks would balk at taking money now dedicated to the Pentagon for aircraft, weapons and improvements to the armed forces' readiness and instead steering it toward construction of the wall.

can tell you that the continuation of building the wall is ongoing, and we're going to continue moving forward in that process," Sanders told reporters.

"Build WALL through M!" Trump recently wrote on Twitter. He retweeted those words Tuesday, noting that "our Military is again rich." Two advisers said "M" stood for "military."

The president has suggested to Mattis that his department, instead of the Department of Homeland Security, could fund the construction, two Trump advisers said. But the military is not likely to fund the wall, according to White House and Defense Department officials.

The Pentagon has plenty of money, but reprogramming it for a wall would require votes in Congress that the president does not seem to have. Taking money from the current 2018 budget for the wall would require an act of Congress, said a senior Pentagon official.

To find the money in the 2019 defense budget, Trump would have to submit a budget amendment that would require 60 votes in the Senate, the official said.

Democrats in Congress would probably chafe at military spending going to the construction of a border wall, and military officials may also blanch, White House advisers said.

Defense hawks in the Republican ranks would balk at taking money now dedicated to the Pentagon for aircraft, weapons and improvements to the armed forces' readiness and instead steering it toward construction of the wall.

"First Mexico was supposed to pay for it, then U.S. taxpayers, and now our men and women in uniform? This would be a blatant misuse of military funds and tied up in court for years. Secretary Mattis ought not bother and instead use the money to help our troops, rather than advance the president's political fantasies," Senate Minority Leader Charles Schumer, D-N.Y., said in a statement to the *Washington Post*.

Trump has grown frustrated watching constant TV criticism of the spending package and is determined to find a new way to fund the wall, several advisers said, privately grousing that his political supporters could become disenchanted without progress. After a recent trip to see prototypes of the wall in California, Trump has grown more animated by the issue, advisers said.

The president's comments raising the possibility of using Pentagon funds to build the wall came after the collapse of negotiations with Democrats to secure $25 billion in long-term wall funding in exchange for protections for young immigrants at risk for deportation because of Trump's cancellation of the Deferred Action for Childhood Arrivals (DACA) program.

The White House offered three years of protections for DACA recipients, according to multiple congressional aides, but Democrats demanded protections for a larger group of "dreamers," including those who never applied or are ineligible for DACA. The negotiations fell apart before the spending bill was drafted and passed last week.

The urgency to strike a deal reflected the growing sense that the spending bill represented the last chance for the Trump administration to secure substantial wall funding, at least in the president's first term. Top Republicans believe it is all but certain that Democrats will gain House seats in November's midterm elections—and perhaps take the majority—greatly enhancing their bargaining position in future spending negotiations.

Only $641 million is earmarked for new primary fencing in areas that currently have no barriers, and most of the money can be spent only on "operationally effective designs" that were already deployed as of last May. That means the prototype designs the Trump administration is exploring cannot be built, except along a stretch of the border near San Diego where a barrier is already in place.

Print Citations

CMS: Dawsey, Josh, and Mike DeBonis. "Trump Privately Presses for U.S. Military to Pay for Border Wall." In *The Reference Shelf: The National Debate Topic 2018–2019 Immigration,* edited by Betsy Maury, 127-129. Ipswich, MA: H.W. Wilson, 2018.

MLA: Dawsey, Josh, and Mike DeBonis. "Trump Privately Presses for U.S. Military to Pay for Border Wall." *The Reference Shelf: The National Debate Topic 2018–2019 Immigration.* Ed. Betsy Maury. Ipswich: H.W. Wilson, 2018. 127-129. Print.

APA: Dawsey, J., & M. DeBonis. (2018). Trump privately presses for U.S. military to pay for border wall. In Betsy Maury (Ed.), *The reference shelf: The national debate topic 2018–2019 immigration* (pp. 127-129). Ipswich, MA: H.W. Wilson. (Original work published 2018)

In 2006, Democrats Were Saying "Build That Fence!"

By Annie Linskey
Boston Globe, **January 27, 2017**

WASHINGTON—As a senator, Barack Obama once offered measured praise for the border control legislation that would become the basis for one of Donald Trump's first acts as president.

"The bill before us will certainly do some good," Obama said on the Senate floor in October 2006. He praised the legislation, saying it would provide "better fences and better security along our borders" and would "help stem some of the tide of illegal immigration in this country."

Obama was talking about the Secure Fence Act of 2006, legislation authorizing a barrier along the southern border passed into law with the support of 26 Democratic senators including party leaders like Hillary Clinton, Joe Biden, and Chuck Schumer.

Now it's become the legal mechanism for Trump to order construction of a wall between the United States and Mexico, attempting to make good on a key promise from the campaign trail. Trump specifically cited the law in the first sentence of Wednesday's executive order authorizing the wall.

The episode shows how concerns over border security occupied Washington well before Trump made it the centerpiece of his candidacy, and that Democrats were more than willing to offer big sums of taxpayer money to keep Mexicans and other Latino immigrants out of the United States. The border fence called for in the 2006 law was far less ambitious than the wall Trump envisions, and, as he is apt to do, he has made the issue bigger, more explosive, and far more disruptive to US diplomacy.

Trump has also added his own twist that was never a part of the 2006 legislation, a promise that the Mexican people would pay for the wall. But on Thursday White House spokesman Sean Spicer, in a briefing aboard Air Force One, said that Trump would levy a 20 percent tax on all imports from Mexico to fund construction of the barrier.

He estimated that the 20 percent tariff would bring in $10 billion a year and "easily pay for the wall." Later, the White House appeared to back away from the idea of an import tax.

Even before the highly controversial proposed funding mechanism was made public Thursday afternoon, Mexican President Enrique Peña Nieto announced that he was canceling his planned trip to the United States next week, citing the new administration's focus on the wall.

Former Mexican president Vicente Fox, who opposed the measure in 2006 when he was in office, had even harsher words for Trump. "Donald, don't be self-indulgent," he posted on his Twitter feed Thursday. "Mexico has spoken, we will never ever pay for the #[Expletive]Wall."

For Democrats who generally support relaxed rules that offer a path to citizenship for immigrants, the 2006 law was seen as the better of two evils. The House had recently passed legislation immigration advocates viewed as draconian because it would make any undocumented immigrant a felon.

By comparison, the border fence didn't seem so bad. Moreover, immigration reform advocates were beaten down after a wider overhaul had stalled.

"It didn't have anywhere near the gravity of harm," recalled Angela Kelley, who in 2006 was the legislative director for the National Immigration Forum. "It was hard to vote against it because who is going to vote against a secure fence? And it was benign compared with what was out there."

The law flew through the Senate with a vote of 80 to 19. (One senator, Edward Kennedy of Massachusetts, was not present. John Kerry, the state's other senator, voted against it.) In the House, the measure passed 283 to 138, with 64 Democrats supporting it. (The Massachusetts delegation was split.) From there it went to then-President

> **Trump has also added his own twist that was never part of the 2006 legislation, a promise that the Mexican people would pay for the wall.**

George W. Bush, who signed it 12 days before the 2006 mid-term elections.

The number of illegal immigrants in the United States reached about 12 million in 2007, and has since dropped off.

The plan was not nearly as expansive as Trump's promise for a wall along the entire border. It allowed for about 700 miles of fencing along certain stretches. Congress put aside $1.4 billion for the fence, but the whole cost, including maintenance, was pegged at $50 billion over 25 years, according to analyses at the time.

The government had constructed about 650 miles of fence by 2015, most of it after passage of the act, according to a report last year by the US Government Accountability Office.

In his 2006 floor speech, Obama nodded to the prevailing belief in Washington that the bill wasn't going anywhere. "This bill, from my perspective, is an election-year, political solution," he said. "It is great for sound bites and ad campaigns."

Clinton also voted for the bill, though in a floor speech during the debate she completely ignored the fence issue and heaped praise on an amendment to it that would help New York farmers by expanding the number of visas allowed for agricultural workers.

During her recent failed presidential campaign, however, she referred to the vote.

"I voted numerous times when I was a senator to spend money to build a barrier to try to prevent illegal immigrants from coming in," Clinton said at November 2015 town hall in New Hampshire, "and I do think that you have to control your borders."

Immigration reform advocates who worked on the bill—and opposed it—remembered thinking the fence would never actually be built.

"There was a lot of analysis done that said you just can't do it," said Kelley, who worked on the bill and is now the Executive Director of Center for American Progress Action Fund. "It was more a political statement than a sound policy proposal."

"A lot of people owned land [where the fence would go]. There were endangered squirrels. None of that was being dealt with. It really did feel like this was more of a slogan than a solution," said Kelley.

Only one current Democratic leader voted against the bill: That's Bernie Sanders, who was in the House of Representatives at the time. He didn't make a statement about it one way or the other, and his spokesman, Michael Briggs, declined to comment Thursday.

Leading the opposition in the Senate was Kennedy, though he was not present for the final vote.

From the floor he bemoaned the death of a larger bipartisan overhaul to the immigration system and mocked the Republicans for coming up with legislation he felt would do little to fix the problem.

"Republican leaders wasted time, opportunity, and your money," Kennedy said. "For a $9 billion fence that won't do the job. That is just a bumper sticker solution for a complex problem. It's a feel-good plan that will have little effect in the real world."

But outside the halls of Congress, constituents took the legislation very seriously.

Republicans held a series of field hearings about the fence around the country, stirring up support for it.

Advocates jammed the phone lines, and even sent members of Congress bricks that were intended to symbolize the wall they wanted constructed on the southern border, according to a *Washington Post* story from the time.

They were led by a senator who did always argue for the wall: Jeff Sessions, whom Trump has selected to be the attorney general.

"We do not have operational control of the border," Sessions said during the 2006 debate. "Fencing on the southern border is and should be a part of our plan to recapture a legal system of immigration in America. It remains one of our important priorities."

Print Citations

CMS: Linskey, Annie. "In 2006, Democrats Were Saying 'Build That Fence.'" In *The Reference Shelf: The National Debate Topic 2018–2019 Immigration,* edited by Betsy Maury, 130-133. Ipswich, MA: H.W. Wilson, 2018.

MLA: Linskey, Annie. "In 2006, Democrats Were Saying 'Build That Fence.'" *The Reference Shelf: The National Debate Topic 2018–2019 Immigration.* Ed. Betsy Maury. Ipswich: H.W. Wilson, 2018. 130-133. Print.

APA: Linskey, A. (2018). In 2006, Democrats were saying "build that fence." In Betsy Maury (Ed.), *The reference shelf: The national debate topic 2018–2019 immigration* (pp. 130-133). Ipswich, MA: H.W. Wilson. (Original work published 2017)

Landowners Likely to Bring More Lawsuits as Trump Moves on Border Wall

By John Burnett
NPR, February 23, 2017

President Trump has promised to build a wall along the 2,000 miles of the U.S.-Mexico border.

A third of that border already has a barrier, thanks to the Secure Fence Act of 2006, which was signed by then-President George W. Bush. That initiative ran into issues with landowners near the Rio Grande. If the wall goes forward as Trump promises, more lawsuits may be coming.

Out on the Western border between the U.S. and Mexico, straight-line fencing cuts through public lands and big ranches. But down in South Texas, the imposing, rust-colored barrier runs into a thicket of private property rights.

Hundreds of irate landowners along the river have protested what they call a government land grab to install the controversial fence. Their cases landed before U.S. District Judge Andrew Hanen in Brownsville. He calls himself "the fence judge."

President Bush—who appointed Hanen—signed the law ordering the erection of 700 miles of physical barriers along the border.

Unlike the sparser population upriver, the lower Rio Grande Valley is dense with people and history. Some of the acreage goes back to Spanish land grants. To purchase property rights for the construction, Border Patrol had to contact landowners near the serpentine river. Most of them settled out of court, but other cases have gotten into the weeds.

Some landowners want more money. Some want a gate in the fence to be able to access their land on the other side. In other cases, Hanen says government lawyers ran into complex family trees.

"Finding out even who owns the land that's being condemned has been a real problem for the government," he says.

When negotiations fail, the Justice Department sues. In all, 320 eminent domain cases have ended up in Hanen's court. The judge has made national news as an outspoken critic of President Barack Obama's more lenient immigration policies. This is the first interview he has given on the years-long legal morass surrounding the border fence.

"You have to realize these are everyday people living their ordinary life, and all of a sudden the government knocks on their door and says, 'We want your backyard,'

" Hanen says. "I mean, all of a sudden they're facing the might of the Department of Homeland Security and the Department of Justice, and all of a sudden, they're a defendant in a lawsuit through no fault of their own."

The 63-year-old judge grew up in Central Texas, but he knows the border—his daughter was baptized in the Rio Grande.

On several occasions, Hanen even left the courthouse to inspect the contested borderlands firsthand, while his U.S. marshal escort worried about cartel violence just across the river.

One of the properties Hanen walked belongs to Eloisa Tamez, 81, who is perhaps the valley's loudest fence opponent. The 18-foot-tall barricade bisects her 3 acres in the community of Calaboz, which is west of Brownsville.

"In order for me to move around in the rest of my property, that which is south of the wall, I have to insert a code so that this monstrous gate can open and then I can go through," she says.

The iron gateway rolls away, giving Tamez access to the other half of her ancestral property, choked with cactus and mesquite.

Her case—*United States of America v. .26 Acres of Land*—dragged on in Hanen's court for seven years. She knew how it would end. In federal condemnation cases, whether for dams, highways or national parks, the government almost always wins.

Ultimately, Tamez got a check for $56,000 for the quarter-acre of land under the fence and the inconvenience. Sitting in her office at the Brownsville campus of the University of Texas Rio Grande Valley, where she is a professor of nursing, Tamez is still not satisfied.

"I wasn't looking for the money," she says. "I don't want to lose the land. I want the land back. I don't believe in the barriers."

NPR looked at the more than 300 fence cases in Hanen's court. Two-thirds of them have been resolved. Most of them took about 3 1/2 years, and most were under an acre. The median settlement works out to $12,600. On the high end, the Nature Conservancy got $1.1 million for 8 acres.

But not everybody ended up in court.

An 84-year-old retired schoolteacher named Arnaldo Farias lives next to Tamez. He was happy to accept the government's offer of $8,000, though he says he still hasn't been paid four years later.

Unlike his firebrand neighbor, Farias says he is glad to have the steel barrier running through his backyard. He says it stops unauthorized immigrants from walking across his property and taking showers in his outbuilding.

"I wanted to sell because I wanted security," he says. "You don't know what kind of people are coming. That's the bottom line."

Hundreds of irate landowners along the river have protested what they call a government land grab to install the controversial fence.

Large federal land acquisition projects typically take years. Today, 91 of the landowner cases in South Texas remain open and even more are expected. When Trump signed his executive order last month calling for his "big beautiful wall," Hanen knew what that would mean.

"What I thought was, 'Oh, this is going to be a lot more work for us,' " Hanen says. "It's gonna be a lot of headache. The people in South Texas, there are a lot of hard feelings about the wall."

Details of the next phase of the wall are unclear. For instance, there's no word whether the federal government is trying to get Mexico to reimburse it to pay for the land along the Rio Grande.

Print Citations

CMS: Burnett, John. "Landowners Likely to Bring More Lawsuits as Trump Moves on Border Wall." In *The Reference Shelf: The National Debate Topic 2018–2019 Immigration,* edited by Betsy Maury, 134-136. Ipswich, MA: H.W. Wilson, 2018.

MLA: Burnett, John. "Landowners Likely to Bring More Lawsuits as Trump Moves on Border Wall." *The Reference Shelf: The National Debate Topic 2018–2019 Immigration.* Ed. Betsy Maury. Ipswich: H.W. Wilson, 2018. 134-136. Print.

APA: Burnett, J. (2018). Landowners likely to bring more lawsuits as Trump moves on border wall. In Betsy Maury (Ed.), *The reference shelf: The national debate topic 2018–2019 immigration* (pp. 134-136). Ipswich, MA: H.W. Wilson. (Original work published 2017)

The Taking: How the Federal Government Abused Its Power to Seize Property for a Border Fence

By T. Christian Miller (*ProPublica*), Kiah Collier, and Julian Aguilar
The Texas Tribune, December 14, 2017

BROWNSVILLE—The land agents started working the border between Texas and Mexico in the spring of 2007. Sometimes they were representatives from the U.S. Army Corps of Engineers. Other times they were officers from the U.S. Border Patrol, uniformed in green, guns tucked into side holsters. They visited tumbledown mobile homes and suburban houses with golf course views. They surveyed farms fecund with sugar cane, cotton and sorghum growing by the mud-brown Rio Grande. They delivered their blunt news to ranchers and farmers, sheet metal workers and university professors, auto mechanics and wealthy developers.

The federal government was going to build a fence to keep out drug smugglers and immigrants crossing into the United States illegally, they told property owners. The structure was going to cut straight across their land. The government would make a fair offer to buy property, the agents explained. That was the law. But if the owners didn't want to sell, the next step was federal court. U.S. attorneys would file a lawsuit to seize it. One way or the other, the government would get the land. That, too, was the law.

The visits launched the most aggressive seizure of private land by the federal government in decades. In less than a year, the U.S. Department of Homeland Security filed more than 360 eminent domain lawsuits against property owners, involving thousands of acres of land in the border states of Texas, New Mexico, Arizona and California.

Most of the seized land ran along the Rio Grande, which forms the border between Texas and Mexico. All told, the agency paid $18.2 million to accumulate a ribbon of land occupying almost half the length of the 120 miles of the Rio Grande Valley in southernmost Texas.

Years before President Donald Trump promised to build his wall, Homeland Security erected an 18-foot-high fence here in a botched land grab that serves as a warning for the future.

An investigation by *ProPublica* and the *Texas Tribune* shows that Homeland Security cut unfair real estate deals, secretly waived legal safeguards for property owners, and ultimately abused the government's extraordinary power to take land from private citizens.

The major findings:

- Homeland Security circumvented laws designed to help landowners receive fair compensation. The agency did not conduct formal appraisals of targeted parcels. Instead, it issued low-ball offers based on substandard estimates of property values.

- Larger, wealthier property owners who could afford lawyers negotiated deals that, on average, tripled the opening bids from Homeland Security. Smaller and poorer landholders took whatever the government offered—or wrung out small increases in settlements. The government conceded publicly that landowners without lawyers might wind up shortchanged, but did little to protect their interests.

- The Justice Department bungled hundreds of condemnation cases. The agency took property without knowing the identity of the actual owners. It condemned land without researching facts as basic as property lines. Landholders spent tens of thousands of dollars to defend themselves from the government's mistakes.

- The government had to redo settlements with landowners after it realized it had failed to account for the valuable water rights associated with the properties, an oversight that added months to the compensation process.

- On occasion, Homeland Security paid people for property they did not actually own. The agency did not attempt to recover the misdirected taxpayer funds, instead paying for land a second time once it determined the correct owners.

- Nearly a decade later, scores of landowners remain tangled in lawsuits. The government has already taken their land and built the border fence. But it has not resolved claims for its value.

The errors and disparities played out family by family, block by block, county by county, up and down the length of the border fence.

The Loop family spent more than $100,000 to defend their farmland from repeated government mistakes about the size, shape and value of their property. The government built a fence across Robert De Los Santos' family land but almost a decade later has yet to reach a settlement for it. Ranch hand Roberto Pedraza was accidentally paid $20,500 for land he did not even own.

Retired teacher Juan Cavazos was offered $21,500 for a two-acre slice of his land. He settled for that, figuring he couldn't afford to hire a lawyer.

Rollins M. Koppel, a local attorney and banker, did not make the same mistake. A high-priced Texas law firm negotiated his offer from $233,000 to almost $5 million—the highest settlement in the Rio Grande Valley.

"We got screwed," said Cavazos, 74.

Homeland Security and the U.S. Army Corps of Engineers referred questions to the Justice Department.

A Justice Department official, who insisted on anonymity, said all agencies involved in the land seizures followed proper procedures. He declined to respond to specific questions.

"[F]or any large public works project impacting hundreds of properties, the values are likely to cover a large range because so many different kinds of property are being acquired," the official said. "It is these very differences in uses that cannot be captured in a cursory statistical analysis of the properties acquired and the prices paid for these lands."

Michael Chertoff, the former secretary for Homeland Security under President George W. Bush who personally approved the condemnations in Texas, declined to comment.

Greg Giddens led the fence building project at Homeland Security. Now retired, Giddens said his team faced pressure from both U.S. Customs and Border Protection, which wanted the fence built quickly to benefit law enforcement, and from Congress, which set a deadline to complete the structure.

"Everybody wanted to do this right. But it was clear that the mission was to get this done," Giddens said.

Hyla Head, the former Army Corps official who oversaw the condemnation process for the agency, said the government did everything according to regulation.

"There is a process that we have to follow and we followed that," said Head, now retired. "I think we did a damn good job with the constraints that we were under."

The fence was born in the middle of a fierce national debate on immigration reform. In 2006, Rep. Peter King, a New York Republican, introduced a plan to build hundreds of miles of a physical barrier along the southern border. Although controversial, the proposal won bipartisan support. Then Sen. Jeff Sessions, the Alabama Republican, led the fight for its passage. Yea votes came from Democratic Sens. Hillary Clinton and Barack Obama.

On Oct. 26, 2006, President Bush signed the Secure Fence Act. President Obama oversaw the fence's construction. All told, Homeland Security built 654 miles of fence—just short of the 700 mile goal set by Congress—at a cost of $2.4 billion.

Now Trump has promised to finish the job with a much larger wall—nearly twice the height of the current fence, made of concrete, and occupying much of the remaining 1,300 miles of southern border unguarded by a physical barrier. His administration has declared its intent to take more land to build the wall in the central Rio Grande Valley, where much of the property remains in private hands.

For Trump to succeed, the federal government will have to file more eminent domain lawsuits using the same law that resulted in uneven payments the last time. Many of the players who oversaw construction of the fence are now working on making Trump's wall a reality.

Mauricio Vidaurri's voice catches when he envisions a wall running across his family farm south of Laredo on the banks of the Rio Grande.

A rancher, Vidaurri strongly supports better border protection. Border crossers constantly trespass on his land, and drug couriers have broken into a home on the ranch.

But a wall would almost certainly split the ranch that has been in his family since the 1700s. If Homeland Security wants to build a wall, Vidaurri knows he will be almost helpless to stop it.

"That's a battle that we can't win," he said.

A Sovereign Power

"Eminent domain" probably exists as a phrase in the consciousness of most Americans in some way or another. Maybe you heard it when the government was building a highway, or clearing a route for gas pipelines.

The sovereign power to seize land—and the need to protect property owners from its abuse—dates to the beginning of modern democracy.

In 1215, the Magna Carta limited royal power—including curtailing the sovereign's ability to take property from his nobles. "No free man shall be seized or imprisoned, or stripped of his rights or possessions," it read. A man's castle was his home, and not even a king could take it without due process. The language survives unaltered in modern British law.

More than five centuries later, America's earliest lawmakers enshrined private property rights in the U.S. Constitution. The Fifth Amendment required that the government provide "just compensation" if it took property through eminent domain—the English rendering of a Latin phrase meaning "supreme lordship." If the government was going to appropriate property, it had to pay for it, fairly and fully.

Over the decades, eminent domain transformed the American landscape. The U.S. Interstate Highway System and some national parks, NASA's Cape Canaveral and the U.S. Supreme Court building itself—none would have been possible without federal land condemnation. During World War II, the Justice Department boasted of being the largest real estate broker in the nation. The federal government acquired more than 20 million acres of land to build bases and other military sites—an area the size of South Carolina.

At the same time, the potential for abuse inspired deep-seated fear. An early Supreme Court justice described eminent domain as a "despotic power." Property owners—from gigantic timber companies to people evicted from their homes—have fought bitterly to stop the government from taking their land, or to ensure a fair market price.

Politically, an unusual coalition of the right and the left has resisted the use of eminent domain.

Progressives have argued that disadvantaged groups feel the pain of condemnation more than most. In the 1950s and 1960s, officials deployed eminent domain to bulldoze mostly minority, mostly poor inner-city neighborhoods in the name of urban renewal. Government planners called it "blight removal." Writer James Baldwin had another term: "It means negro removal," he said after a meeting with U.S.

Attorney General Robert Kennedy in 1963. "And the federal government is an accomplice to this fact."

On the right, conservatives have warned of the so-called "grasping hand" of bureaucratic attacks on private property rights. That concern rose to national prominence in 2005, when the U.S. Supreme Court ruled against private property owners in the landmark case *Kelo v. City of New London*.

The Connecticut city condemned the homes of Susette Kelo and her neighbors to turn the land over to a private developer. The developer planned to build a hotel, housing, and office space to complement a new research center by Pfizer Corp., the pharmaceutical giant. The city determined the new development would generate jobs and tax revenue.

In a 5-4 decision, the court decided that taking land from one set of private property owners to give to another private entity was permissible as a "public use." Kelo's small pink house was relocated and her neighborhood was bulldozed, but nothing was ever built.

The ruling united ideological enemies. Ralph Nader blasted it. So did Rush Limbaugh. A few property rights activists were so angry they sought to condemn the New Hampshire home of Justice David Souter and replace it with the "Lost Liberty Hotel."

One of the few high-profile supporters of the ruling was Donald Trump, then a New York developer. "I happen to agree with it 100 percent," he said. His opinion was informed by experience. In the 1990s, he lost an eminent domain battle when a local agency failed in its bid to tear down an elderly woman's home in Atlantic City to make room for a limousine parking lot for Trump's casino.

Trump's enthusiasm for taking land endures. During a February 2016 presidential debate, Trump described it as almost like winning the lottery. "When eminent domain is used on somebody's property, that person gets a fortune," he told the audience. "They get at least fair market value, and if they are smart, they'll get two or three times the value of their property."

In response to the *Kelo* decision, 45 states, including Texas, passed new laws to improve landholder protections. Some states banned private-to-private takings. Others required "supercompensation" —payments at greater than the fair market value. Those reforms built on others passed over the years. California pays out up to $5,000 for property owners to hire their own appraisers. Texas provides special commissions to review land seizures before the start of costly legal proceedings. Utah created an independent ombudsman to help landowners navigate the process.

But the furor to fix eminent domain abuse bypassed one important entity: the federal government. After *Kelo*, President Bush issued an executive order requiring agencies to better monitor land seizures. Congress passed no meaningful legislation.

And so, by the time the land agents had finished knocking on doors in the Rio Grande Valley at the end of 2007, the property owners faced a federal government armed with powerful legal tools, many created decades earlier for a very different purpose than building a border fence.

Tools for the Taking

The Homeland Security officials in charge of building the border fence were getting nervous.

Congress had set a deadline to complete the project: Dec. 31, 2008. In little more than a year, Homeland Security, working through its U.S. Customs and Border Protection division, needed to issue millions of dollars' worth of government contracts, buy 145,000 tons of steel, and build hundreds of miles of fence across unforgiving terrain.

"The clock is ticking," Giddens, head of the fence task force, warned colleagues in a September 2007 email.

The biggest problem was Texas. Unlike other border states, most of the land where the fence was going rested in private hands. And people in the Rio Grande Valley were refusing to sell. The land agents would close only 22 deals.

On Dec. 7, 2007, Chertoff announced his decision: If landowners wouldn't cooperate, the government was going to take the land. They had 30 days to decide. "We would of course like to reach an agreement with the landowner," he said. "But if we are unsuccessful, we are prepared to use eminent domain," he told reporters.

Over the following seven months, Homeland Security filed hundreds of lawsuits against scores of landowners along the Rio Grande. Most of the targeted acreage was farmland. But homes, golf courses, businesses and even nature preserves were sliced into pieces.

Alberto Garza, 91, lost 10 acres that provided access to the sugar cane farm he had worked for 50 years. The De Leons were disowned of four separate tracts that had been in their family since the 1790s, when Spain ruled the region. Ray Loop was forced to give up a swath of property that ran in front of his home near the Rio Grande. The Nature Conservancy, one of the country's leading environmental organizations, surrendered eight acres of its preserve. The University of Texas-Rio Grande Valley was cut off from the golf course where its team practiced.

All told, the agency built 50 miles of fence in disconnected strips 40 to 60 feet wide—and seized a total of 564 acres. A process that can take years for a single parcel had been compressed into months.

The seizures were made possible by a piece of paper called a Declaration of Taking.

The Taking Act was passed by Congress during the Great Depression to help stimulate the economy. It was designed as an alternative to traditional, slow-moving eminent domain lawsuits. The idea was to expedite land seizures, allowing the federal government to quickly build public works projects and generate new jobs.

By using a so-called quick-take, a federal agency gained title to a person's property on the same day it filed a declaration of taking in court. The bulldozers could roll as soon as a judge approved an order to possess the land. The landowner was almost powerless to stop the process.

To balance this muscular exercise of sovereign power, the law required the government to immediately deposit a check with the court to pay the landholder. The amount was supposed to be the fair market value, the amount that a willing buyer would pay a willing seller. The landowner could take the money, or try to convince the government to pay more—a process that could take years.

"They can just grab the property now and worry about the price later," said Robert H. Thomas, past chair of the American Bar Association's eminent domain committee. "It's a pretty potent tool."

But not powerful enough for Homeland Security. The agency deployed a second tool to make it easier and faster to seize land. It issued a waiver that eviscerated a federal law designed to protect property owners from unfair seizures.

The so-called Uniform Act required the government to negotiate with the owners before seizing land. An agency couldn't take coercive action to force a sale, and owners would receive a detailed description of the property to be seized.

Perhaps the most important provision was that the government had to formally appraise land worth more than $10,000 before taking an owner to court. The appraisal had to be done according to the exacting standards spelled out in the 262-page Yellow Book—the federal government's bible for pricing land.

The idea was to prevent lowballing. The government's initial offer to buy property was not an opening bid in a negotiation. It was supposed to be as close as possible to the final, full value of the land, priced at its "highest and best" economic use. So, for example, if you had fallow land that could be planted with crops, an agency was supposed to pay as though your fields were abundant.

There was an exception to the law. An agency could bypass any of the law's requirements, so long as doing so would "not reduce any assistance or protection provided to an owner."

With virtually no public notice, Homeland Security took advantage of the loophole. It waived the law's requirements for negotiation and eliminated conflict-of-interest provisions. The agency also increased the appraisal threshold to $50,000 for property seized along the border.

In practice, the higher threshold meant that the agency did not have to formally appraise most of the property it wanted. Land is cheap in the Rio Grande Valley, and the government was appropriating only small strips for the fence. Of 197 tracts seized by Homeland Security, 90 percent were valued at less than $50,000.

In place of formal appraisals, Homeland Security directed the Army Corps to assign values to targeted land. Army Corps evaluators did not have to be certified appraisers. They did not have to abide by Yellow Book standards. They did not have to identify the owners, and they didn't need precise legal descriptions, called metes and bounds, to spell out property lines.

Homeland Security worried that the Army Corps did not have the expertise or manpower to complete the job, according to a September 2007 report. Giddens, head of the fence project, said Homeland Security directed the agency to gather real estate experts from other Army Corps offices and hire contractors to do the work as fast as possible.

It was not worth waiting long to conduct the condemnation process, given strong opposition by landowners in the Valley, Giddens said.

"This was not going to get better with time. None of us thought if we waited six months, people were going to say, 'Hey, I get it now,' " he said. "There was no use in prolonging it."

In the spring of 2008, the Army Corps representatives fanned out across the Rio Grande Valley to conduct negotiations with holdout land owners.

They were met with confusion and anger, according to an Army Corps report of the negotiations. Landowners wanted to know where the fence would go, how it would affect their property. They asked for more time to consider the offers. The contractors told them they had just weeks to sign a deal or the federal government would sue them.

One negotiator described a farmer's distress at being pressured to make a decision in less than two weeks in the middle of his onion harvest.

"He takes this a little more to heart and is a little more emotional about the acquisition than some others," an Army Corps realty specialist wrote. "He had lost confidence that Congress had any common sense."

Tudor Uhlhorn, 58, a local politician, farmer and business owner, was perplexed by the federal offer to buy land he owned along the Rio Grande. He had been involved in land condemnation cases filed by the state of Texas, and in those cases the state's attorneys had provided detailed property descriptions and construction plans.

Homeland Security sent him a map that appeared to be taken from Google Earth, with a red rectangle drawn around the targeted tract. When he asked for more information, the Army Corps sent a letter: "The accelerated schedule that is necessary to meet the Congressional mandate will not permit the completion of the ground survey before acquisition," it read.

Homeland Security would take first, and measure later.

Neither Uhlhorn nor his attorney was informed that Homeland Security had gutted landholder protections, until they argued the case in court.

"They were building the fence on me without a full set of plans. They had no plans they could show me," Uhlhorn said. "They just said it starts sort of in this area here and it ends sort of over there."

Homeland Security's decision—changing a single digit in an obscure line of the federal code—left landowners in the Valley vulnerable to the caprice of federal agencies more focused on fence construction than fair compensation.

That's because the Uniform Act contained a final weakness. Even if a property owner could show that Homeland Security had violated the law's requirements, there was nothing the court—or anyone else—could do to fix it.

Buried deep in the law, Congress had included a sentence that said the Uniform law "creates no rights or liabilities and shall not affect the validity of any property acquisitions by purchase or condemnation."

In other words, there was a law. But there was no way to enforce it. In legal terms, it was "nonjusticiable" —beyond the reach of the federal court.

"This is pretty much a very dark corner of the law," said Gideon Kanner, a professor emeritus at Loyola Law School in Los Angeles and a longtime champion of private property rights. "Any notions of due process that you may have will have to be re-examined."

Out of Commission

Delia Perez Weaver, 74, started working on her grandfather's farm near San Benito in the fourth grade. Back then, Mexican workers would come across the Rio Grande under temporary work permits granted under the *bracero* program. They would pick okra and cotton, green beans and tomatoes.

When the Army Corps came to talk with her, Weaver had rented out the farmhouse and the land. They told her they needed an acre to construct the fence and secure an access road. As compensation, she would receive almost $15,000.

To Weaver, the offer seemed low. A relative told her she'd received a larger payment for a similar piece of land up the road. The 18-foot-high fence was an eyesore that would drop the land's value. And so much of her life, and her family's life, was wrapped up in her grandfather's farm. She asked the Army Corps representative for more money. He told her no. So she took the offer.

"This is it," she remembered him saying. "If you want some more you need to go to court and that's going to cost you more money."

The Army Corps official was right. Property owners sued by the government have no right to be assigned an attorney. They must hire their own, or find one willing to work on a contingency fee. That's not easy. By tradition, private eminent domain lawyers take roughly 30 percent of the increase over the initial offer. Few will take on cases where the property is worth less than $100,000—it's not worth their time.

The federal courts, however, had developed a solution for owners like Weaver. In projects involving many owners of inexpensive tracts spread out over a large area, a judge could appoint a land commission composed of local real estate experts to determine property values. The commissions allowed small landowners to plead their cases without the expense or formal procedures involved in a judicial hearing.

Commissions were used in the two largest eminent domain cases in U.S. history: the creation of Florida National Everglades Park, which involved more than 40,000 lawsuits over three

> Property owners—from gigantic timber companies to people evicted from their homes—have fought bitterly to stop the government from taking their land, or to ensure a fair market price.

decades, and the Tennessee Valley Authority, a congressionally chartered hydroelectric power company that required acquiring hundreds of thousands of acres of land. Such commissions have also been used in much smaller condemnation projects, some involving as few as 16 properties.

As the lawsuits started, the Justice Department, representing Homeland Security, urged the federal judge overseeing most of the cases in the Valley to appoint such a commission.

Virginia Butler, the chief of the Justice Department's real estate acquisition section, warned in a motion to Judge Andrew S. Hanen that failure to do so would "result in protracted litigation of these matters and disparate awards to claimants—a very unsatisfactory result for all parties involved."

"In order to achieve fair, uniform compensation awards expeditiously for all affected owners (represented and unrepresented) in the Rio Grande Valley, appointment of a commission is required," she wrote.

Hanen is best known now as the judge who blocked an Obama order to ease immigration laws. But before, he was the "fence judge" —handling nearly all of the cases along the Rio Grande. Hanen rejected Butler's request. A jury trial, he said, was the best forum for the cases. And there was no need to worry about defendants without legal counsel, according to Hanen, because all the cases before him already had lawyers.

When it came to negotiations between the government and landowners, Hanen declared that he would be "hands off."

Hanen's confidence was misplaced. As the lawsuits played out in court instead of before a commission, Butler's dire predictions came true. Payments were unequal and lawsuits dragged on for years, according to a review by *ProPublica* and the *Texas Tribune* of 197 cases in the Rio Grande Valley where the government took possession of property from landowners. The review did not include cases which remain open, or temporary land seizures.

The Justice Department takings lawsuits resulted in splitting the community into three groups, not on the basis of the land they owned, but on their ability to retain an attorney.

The biggest group was made up of landholders of modest means, many elderly, some Spanish-only speakers. They didn't hire attorneys and took the government's initial offer. Half the lawsuits had that result. The median settlement was $8,000. The median seizure was just over one-third of an acre.

Those who settled were people like Otalia Perez, 81, and her 85-year-old husband Tomas. They lived in a modest brick home across from their farmland. When the Army Corps approached them, Tomas had long ceased working the land himself, instead renting it out to tenant farmers. Neither he nor his wife felt like fighting the government. They accepted $21,000, and the government took two acres of land.

"My folks are old and didn't need to be in that legal battle, so we said, "Look, just take whatever they give you now 'cause it's gonna happen anyway," said Joe Perez, their son who handled discussions with the government.

Jack Coleman, 77, was a military veteran who retired from the Naval Space Command in 1996. When the government offered him $10,600 for a piece of overgrown land that he used as a personal firing range, it seemed like a good deal. It was almost the same amount that he'd paid for the entire five-acre tract years before. "They offered a more than fair price," he said.

But when taking slices of land from larger parcels, as happened in the Rio Grande Valley, the government didn't price property in the way that real estate transactions are typically valued.

Under federal guidelines, Homeland Security was supposed to evaluate the worth of a piece of land before building the fence, and do so again after construction. Subtracting the second figure from the first produces an estimate of the damage inflicted on the property by the construction of the fence. The formula is designed to capture price differences caused when land is severed from a parent tract.

But many in the Valley weighed the offer on a price-per-acre basis at a time when the best irrigated cropland was selling for $10,000 an acre. To those who didn't know about the formula, the government offers seemed generous—at first.

The Cavazos family lived in a home on 30 acres wedged between the Rio Grande and Oklahoma Avenue, a two-lane stretch of blacktop on the eastern edge of Brownsville. Much of the land was between the river and a levee—good only for crops.

The Cavazoses kept cattle, horses and chickens that roamed the thick grassland and pastures behind their single-story tan brick ranch house. The area is rural: horses graze on tall grass on the sides of roads. There are no street lights, and fields of cotton, corn and citrus trees line the road.

The Army Corps told the family that it would build a fence to run just behind the house, and also put in a gravel side road. To compensate them for the loss of two acres to the project, Homeland Security offered $21,500 and promised to install a gate with a security code that would give them access to their land remaining on the other side.

Juan Cavazos was a teacher. His wife worked as a secretary for the school district. They didn't want the fence. They thought there were smarter ways to stop the crossers and smugglers who darted across their land. But who were they to fight the government? They figured an attorney would just take a big contingency fee.

"Regardless of whether we were going to be opposed or in favor of it, they were going to build it," Cavazos said. "We were totally against building the border wall but we couldn't do anything about it."

They took the money. Homeland Security built the barrier. It looms in the backyard, sharp and jagged, like a giant's picket fence. The gate in the middle lets Cavazos stroll the back portion of his property. Border patrols officers race past on the gravel road.

Had he known anything about the law, Cavazos could have argued for more money. For instance, he could have insisted that his land be valued for its farming potential—its highest and best use. Or he could have hired an appraiser to counter the government's estimate. Cavazos didn't know any of that, though. The sole burden to prove the full market value lies upon the owner—not the government.

He learned later that nearby landowners got higher payments than he did for similar parcels of land. He also believes the barrier has permanently reduced the resale value of the land now caught between the river and the fence.

"At the time, we thought it was a fair offer," Cavazos said. "The people who didn't hire the lawyers got screwed."

People didn't have to have a lawyer to prove the government's offer was too low—in some cases, all they had to do was pick up the phone.

The De Leons fell into a second group of property owners. Like the first group, they, too, faced Homeland Security without counsel. But they were able to negotiate an increase in their final settlement. Of the 131 lawsuits in which landowners had no attorney, 30 settled for an increase of 33 percent higher than the median government offer. The payment for a median one-third acre tract increased from a median of $6,000 to just under $8,000.

Many of these landowners had some familiarity with the workings of government—they were local, state or federal employees. Or they had connections to power brokers like local attorneys or politicians. Or they were simply comfortable negotiating directly with the U.S. Attorney's Office.

Frequently, it did not take much to get a higher offer. Landowners who contacted the Justice Department often described a quick, cordial discussion. While few got what they were asking, they usually received some additional money or an agreement to reduce the effect of the fence on their land. For instance, farmers negotiated deals to install electronic gates to allow them to get farm equipment to their fields.

The government informed Rosalia Gonzalez that it would pay $700 for a little more than a tenth of an acre from a 1.4-acre lot she owned in Brownsville near the Rio Grande. Gonzalez asked for $60,000. "The United States is not aware of any land in the area of your property that has a fair market value as high as what you have requested," a federal attorney wrote back. He did, however, boost the offer to $1,000. Gonzalez took it.

Retired teacher Josephine Weaver, 80, saw her offer for a little more than a tenth of an acre of her 3.5 acre lot near Los Indios increase from $1,150 to $3,000 after she protested. "They were doing the right thing," she said.

In the De Leons' case, the family had deep roots—historically and politically. The De Leons traced their presence in the Rio Grande Valley to the days of the Spanish empire. One De Leon has a gold-framed family tree on the wall of his home with dates going back to the 1790s, when the family's ancestors received a Spanish land grant in the Brownsville area.

At 82, Ernesto De Leon was the family's patriarch. He once served as a city commissioner in Brownsville. He helped raise money for former Texas Gov. Rick Perry, a Republican who is now Trump's energy secretary.

When the land agents came around, they wanted five different parcels of land owned by the family. De Leon picked up the phone and started making calls.

"I got on it and talked to my congressman. Talked to my state representative and county judge, and all the people that could help," De Leon said. "By the grace of God we were able to make them understand."

De Leon wound up speaking to the assistant U.S. attorney assigned to the family's cases. On one plot of farmland, he convinced the government to raise its offer from $13,700 to $17,000—a modest 24 percent boost.

But on another piece of agricultural land—this one closer to Brownsville—he more than quadrupled Homeland Security's offer from $11,300 to $48,120 for the damage of losing a little more than an acre and a half from a 50-acre tract. He also worked out a deal to ensure that Homeland Security installed an electronic security gate to provide continued access to the land.

"I say, don't rock the boat. In other words, what they offer you, see if you can negotiate a better price." De Leon said. "Don't be greedy, get a reasonable price for your property and move forward."

For most people who had the money, hiring a lawyer proved a smart investment. Not everyone with an attorney got more money—but those who did reaped significant returns.

For about 30 landowners represented by attorneys, the jump between the government's median opening bid and its final offer was 207 percent—from a median offer of $13,100 to a settlement of $40,305. (In another 20 cases, the final settlement included additional land, making direct before-and-after comparisons difficult.)

The reason for the huge jumps became apparent during the battles between landholders and government attorneys: The Army Corps' evaluators had consistently undervalued the land.

As part of the government's defense preparations, the Justice Department hired independent appraisers to evaluate the targeted land. In the few lawsuits where those appraisals were made public, the government's outside experts invariably priced the land higher than the Army Corps' evaluators.

Take the case of Rollins Koppel. In 2002, Koppel and his investors bought 420 acres of vacant land wedged in a prime location between Brownsville and Matamoros, its sister city across the river in Mexico. They planned a neighborhood of affordable homes that would be surrounded by a park overlooking the Rio Grande. Koppel successfully lobbied the Brownsville City Commission to establish a special taxing district for the development.

By 2007, Koppel had managed to install sewer and water lines, and he had platted the subdivision. But it was still just vacant land.

Then the federal government showed up with a Declaration of Taking. The border fence cut up the development and destroyed any chance for a riverfront park. Homeland Security made him an offer: $233,000 in return for a little more than six acres of land.

Perhaps no property owner along the Rio Grande was more savvy about the value of his land than Koppel. With deep roots in Brownsville, Koppel had practiced law in the area for more than 45 years. He had partnered with some of the biggest developers in Texas to build the project.

So when the Justice Department filed its Declaration of Taking, Koppel hired one of Texas' top law firms, Vinson & Elkins, renowned for its ferocious litigators, to fight back.

Over the next three years, the two sides faced off in court, even as Homeland Security built the fence. Koppel's attorneys attacked the integrity of the government's appraiser.

Justice attorneys argued that Koppel's appraiser had not properly followed government standards. And Koppel, they said, was overvaluing the market for his development in one of the most economically depressed parts of Brownsville.

On one point, though, both sides agreed. The government's initial evaluation had vastly underestimated the damage the fence would do to Koppel's development. Koppel's attorneys put the total price at more than $14.6 million. The government's attorneys said it was $1.4 million.

When the two sides finally settled, Homeland Security paid Koppel $4.9 million. That was the highest payout for any property in the Rio Grande Valley, and it represented a 2,043 percent increase from the government's initial estimate of fair market value.

In the end, even that might not have been enough. Koppel was never able to get the subdivision built. He died earlier this year at 88. His attorney did not return phone calls seeking comment.

Equal but Different

U.S. courts have held that appraisals are more art than science. Actual market sales are the single most important component in most appraisals—but real estate in the Rio Grande Valley did not turn over often. Nor had anyone ever sold property with a border fence on it. The government's experts were left guessing at values—and often getting them wrong.

A close look at the Loop family's case exposes the inequity of the government's work in the Rio Grande Valley.

The Loops have been farming at the very edge of America since the early 1900s. The family's land runs along the Rio Grande at the southernmost tip of Texas, just a few miles before it unspools into the Gulf of Mexico. Loop brothers, uncles and cousins grew navel oranges and tangerines, cabbages and corn, green peas and cotton—pretty much anything they wanted to put in the ground. The rich soil, bottomland, is blessed with yearlong sunshine and warmth.

The family lived the border's problems. Drug couriers hauling duffel bags stuffed with narcotics hiked across their farm. People from Mexico, elsewhere in Central America, as far away as Romania, illegally crossed the border into their land. Every once in a while, dead bodies floated past in the river.

When the government came looking to build the border fence in 2007, Ray and Frank and their cousins, Tim and Paul, were working more than 5,200 acres on contiguous properties. Though the barrier didn't make much sense to them, they welcomed the idea of better border control.

"Good fences make good neighbors; isn't that what Robert Frost said?" Ray Loop remarked.

The border fence cutting across the Loops' land was going to trap most of it between the river and the fence. It would also strand Tim's home and Ray's home in the no man's land that remained. The Loops' biggest concern was their farms: How would they be able to get to them?

Both pairs of brothers talked with the land agents sent out by the Army Corps. To a person unfamiliar with the finer points of eminent domain law, the offers looked awfully generous.

In Ray and Frank's case, the government announced its intention to take 5.5 acres. The compensation would be $210,000.

But issues beyond the amount of money bothered Ray Loop. He was having trouble nailing down answers to questions. Was Homeland Security going to build a gate? Would the road be wide and durable enough to accommodate his 42,000-pound, 26-foot-wide John Deere combine? And what about his family? He had three daughters. If they had a code to the gate, wouldn't they become targets for drug dealers who wanted access?

"The safety issues were terrible," he said. "I was worried all the time."

Ray Loop talked it over with his family. He decided to fight. He hired one of the best-known eminent domain law firms in Texas, a boutique outfit called Barron Adler. Steve Adler, the politically connected co-founder, would become Austin's mayor. (Adler also provided initial funding for the launch of the *Texas Tribune*.)

Kim Loessin, the Barron Adler lawyer who handled the Loops' case, believed the government offer ignored key facts. Loop got money from his farm, and from a sand mining operation and a hunting camp. How would the value of the land between the fence and the Rio Grande be affected?

Loessin hired a professional appraiser to judge the property's value. Using the government's formula, the Loops' appraiser put the total damages across the 630-acre farm at $1.4 million. The damage tally included an additional four acres of land for fence construction, troubles with access to the farmland, and the effect of the fence on the resale value of Ray Loop's home.

The government hired its own appraiser. Unlike the Army Corps, he was required to carry out a full assessment using Yellow Book standards. His estimate of the harm done to the Loop farm was just under $1 million.

The two professional estimates differed—not unusual in a court battle. But both soared far above the Army Corps' initial estimate of $210,000.

"It was one of the only projects that I had ever encountered in this area of practice where the government just skated on so many things," said Loessin, who wound up representing dozens of owners in the Rio Grande Valley. "I'm not just generally an anti-government person, but that just infuriated me, with regard to property rights in particular."

Tim and Paul Loop took a different path. They did not respond to requests for an interview, but Tim submitted a sworn affidavit in court files that tells their story.

Tim and Paul Loop decided to accept the Army Corps' initial offer—a payment of $160,000 for the damage to their farming operation caused by the fence. It would run across seven acres on scattered strips of land. The price seemed right.

"It was our desire to not be an obstruction to our government's getting a job done," Tim Loop declared in his affidavit. "We wanted to do our patriotic duty." Nobody told the family that the money was supposed to represent all the losses to their farming operation.

Only after Ray and Frank's experience did they realize the government had short-changed them. After all, they farmed similar crops, on the same land—the Loops' farms bumped up against each other. Why were the two sets of cousins being compensated so differently? Tim and Paul tried to reopen negotiations. But by then, it was too late. The government already owned the land.

"We trusted our government to treat us fairly," Tim Loop wrote. "We trusted the representatives of the government to be honest and forthright when dealing with us."

In the end, the government took additional land to build the fence. By then, Tim and Paul had hired Loessin. The brothers' final compensation was $400,000, with a loss of 20 acres.

Ray and Frank Loop, on the other hand, received $1.4 million for the loss of 11 acres.

In the years after construction, Ray Loop learned to live with the fence. Sometimes the gates broke down, but the government sent a contractor to fix it. The added border control was hardly perfect. Homeland Security never closed up access at an old farm road, leaving a yawning, 40-foot-wide gap in the fence where anyone could walk through.

But earlier this year, one of Ray's nightmares became real.

Rising early one morning in January, he smelled smoke. A few minutes later, a Border Patrol officer texted him: "Sir, your barn is on fire I believe," it read.

The barn was actually the Loops' home—they lived on the second floor, above a space that housed some of their animals. He rushed to wake his daughters and his wife. The family escaped unharmed, but the animals did not. Four of the family's dogs and a goat burned alive, their cries haunting the family.

Ray believes that the fire engines that raced to his home were hindered by the gate. Fire officials dispute that. But Ray is certain that the engines would have been able to respond faster had they not had to negotiate the fence that was meant to block border crossers—not emergency vehicles.

Ray and his family have rebuilt their home. They are again living in no man's land, that slice of America between the fence and Mexico.

"What else are we going to do?" he asked.

Comedy of Error

It was Feb. 3, 2009, and Assistant U.S. Attorney Eric Paxton Warner had a confession to make.

For more than a year, Justice Department attorneys had been seizing property. And for more than a year, they had been paying the landowners for their losses. They had beaten the Dec. 31, 2008 deadline set by Congress. Contractors were digging wide trenches and pouring concrete for the fence.

But it was only now, in the middle of litigating a case against the Borzynski brothers, two farmers known as the Cabbage Kings of America, that the government realized that it had erred in nearly every single case, Warner told the court.

"I have made a mess of the Borzynski case," Warner told the court.

The government had not finished title work on many of the properties until Christmas. In the rush, the attorneys had not realized that they had failed to compensate the owners for water rights to their land.

It was an almost unbelievable mistake for anybody who knew anything about the American West.

In Texas, as in many states west of the Mississippi, water rights can be worth more than the land itself. The rights give landowners control over a certain amount of water from the Rio Grande. That allocation can be sold to farmers who need water for their crops. Without water rights, there is no agriculture.

Now, Warner told the judge, the government was going to refile all of its taking cases to ensure that the landholders would retain those rights.

The congressional deadline "required us to kind of, I guess, essentially work backwards from the way a normal condemnation would have been done," Warner explained.

Justice Department attorneys discovered another giant mistake. Much of the fence had been built on top of an earthen levee running parallel to the Rio Grande. Only after construction did the government realize that property owners actually had title to the land beneath the levee. The government had not paid for any of it.

Daniel Hu, the U.S. attorney overseeing the condemnation lawsuits, offered an apology.

"We actually built the fence on land that we haven't finished taking yet," Hu told Hanen at a hearing.

Yet another problem: The Rio Grande Valley was famous in Texas for murky land claims—the river shifted constantly, changing property lines. Records were missing. Families often had multiple members claiming ownership. But nobody at Homeland Security or the Justice Department appeared to have prepared for the complexity involved. Years would pass before the government would even know who it was suing.

In one case in the small town of Eagle Pass, Justice lawyers found 24 heirs to a half-acre tract overlooking the Rio Grande. The case took almost five years to unravel, with a plot worthy of a Gabriel García Márquez novel. The lawsuit involved the Roman Catholic Church, a competing land claim from another family, and a handwritten deed from 1894 that referred to the property line as "beginning at a mesquite tree eight inches in diameter on the east bank of the Rio Grande."

When pressed about problems or delays, U.S. attorneys continually blamed the deadline set by Congress for their mistakes.

"The government had to rush," Warner explained in defending himself from a sanctions motion.

The Justice Department, "working within the parameters set by the realities of the world we live in, rather than as we wish them to be, took the subject properties with the information then available."

Sometimes, the mistakes seemed farcical. In one case, Homeland Security offered to pay the city of Brownsville $123,100 for nearly 16 acres abutting the Rio

Grande. It turned out the land was owned by the city—but 257 other people also had claim to the property.

What's more, Homeland Security had relied on a mistaken land survey to seize the tract. The new property line had been drawn to cut through the middle of an irrigation pump house owned by Brownsville.

"[W]e inadvertently took half of a pump house that belongs to the city," Hu told Hanen. "The federal government doesn't want it. We want to give it back to the city."

"Why did you only take half? You didn't want the whole pump house?" Hanen joked.

"We didn't even want half actually," Hu said.

More than nine years later, the case remains open. Justice Department attorneys continue to locate and pay the additional landholders. Just this September, the agency disbursed a payment of $5,750 to two owners.

The circumstance is not unusual. Pamela Rivas is one of more than 40 property owners who have waited almost a decade for their cases to resolve. Many involve complex ownership claims. The government had to untangle who owned a small tract of land in Rivas' case.

That dispute, however, was settled years ago. The United States now owns about an acre of her land near a border crossing. But it has yet to agree with Rivas on a final payment..

"I'm just a nobody and they're going to do what they want to do," Rivas said. "I don't think that's right."

Roberto Pedraza, meanwhile, hit the jackpot—just not the way he ever imagined.

Pedraza was one of several property owners who were paid by the government for land that they did not own.

Pedraza spent most of his life working as a farmer and foreman for rancher Rex McGarr, whom Pedraza affectionately still calls "my boss man." When McGarr died, he willed 114 acres of Hidalgo County farmland to Pedraza and his wife, Olivia.

But McGarr's death led to decades of legal wrangling between other beneficiaries and attorneys for the estate. In 2008, the year Pedraza was first approached by an Army Corps land agent, he still wasn't clear on what was legally his. But the federal government seemed to have figured that out for him.

"I told him, that person from the government, that [there] was a legal matter on this property," Pedraza said. "And [the government official] said, 'Well, according to the records… you own it.'"

In September 2008, Pedraza was paid $20,500. He and his wife used the money to pay off longstanding bills.

More than six years passed. Then, one day in 2014, a government representative contacted them. After completing title research, the Justice Department realized that the land had not belonged to him.

The government offered him a deal. Pedraza could keep the money, so long as he signed a document disclaiming ownership to the land.

"The government came in and said, 'Look if you give the right of way … then you don't have to pay,'" he said. "I said, 'Fine,' because I knew this thing was a big mess."

The real owner of the land was Pedraza's next-door neighbor: Alberto Garza, the 91-year-old sugar cane farmer.

Homeland Security had already paid Garza $45,000 for a total of 3.4 acres from Garza's sugar cane farm, which stretches on both sides of a highway that parallels the Rio Grande near the hamlet of San Benito.

Border Patrol officials promised to build a gate in the border fence to give Garza continued access to the land that he had farmed for five decades. But when Homeland Security's contractors showed up, they ignored the promise, according to his daughter, Norma Longoria.

"When we saw that they were putting the poles up, we tried to stop them," Longoria, a 62-year-old retired state worker, remembered. "They told us no."

When the government returned years later to pay the family for land that they thought had belonged to Pedraza, it seemed a recompense for the oversight of not installing the gate. Garza got an additional $10,500 out of the deal.

But Longoria said her father never fully recovered from the shock of being shut off from his own farm. Before, he followed a dirt road behind his house to get to his sugar cane fields or visit his beloved cattle. Now he must drive a mile down the highway until he reaches a gate, then double back. He still visits his land. But not as often as he used to.

"It's very inconvenient now," Longoria said. "We didn't feel it was fair."

The Justice Department spokesman explained that the government is not required to provide exact property descriptions or have done research prior to seizing land using a Declaration of Taking.

The spokesman said that many of the condemnation lawsuits in the Valley were filed to clean up problems with property tiles. In a so-called "friendly" take, the seller makes no objection, but the government files a condemnation suit to make sure that legal ownership is clear and no debts are attached to the property when the federal government takes possession.

The spokesman declined to comment on any open cases.

Past as Present

About 20 miles south of Laredo, Texas, lies a forgotten town.

Four crumbling structures cluster around a soft dirt road. The roofs are gone. The stucco has peeled off the walls, revealing hand-carved blocks of dun-colored sandstone. Mesquite trees and thick grass grow all around. Butterflies flit about.

The ruins are what remain of a town once called Dolores. It was an early settlement north of the Rio Grande, built in the summer of 1750 under the command of José de Escandón, the Spanish conquistador who colonized the region.

For Mauricio Vidaurri, it is home.

Vidaurri is a descendant of one of the pioneers who founded the town. Vidaurri's family once owned thousands of acres around this spot off a lonely stretch of highway between Laredo and Zapata. Now, they farm some 1,300 acres of watermelon, cucumbers and grazing hay. A power company rents the land to extract natural gas. An irrigation pump draws water from the Rio Grande.

Vidaurri likes to come here sometimes and just sit—there is a mystery, a power, about the place that fills him.

"We've been here since before the United States," he said. "One owner."

These days, another feeling haunts him: worry. Since the presidential campaign began, Vidaurri has paid close attention to Trump's promises about building a wall between the U.S. and Mexico. It would be 40 feet high and be made of concrete. It would stretch from the Gulf of Mexico to the Pacific Ocean.

If Trump were to build that wall, it would run straight through Vidaurri's ranch, which lies north of the Rio Grande Valley. When constructing the border fence, Homeland Security skipped much of the area around Laredo, deciding it was not a high enough priority.

Trump has not announced any plans to build the wall here—but Homeland Security officials have indicated that the agency will be taking land and erecting a fence about 50 miles to the south, around Rio Grande City.

Mark Borkowski, the top contracting official for Customs and Border Protection, told a conference in San Antonio in April that the agency would return to finish what it had started a decade ago. "We're going to seize more land," Borkowski said. "We are going to do it."

Vidaurri is a strong proponent of better border protection. Border crossers trespass on his land constantly. Drug couriers have broken into a home on the ranch.

But Vidaurri thinks the solution lies in the better deployment of technology, like the hidden cameras that Border Patrol has installed throughout his ranch, or the static blimps that hover silently in the sky above, scanning the border.

With Trump still promising the wall, Vidaurri figures it's only a matter of time until Homeland Security arrives with bulldozers and pile drivers. When the time comes, he knows there will be no stopping the government. And he doesn't think any amount of compensation will make him whole.

"We can't say our land is worth so much. Our land was bought with our blood, sweat and tears," Vidaurri said.

Vidaurri's concerns are especially personal.

From Dolores' ruins, Vidaurri can walk a few hundred yards to a small, fenced graveyard on a bank overlooking the Rio Grande. Simple white crosses mark some graves. Others are surrounded by elaborate wrought iron fence. Many of the markers date from the early 1800s. In one corner, two flags fly: that of the United States and that of the U.S. Marine Corps.

Vidaurri stops by the grave of his father, Roberto J. Vidaurri. He served in the Marine Corps during World War II, and was twice wounded in Iwo Jima. The wall would slice right through here, Vidaurri figures, cutting him off from his land, from his father.

It would be like building a wall through his heart.

"You'll build a wall on our land and destroy sacred ground for us and tear away our history," he said. "What good will it do?"

Print Citations

CMS: Miller, T. Christian, Collier, Kiah, and Julian Aguilar. "The Taking: How the Federal Government Abused Its Power to Seize Property for a Border Fence." In *The Reference Shelf: The National Debate Topic 2018–2019 Immigration,* edited by Betsy Maury, 137-157. Ipswich, MA: H.W. Wilson, 2018.

MLA: Miller, T. Christian, Collier, Kiah, and Julian Aguilar. "The Taking: How the Federal Government Abused Its Power to Seize Property for a Border Fence." *The Reference Shelf: The National Debate Topic 2018–2019 Immigration.* Ed. Betsy Maury. Ipswich: H.W. Wilson, 2018. 137-157. Print.

APA: Miller, T.C., Collier, K., & J. Aguilar. (2018). The taking: How the federal government abused its power to seize property for a border fence. In Betsy Maury (Ed.), *The reference shelf: The national debate topic 2018–2019 immigration* (pp. 137-157). Ipswich, MA: H.W. Wilson. (Original work published 2017)

5
Sanctuary

Protesters at a pro-immigration rally where organizers called for a stop to the Immigration and Customs Enforcement (ICE) raids and deportations of illegal immigrants and to officially establish Los Angeles as a sanctuary city. Los Angeles, California February 18, 2017.

The Politics of Sanctuary

One of the biggest immigration controversies in 2018 is the Sanctuary Movement debate. A sanctuary city, state, or other territory is a municipality with policies in place that limit cooperation with or involvement in federal immigration enforcement. One of the most common sanctuary policies involves states or cities that refuse to detain individuals based on immigration status alone or refuse to withhold city or municipal services from noncitizens. A sanctuary municipality may argue that complying with federal policies places an undue burden on their government or may justify sanctuary policies based on ethical or moral concerns.

The federal government is supposed to create policies that reflect the needs and wishes of the entire US population, though not all federal legislators and politicians adhere to this approach. Local leaders, by contrast, are responsible for reflecting the priorities and views of their immediate constituents, which may differ from state to state. Cities and states therefore pass laws, at times, that are at odds with the priorities of a federal executive or a national political party and this balance between local and central power is a constitutionally-enshrined and essential part of American culture and politics. On same-sex marriage, for instance, states and municipalities adopted laws in support of same-sex marriage well before the federal government adopted the same policy, which reflects the fact that populations in some states and some cities especially, tend to be more progressive and liberal than the population as a whole. The sanctuary movement is a reflection of this same feature of American society in which local populations have embraced policies at odds with federal policy, but, in some cases, better reflect the views of citizens in those communities.

Origins of the Sanctuary Movement

Some Americans believe that the United States has a moral responsibility to use its wealth, abundant space and natural resources, and global influence to help populations in need. Others disagree and believe that America should look out for itself, primarily, and does not have a responsibility to take an active role in global humanitarianism. These different attitudes about the priorities of the American government, with regard to the nation's relationship with the world, play a major role in determining immigration policies and how those policies are received by the American people.

During the Cold War, the United States engaged in numerous clandestine activities to support regimes favorable to US interests and to weaken or oppose regimes favoring communism or socialism. Declassified documents show that, during the Ronald Reagan administration, the US government funded violent dictatorships in Central America that were facing pressure from internal socialist rebellions. These civil wars led to millions of civilian casualties and hundreds of thousands of refugees fleeing Guatemala, El Salvador, and Nicaragua to escape fighting between rebels and US-supported dictatorships. Thousands of migrants from these countries attempted to seek asylum in the United States, which put the Reagan administration in a difficult position. If the administration embraced the refugees as victims of violence and war, then the United States would have to admit that the regimes they funded in Central America were violent, dictatorial regimes. The controversial US approach was to secretly round up and expel the asylum seekers under the basis that they were "economic refugees" rather than victims of violence.[1]

In the early 1980s, a collection of religious congregations in and around Tucson, Arizona began taking in Guatemalan and Salvadoran migrants, attempting to help them establish legal status as refugees fleeing violence. Most of these refugees were refused refugee status and rejected for political reasons, and this network of religious leaders decided that they still had a duty to aid the then-illegal Central American arrivals to their communities. These religious leaders then partnered with social and political activists to create a network that would help to provide services, shelter, and employment for the refugees, in violation of federal law. The controversial sanctuary movement became the subject of a major 1985 trial after federal agents infiltrated the churches and collected information on the activities of the groups involved.[2] Father Luis Olivares, a Roman Catholic priest who used his Los Angeles church to shelter Central American refugees during the 1980s movement is quoted in a 2009 study on the movement as:

"You cannot be witness to human suffering and not be convinced of the condition of social sin. We are all responsible unless we take a stand and speak against it."[3]

The Modern Sanctuary Cities Debate

Sanctuary cities, towns, and states have existed since the 1980s and, in the 2010s, these communities take many forms with many different types of sanctuary policies. For instance, San Francisco has set aside city funds to provide legal aid to immigrants, without discriminating on the basis of legal status. Los Angeles has a policy in place that prohibits police officers from detaining individuals for the sole purpose of determining the individual's immigration status, and Chicago, under Mayor Rahm Emanuel, has adopted a "Welcoming City Ordinance" under which the city will not investigate the citizenship status of individuals unless specifically mandated by law or a court ruling.[4]

In January of 2017, President Donald Trump signed an Executive Order (EO) that would restrict federal funding to cities, counties, and states that refused to comply with federal immigration law. Sanctuary cities like San Francisco, Los Angeles, and Chicago announced that they would not comply, despite the administration's threats of withdrawing federal funding. For over a year, this debate continued sporadically, with frequent news articles exploring the history of the sanctuary movement and presenting views on both sides of the debate. On April 19, 2018 a panel of three justices from the United States Court of Appeals for the Seventh Circuit ruled unanimously against the Trump administration on the basis that the

EO violated the separation of powers established in the US Constitution. Judge Ilana Rovner, appointed by Reagan and elevated to the circuit court by George H.W. Bush, penned a 35-page rebuke of the policy, stating:

> The founders of our country well understood that the concentration of power threatens individual liberty and established a bulwark against such tyranny by creating a separation of powers among the branches of government. If the Executive Branch can determine policy, and then use the power of the purse to mandate compliance with that policy by the state and local government, all without the authorization or even acquiescence of elected legislators, that check against tyranny is forsaken.[5]

Public opinion on sanctuary cities is mixed. In a February 2017 poll from Harvard University, 80 percent of respondents agreed that cities that arrested illegal immigrants for crimes should be required to turn them over to immigration authorities. This survey has repeatedly been cited by critics of the sanctuary movement who claim that this study indicates that 80 percent of Americans disapprove of the sanctuary movement. This is an incorrect assessment of available data as the study cited asks specifically about how a city or state should handle an undocumented migrant who has been arrested for committing a crime. In general, Americans believe that undocumented migrants who have committed crimes (other than the crime of residing in the nation illegally) should be turned over to immigration authorities. This does not, however, mean that 80 percent of people, or even a majority of people, disapprove of the sanctuary movement. For instance, a *Fox News* poll in March of 2017, found that 53 percent opposed withholding funding for sanctuary cities, as opposed to 41 percent in support of the financial penalties as Trump's EO would require.[6]

Trump allies have also claimed, in statements to the press, that a majority of California residents disapprove of sanctuary policies. A November 2017 USC/*Los Angeles Times* poll, however, asked about a California law that would mean law enforcement would not hand over an unauthorized immigrant to US immigration agents unless the person had committed a serious crime; 53 percent approved of the policy, while only 29 percent opposed the policy. Even among those opposed, only 18 percent strongly disapproved of local authorities not handing over an otherwise law-abiding unauthorized migrant to authorities. What this poll shows is that Americans are concerned about crime and believe that, if an immigrant, illegal or legal, is arrested for a crime than that individual should be handed over to immigration authorities. When it comes to policy regarding otherwise law-abiding individuals, however, California residents are generally in support of the state's sanctuary policies. This same general result can be seen in a May 2017 Public Policy Institute poll and a March 2017 UC Berkeley poll, both indicating a majority in support of sanctuary policies for California.[7]

Civil Disobedience and the Morality of Law

In 1850, President Millard Fillmore signed the Fugitive Slave Act into law. The law made it a federal crime to either aid fugitive slaves or to refuse to assist federal authorities in recapturing slaves who had escaped their bondage. This controversial law became the subject of intense debate in the 1850s and was a precursor to the Civil War that followed. Essentially, there were many Americans who viewed slavery as immoral, whether because of religious beliefs or secular moral principles, and who refused to obey any law that would force them or their communities to willingly participate in the institution. In addition, it wasn't only individuals who fought against the Fugitive Slave Act, but also states and communities united against the law and the immoral institutions they believed it supported. For instance, the Wisconsin state government invalidated the Fugitive Slave Act and the Wisconsin state Supreme Court ruled the law unconstitutional, though this ruling was later overturned by the US Supreme Court.[8] The Fugitive Slave Act was ultimately a failure and actually resulted in increasing opposition to slavery as northern citizens objected to being forced, by federal policy, to take part in an institution that their communities had already rejected and refused to embrace.

There are many examples from history of situations in which a portion of the population, whether simply a few individuals or even millions, have objected to the laws and policies that the government has put into place. The marriage rights debate provides an example. While federal laws allow same sex marriage and require that all state governments recognize same-sex legal marriages, there are many Americans who disapprove whether because of their religious or personal beliefs. *Citizen Times* noted in 2017 that 5 percent of North Carolina justices were refusing to perform marriage ceremonies for same sex couples, despite the fact that this is a violation of federal law.[9] President Trump has supported the idea that persons (even government employees) should have the right to refuse providing services to individuals based on their personal religious beliefs, and should be protected, by law, from suits or punishment for discrimination. The Sanctuary Movement and the "religious choice" movement are examples of situations in which federal policy runs contrary to the moral, ethical, or spiritual beliefs of a certain facet of the American public.

Works Used

Chinchilla, Norma Stoltz, Hamilton, Nora, and James Loucky. "The Sanctuary Movement and Central American Activism in Los Angeles." *Latin American Perspectives*. Issue 169, Vol. 36, No. 6 (Nov 2009). http://sanctuaryweb.com/Portals/0/2017%20PDFs/Sanctuary%20Movement/2009%20Chinchilla%20The%20Sanctuary%20Movement%20and%20Central%20American%20activism%20in%20LA.pdf.

"City of Chicago v. Jefferson B. Sessions III, Attorney General of the United States." *US Courts*. United States Court of Appeals for the Seventh Circuit. Apr 19, 2018. http://media.ca7.uscourts.gov/cgi-bin/rssExec.pl?Submit=Display&Path=Y2018/D04-19/C:17-2991:J:Rovner:aut:T:fnOp:N:2142410:S:0.

Foner, Eric. "What the Fugitive Slave Act Teaces Us about How States Can Resist

Oppressive Federal Power." *The Nation*. Feb 8, 2017. Web. https://www.the-nation.com/article/what-the-fugitive-slave-act-teaches/.

García, María Cristina. "America Has Never Actually Welcomed the World's Huddled Masses." *The Washington Post*. The Washington Post Co. Nov 20, 2015. Web. https://www.washingtonpost.com/opinions/america-has-never-actually-welcomed-the-worlds-huddled-masses/2015/11/20/6763fad0-8e71-11e5-ae1f-af46b7df8483_story.html?utm_term=.2e075ad24247.

Guthman, Edwin. "Underground Railroad, 1980's Style." *The New York Times*. The New York Times Co. Sep 25, 1988. Web. https://www.nytimes.com/1988/09/25/books/underground-railroad-1980-s-style.html.

Gzesh, Susan. "Central Americans and Asylum Policy in the Reagan Era." *MPI*. Migration Policy Institute. Apr 1, 2006. Web. https://www.migrationpolicy.org/article/central-americans-and-asylum-policy-reagan-era.

Kopan, Tal. "What Are Sanctuary Cities, and Can They Be Defunded?" *CNN Politics*. CNN. Mar 26, 2018. Web. https://www.cnn.com/2017/01/25/politics/sanctuary-cities-explained/index.html.

Myrick, Gayle. "You Can't Make Me Perform Same-Sex Marriages." *News Observer*. Feb 14, 2018. Web. http://www.newsobserver.com/opinion/op-ed/article200224229.html.

Nichols, Chris. "No, Californians Do Not Overwhelmingly Oppose Sanctuary Policies." *Politifact*. Politifact. Jan 9, 2018. Web. http://www.politifact.com/california/statements/2018/jan/09/travis-allen/no-californians-do-not-overwhelmingly-oppose-sanct/.

Tharoor, Ishaan. "What Americans Thought of Jewish Refugees on the Eve of World War II." *The Washington Post*. The Washington Post Co. Nov 17, 2015. Web. https://www.washingtonpost.com/news/worldviews/wp/2015/11/17/what-americans-thought-of-jewish-refugees-on-the-eve-of-world-war-ii/?noredirect=on&utm_term=.0de0aa7925a7.

Ye Hee Lee, Michelle. "Do 80 Percent of Americans Oppose Sanctuary Cities?" *The Washington Post*. The Washington Post Co. Mar 28, 2017. Web. https://www.washingtonpost.com/news/fact-checker/wp/2017/03/28/do-80-percent-of-americans-oppose-sanctuary-cities/?noredirect=on&utm_term=.fe46550cbe47.

Notes

1. Guthman, "Underground Railroad, 1980s Style."
2. Gzesh, "Central Americans and Asylum Policy in the Reagan Era."
3. Chinchilla, Hamilton, and Loucky, "The Sanctuary Movement and Central American Activism in Los Angeles," *101*.
4. Kopan, "What Are Sanctuary Cities, and Can They Be Defunded?"
5. "City of *Chicago v. Jefferson B. Sessions III*, Attorney General of the United States," *US Courts*.
6. Ye Hee Lee, "Do 80 Percent of Americans Oppose Sanctuary Cities?"
7. Nichols, "No, Californians Do Not Overwhelmingly Oppose Sanctuary Policies."
8. Foner, "What the Fugitive Slave Act Teaches Us About How States Can Resist Oppressive Federal Power."
9. Myrick, "You Can't Make Me Perform Same-Sex Marriages."

The False Promise of Sanctuary Cities

By Daniel Denvir
Slate, February 17, 2017

In the wake of President Trump's nativist crackdown, mayors in left-leaning cities have defiantly proclaimed that their cities will remain "sanctuaries" where immigrants can find refuge. The definition of a sanctuary city is somewhat murky: At minimum, it is a locality that won't hold suspects for Immigration and Customs Enforcement or allow their police officers or sheriffs' deputies to do the work of federal immigration agents. But for many immigrants, such protections mean nothing at all.

It's not just tough-on-crime Republicans that preside over a criminal justice system that today serves as the front door for a massive deportation pipeline. Every day, police and prosecutors in Democratic Party–controlled cities fuel mass incarceration by arresting and charging people for low-level nonviolent offenses. An arrest for jumping a turnstile or a minor drug charge could result in a person's separation from his or her family forever.

America is the most incarceratory nation in the world—in 2015 alone, police made an estimated 11 million arrests. For undocumented immigrants, an arrest can trigger detention and deportation by ICE. And that's true even if a self-described sanctuary city refuses to detain someone upon federal request. The fingerprints police collect when booking someone into custody are automatically shared with federal immigration authorities, whether that police department wants to share them or not. A fingerprint match alerts ICE that a suspected undocumented immigrant has been arrested. ICE agents can then find that person, detain them, and deport them. If ICE wants to detain someone, they can find and detain them anywhere in the United States regardless of whether local officials are cooperating.

Now, under Trump, a man who has declared that the Mexican government is coordinating the mass migration of rapists to the United States and that Muslims pose an existential threat to the West, things could get far worse. On Friday morning, the *Associated Press* reported the existence of a draft memo that indicates the Trump administration is considering the unprecedented step of deploying 100,000 National Guard troops "to perform the functions of an immigration officer in relation to the investigation, apprehension and detention of aliens in the United States." As of last year, ICE employed roughly 5,800 deportation officers. (The White House has denied it is considering such a policy but did not deny the existence of such a memo.) With more boots on the ground, the imperative for local criminal justice officials is clearer than ever. As long as police and prosecutors continue to arrest and charge people for low-level offenses, sanctuary cities simply aren't safe for undocumented immigrants.

Recently, the administration began an end run around self-proclaimed sanctuary cities. In Travis County, Texas—which includes Austin, the state's liberal mecca—Sheriff Sally Hernandez promised recently to ignore most ICE detainers or requests to detain an immigrant. But according to a news report last week, immigration officials obtained federal arrest warrants for at least 42 immigrants, charging most with federal felonies for illegally re-entering the United States. By using judicial arrest warrants instead of detainers, ICE is now requiring rather than requesting that immigrants be detained—and Hernandez was thus compelled to turn them over to the feds.

ICE also identifies, detains, and deports immigrants after they have been convicted of a crime, including very minor ones. Even lawful permanent residents who have spent their entire cognizant lives in the United States can be deported as the result of a minor drug-dealing conviction. For undocumented immigrants, incarceration in state prison will also tip off the feds: If you're locked up, they'll know exactly where to find you.

Harsh and inhumane federal immigration laws are, of course, the fault of the federal government. But as long as local law enforcement shares information with ICE, everyday policing and prosecution are complicit in Trump's crackdown. For decades, mainstream Republicans and Democrats have turned local criminal justice systems into the grease that smoothes the federal deportation machine's operation. It was

> **Purportedly progressive mayors are offering immigrants a false sense of security.**

legislation passed by the Republican-controlled Congress and signed into law by President Bill Clinton in 1996 that made it so easy to deport lawful permanent residents for minor crimes. And it was the Secure Communities program initiated under President George W. Bush and rolled out under President Obama that has rendered local police de facto immigration agents and made it virtually impossible for states or localities to opt out.

Trump undoubtedly poses a historic threat to immigrants. But local elected officials and prosecutors cannot just shrug their shoulders and blame mass deportations on Washington politicians. Local district attorneys are responsible for the vast majority of prosecutions that result in incarceration. These local prosecutors must also take responsibility for the massive deportation campaign that Trump has pledged to undertake. Simply ignoring federal detainer requests isn't enough to make a city a real sanctuary.

Sanctuary cities were a critical victory won by activists. They were implemented because outraged immigrant communities—with assistance from federal courts that found detentions raised serious constitutional issues—successfully pressured cities to refuse to cooperate with federal detainer requests. In Washington, that pressure led Obama, who had carried out mass deportations, to more narrowly define which immigrants would be prioritized for removal, amongst other reforms. But Obama left the program's basic information-sharing architecture in place and ready for full deployment by the most nativist administration in recent U.S. history.

Purportedly progressive mayors are offering immigrants a false sense of security. The reality is that sanctuary cities are not doing enough to mitigate the immigration threat that Trump poses. The only reason that Secure Communities works is because it affixed the deportation pipeline to the largest policing and imprisonment system on Earth. Cities can and must shrink their contribution to that system by arresting and prosecuting fewer people. While localities can't end drug prohibition, they can pull back from fighting the drug war by ceasing to arrest and prosecute people for drug possession and minor drug-dealing offenses. Prosecutors and police don't make laws, but they have the power of discretion.

Print Citations

CMS: Denvir, Daniel. "The False Promise of Sanctuary Cities." In *The Reference Shelf: The National Debate Topic 2018–2019 Immigration*, edited by Betsy Maury, 167-169. Ipswich, MA: H.W. Wilson, 2018.

MLA: Denvir, Daniel. "The False Promise of Sanctuary Cities." *The Reference Shelf: The National Debate Topic 2018–2019 Immigration*. Ed. Betsy Maury. Ipswich: H.W. Wilson, 2018. 167-169. Print.

APA: Denvir, D. (2018). The false promise of sanctuary cities. In Betsy Maury (Ed.), *The reference shelf: The national debate topic 2018–2019 immigration* (pp. 167-169). Ipswich, MA: H.W. Wilson. (Original work published 2017)

The Trump Administration's First Step to Defund "Sanctuary Cities" Is Surprisingly Cautious

By Dara Lind
Vox, April 21, 2017

On Friday, the Department of Justice sent letters to a handful of jurisdictions that currently receive federal funding for law enforcement, with what seems like an innocuous request: they have 2 months to "provide documentation" proving that they're in full compliance with a federal law about information-sharing, in order to continue qualifying for federal grants in the coming fiscal year.

But that uncontroversial request—asking cities to prove they obey a law that pretty much all of them say they already obey—is the Trump administration's attempt to turn up the heat on so-called "sanctuary cities." And it could lend fuel to a political fight that's much broader than the jurisdictions who got the letters, or the text of the federal law they're being asked to obey.

Most cities—and critics—have defined "sanctuaries" as places where local police and jail officials don't always comply with Immigration and Customs Enforcement requests to hold immigrants in jail (after they'd normally be released) so ICE officers can pick them up.

The Trump administration isn't, so far. The places it's asked to certify compliance are cities that don't just fail to help enforce federal law but, the administration has implied, actually violate it—with policies that could prohibit municipal employees from giving any information about immigrants to federal agents.

The threat is substantial: DOJ's state and local grants include Community-Oriented Policing Services grants, on which many local police departments are heavily reliant. Cities aren't going down without a fight. (Several cities have already filed a lawsuit against the administration to keep their funding; those cities have limited overlap with the jurisdictions being targeted now.)

What's not yet clear is whether the Trump administration is being *so* cautious in defining "sanctuary cities" that they won't end up doing any actual defunding—or whether this is a setup to argue that cities who don't do what the federal government wants with immigrants are inherently violating the law. The latter sounds aggressive, but it's possible the administration might win a court battle—or at least drag it out long enough that cities lose their political appetite for a fight.

The Trump Administration Isn't Defining "Sanctuary Cities" the Way They're Commonly Understood

Debates over "sanctuary cities" have been ongoing for years—including during the debate that unfolded in 2015 after the murder of Kate Steinle in San Francisco, helping propel the fledgling candidacy of long-shot Republican Donald Trump. But the biggest challenge may lie in how the administration defines "sanctuary cities."

When Attorney General Sessions rolled out his department's "anti-sanctuary" policy in March, he implied these were the cities his Department of Justice would now start targeting. "Some states and cities have adopted policies designed to frustrate the enforcement of our immigration laws. This includes refusing to detain known felons," Sessions said. "These policies cannot continue. They make our nation less safe by putting dangerous criminals back on our streets."

His speech was misleading—not just because of the undertones painting all unauthorized immigrants as dangerous criminals. While the Department of Homeland Security and the Department of Justice are reportedly working on a definition of "sanctuary city" to use in future, Sessions' DOJ is moving ahead with an interim policy in the meantime—based on a definition of "sanctuary" that isn't about detention at all.

Under federal law, state and local governments can't prohibit their employees from sharing information with the federal government (if they so choose) about someone's immigration status. (They're allowed to have broad confidentiality policies in place that protect immigration information along with other kinds of personal info.)

In 2016, Republican members of Congress asked the Obama administration's Justice Department to look into whether cities that got federal grants were violating this law. The memo written by the DOJ's inspector general in response—which Sessions referred to on Monday—concluded the answer could be yes: that many of America's biggest cities had policies that, depending on how they were applied, could "restrict cooperation with ICE in all respects."

In Chicago, for example, an ordinance states that "no agent or agency shall disclose information regarding the citizenship or immigration status of any person unless required to do so by legal process or such disclosure has been authorized in writing by the individual to whom such information pertains."

It's not at all clear how many "sanctuary cities" exist under this definition. The DOJ sent letters to nine jurisdictions—including the state of California, the cities of Philadelphia, New Orleans, New York and Chicago (and Cook County, IL, the county associated with Chicago); and the counties associated with Milwaukee, Miami and Las Vegas.

That list is nearly identical to the jurisdictions that the Obama administration looked at in 2016—which makes sense, since Attorney General Sessions cited the Obama administration report in March when announcing a crackdown on "sanctuary city" funding.

The jurisdictions that the Obama-era DOJ looked at represented 63 percent of active (at the time) DOJ grants through three offices. So in theory, the stakes are high.

But in practice, it's not clear whether the letter *does* anything. It just asks the jurisdictions to certify that they're in compliance with the federal information-sharing law. And those jurisdictions argue that they already do.

The Chicago ordinance (and other similar ordinances) has an exception for "applicable federal law"—a clause local officials argue they're fully in compliance with the federal information-sharing law.

The Obama administration memo concluded that city employees might, in practice, think they were prohibited from answering any ICE request for information—even when they might want (and be legally authorized) to do so. The Trump administration is certainly hinting that it agrees with that assessment. But nothing is stopping the jurisdictions targeted by the letters from just sending replies in the next two months attesting that they comply with federal law—and using the clauses in their ordinances as the "documentation."

Then, it'll be up to the DOJ to decide whether they agree—or whether to challenge the cities' interpretation.

Cities Are Already Suing to Keep Their Funding—But the Limited Definition of "Sanctuary Cities" Gives the Federal Government a Stronger Case

The Supreme Court doesn't let the federal government tell cities and states which laws to prosecute, and it can't force them to help enforce federal law. That's called "commandeering," and the Supreme Court has ruled it violates the 10th Amendment. This is why President-elect Trump can't just decree that all police officers in the US have to assist federal immigration agents whenever possible.

If the federal government wants to get states to do something, it has to use funding: making grants to states or cities conditional on certain policies. This is why the legal drinking age is 21 in most states: Thanks to legislation passed in 1984 and pushed by Mothers Against Drunk Driving, the federal government started refusing to give federal highway funds to any state with a lower drinking age.

What the federal government can't do is place conditions on grants that have nothing to do with the grant's purpose. (It couldn't deny Small Business Administration grants, for example, to states that allowed unauthorized immigrants to get

Cities have been defiant, but now the threat of defunding is real.

driver's licenses.) Nor can it put conditions on funding to the point of being "coercive"—even if those conditions are relevant to the purpose of the grant. That, too, courts have judged, runs afoul of the 10th Amendment.

This is why the Supreme Court ruled the Medicaid expansion in the Affordable Care Act unconstitutional—it took existing Medicaid funding that states were already receiving, and declared they would stop receiving that money unless they adopted a new, expanded definition for who ought to qualify for the program.

The Medicaid decision was a defeat for progressives when it came down. But in the wake of Trump's election, many have embraced it—in the belief that Trump's pledge to defund "sanctuary cities" will also be deemed coercive. Indeed, even before Sessions's announcement, San Francisco had already filed a lawsuit against the Trump administration to attack the constitutionality of (as yet hypothetical) defunding.

But the Trump Department of Justice might be on much stronger legal footing than the Obama Department of Health and Human Services was. It can argue it's not putting any new conditions on funding whatsoever—just enforcing existing rules.

As Jessica Vaughan of the Center for Immigration Studies said, according to the inspector general's memo, "If they are violating federal law, then according to the DOJ rules, they are not eligible for certain DOJ grants."

This strategy wouldn't be constitutionally foolproof. (The government would be on much more solid footing, says professor Gabriel Chin of UC Davis, if it replaced existing grants with new ones that had conditions attached—much like Race to the Top grants the Education Department used to pass teacher accountability laws and the adoption of Common Core standards in states—rather than trying to retroactively wedge new conditions into existing funding.) And as we've seen in the litigation over the Trump administration's refugee and visa ban, the judicial branch may be more skeptical of this administration than it has traditionally been of the executive branch.

But even defenders of "sanctuary cities" acknowledged before Trump's inauguration that a defunding strategy along these lines would be harder to challenge in court. "There is some case law supporting the idea that merely requiring communication is not an impairment of a state's rights under the 10th Amendment," says Melissa Keaney of the National Immigration Law Center, which advocates for "sanctuary city"–type policies.

Cities Have Been Defiant: But Now the Threat of Defunding Is Real

So far, many local governments are anything but intimidated by the Trump administration's threats. Dozens of cities that could count as "sanctuaries" have already made it clear that they won't change their policies even at the risk of losing federal funding.

It's a way for blue cities to stand up to a suddenly deep-red federal government, and to do so in the name of protecting some of their most vulnerable residents. It doesn't hurt that because the definition of "sanctuary city" is fuzzy, cities can make it sound like they're saving their unauthorized immigrant residents from getting turned over to ICE and deported, even if that's not how it really works.

But cities and agencies that aren't looking for a big political fight are more cautious. Indeed, the mere threat of defunding has already led one of the targeted jurisdictions—Miami-Dade County—start complying with federal detainers in

February, in the name of turning down the heat from the feds. (This didn't stop them from getting a DOJ letter Friday.)

Some small towns, like Storm Lake, Iowa, plan to keep protecting their immigrant residents—but avoid the term "sanctuary city." "We're getting along just fine, we don't need to take on that," Storm Lake's city manager told Vice's Meredith Hoffman.

And local officials who are most directly under threat from federal defunding—police officers—are even more squeamish.

"I don't think people understand what it would mean to cut off federal assistance," one California police officer told the Intercept. "I'd lose all my (organized crime task force) funding, my investigative assistance, all the resources we use to go after seriously bad dudes."

So far, their anxiety hasn't spilled over to the rest of city governments. But now that the threat of defunding is no longer abstract—even if no jurisdiction has actually lost its grants yet, or been denied requests for new funds—those attitudes could change.

Even cities that respond by challenging defunding in court could lose their appetites over the course of a long and costly legal battle.

And at the end of the day, UC Davis's Chin says, the federal government could win.

Chin compares the situation to the Solomon Amendment, a statute that prevented universities from getting federal money if they didn't allow military recruiters access to its campuses (something many schools were loath to do in the era of legalized anti-LGBTQ discrimination in the military). Universities challenged the amendment, but the Supreme Court upheld it—and most schools gave in.

"The cost of noncompliance was too high," Chin said.

While cities might be willing to fight for the ability to keep both the funding and "sanctuary" policies, if they lose the court case and have to pick one, they might decide they need the former more.

"It's possible that a cleverly drafted and broadly worded statute could put a lot of state and local funding at risk," Chin says. "And if that happens, and it was upheld, then I think states and localities would knuckle under."

That could take years to play out. And it's going to be harder for the Trump administration to win a legal battle if it doesn't have backup from Congress in shoring up Sessions's interpretation of DOJ rules with legislative language. But by choosing the limited definition of "sanctuary," the Trump administration is picking a fight it could hypothetically win.

Print Citations

CMS: Lind, Dara. "The Trump Administration's First Step to Defund 'Sanctuary Cities' Is Surprisingly Cautious." In *The Reference Shelf: The National Debate Topic 2018–2019 Immigration*, edited by Betsy Maury, 170-175. Ipswich, MA: H.W. Wilson, 2018.

MLA: Lind, Dara. "The Trump Administration's First Step to Defund 'Sanctuary Cities' Is Surprisingly Cautious." *The Reference Shelf: The National Debate Topic 2018–2019 Immigration*. Ed. Betsy Maury. Ipswich: H.W. Wilson, 2018. 170-175. Print.

APA: Lind, D. (2018). The Trump administration's first step to defund "sanctuary cities" is surprisingly cautious. In Betsy Maury (Ed.), *The reference shelf: The national debate topic 2018–2019 immigration* (pp. 170-175). Ipswich, MA: H.W. Wilson. (Original work published 2017)

Whom Do Sanctuary Cities Protect?

By Lauren Carasik
Boston Review, March 9, 2017

The furor against sanctuary cities hit a fevered pitch after the July 2015 killing of thirty-two-year-old Kathryn Steinle. She was shot in San Francisco by Juan Francisco Lopez-Sanchez, an undocumented Mexican immigrant who had seven felony convictions and had been deported five times. Lopez-Sanchez had been released when the San Francisco police declined to detain him for immigration authorities after drug charges against him were dropped.

A year later at the Republican National Convention, Donald Trump used her death as a rallying cry: "My opponent wants sanctuary cities but where was the sanctuary for Kate Steinle?" One of his first actions as president was to sign an executive order threatening to strip federal funding from sanctuary cities—an estimated four hundred jurisdictions that limit, in varying degrees, the manner in which their police assist with immigration enforcement.

Trump tells a story of recalcitrant local authorities, violent immigrants, and sanctuary cities as breeding grounds for crime. Apparently many Americans embrace that story. In recent polls, a majority oppose sanctuary cities and want local law enforcement to cooperate with federal authorities. Why then, under the threat of Trump's order, did many sanctuary cities double down on their commitments to immigrants?

While Miami mayor Carlos Gimenez acquiesced to the administration's threat and ordered his jails to comply with federal requests, other jurisdictions have reaffirmed their immigrant-friendly positions and some are considering expanding protections, such as California, which may adopt sanctuary policies statewide, and Washington, D.C., which allocated additional funding to provide legal aid to immigrants facing deportation.

Opponents of sanctuary cities see them as a blight on public safety, but security concerns are one of the reasons that hundreds of jurisdictions think sanctuary cities are a good idea. It all depends on your views of the threat of criminality among immigrants and what policies best serve public safety. Fortunately the record on those issues is well-documented.

Trump's assertion that sanctuary cities breed crime is, like many of his other canards about immigrants, unfounded. An October 2016 study by researchers from University of California, Riverside and Highline College found "no statistically

discernible difference in violent crime rate, rape, or property crime across the cities." They concluded that "sanctuary policies have no effect on crime rates, despite
narratives to the contrary." The report echoes the findings of other studies that do
not bear out increased crime in sanctuary cities. And the societal benefits are not
limited to lower crime: economies are stronger in sanctuary counties.

Moreover Trump's order, in addition to being questionably legal, will undermine,
not enhance, security. Indeed one of the most critical arguments for the necessity
of sanctuary cities is one of public safety: local officials cannot protect communities that do not trust them. Few if any cities refuse to turn over immigrants charged
with serious offenses. Instead they balk at turning over those arrested for minor
infractions or verifying the immigration status of people encountered in the course
of normal policing. In other words, they simply treat immigrants the same way as
everyone else. *The New York Times* points this out in its story about the Steinle
case. While the tragedy was exploited to depict immigrants as dangerous criminals,
Lopez-Sanchez did not have a record of violent crime. There is evidence to indicate
he did not intend to commit murder, since "the bullet he fired was found to have
ricocheted off the pier." And the suggestion that he sought out San Francisco because it was a sanctuary city is also false. In fact federal officials sent him there to
face a minor drug charge, after which he was released—as would be anyone else
with only a minor drug offense. The backstory does not ease the anguish of Steinle's
family, but the grand narrative about immigrants that Trump has consistently sought
to advance is simply not true. Immigration status is not a predictor of criminality.
Quite the opposite: studies have shown that immigrants in the United States commit fewer crimes than native-born citizens.

Misrepresentations also abound about what sanctuary cities actually do and the
nature of their commitments. Sanctuary cities take their name from the sanctuary
movement that sprung up in the 1980s to provide safe haven for Central American refugees desperate to avoid deportation to the violence-stricken countries from
which they fled. Many Americans saw the mayhem as a direct result of Washington's policies supporting repressive regimes in the region, which, compounded by
U.S. hostility to asylum claims from Salvadorans and Guatemalans, motivated a
sense of heightened duty by many houses of worship to shelter immigrants from law
enforcement.

Unlike the sanctuary movement, sanctuary cities are not actively harboring the
undocumented or forgiving crimes when they do commit them; they are refusing
to take on tasks of federal immigration enforcement that were never theirs to begin with. Although sanctuary cities can refuse to cooperate, their ability to impede
federal immigration is fairly limited: they cannot prevent federal authorities from
conducting raids or otherwise enforcing immigration laws themselves.

The number of sanctuary cities grew rapidly in response to the Secure Communities program, implemented under President Bush and continued under the Obama
administration. Under that program, local law enforcement sent the fingerprints of
anyone arrested to a national database and often detained arrestees for immigration
authorities. Numerous complaints—about the program's impact on safety, concerns

> **There is a strong argument that punishing sanctuary cities runs afoul of the Tenth Amendment, which bars the federal government from "commandeering" state and local government to effectuate its policies, as well as spending clause restrictions.**

about due process and racial profiling, and that it ensnared people for minor offenses as well as non-offenders—compelled the Obama administration to curtail the program in 2014. Under its successor, the Priority Enforcement Program, which focuses on immigrants thought to threaten national and border security and public safety, Immigration and Customs Enforcement (ICE) continues to be notified of all arrests. Trump's deportation priorities vastly expand those designated by Obama, and he has ordered the reinstatement of the Secure Communities Program.

Jurisdictions have good reasons to adopt sanctuary policies, some political and some pragmatic. Some municipalities do not want local law enforcement to be active participants in mass deportation and have rallied to the defense of their immigrant communities, in part because the failure of immigration reform has made it impossible for people to stay legally and they abhor the idea of tearing communities apart. Others believe immigration enforcement should be reserved for federal authorities. But the objections extend far beyond jurisdictional and political ones. The primary one is that effective policing is predicated on community trust.

The President's Task Force on 21st Century Policing recognized this: "At all levels of government, it is important that laws, policies, and practices not hinder the ability of local law enforcement to build the strong relationships necessary to public safety and community well-being." The report concludes that "whenever possible, state and local law enforcement should not be involved in immigration enforcement."

This is particularly important to protect the vulnerable, such as victims of domestic and sexual violence or exploitation. For them, the fear that interaction with law enforcement could lead to deportation bolsters the power of abusers and serves to further isolate and silence them. Last month in Texas, a woman was detained by ICE—which was acting on a tip suspected to have come from her alleged abuser—in the courthouse just after obtaining a protective order against him. Although records later showed that the woman may have had her own criminal history, the message to other victims about the risks of seeking protection is chilling. Similarly, witnesses critical to prosecuting crimes or good Samaritans may be reluctant to come forward without assurances that they do not risk being reported to immigration authorities. Compounding the cost to community trust, using police departments' resources to assist in federal immigration enforcement can drain local budgets. Facilitating deportation exacts significant social costs as well, by devastating families and losing immigrants' contributions to community.

As Republican governors threaten to cancel grants to sanctuary jurisdictions and lawmakers propose legislation banning sanctuary policies, Trump's executive order compromises the safety of communities. Its legality is also suspect.

While sanctuary cities do not conflict with federal law, there is a strong argument that punishing sanctuary cities runs afoul of the Tenth Amendment, which bars the federal government from "commandeering" state and local government to effectuate its policies, as well as spending clause restrictions. San Francisco, which has had a sanctuary law since 1989, was the first municipality to sue the Trump administration, claiming the order is unconstitutional. The city has an estimated 30,000 undocumented immigrants and risks losing $1.2 billion in federal funding. Another legal hurdle is that ICE detainers—agency requests that local law enforcement continue to hold someone for forty-eight hours who would otherwise be released—are likely unconstitutional. As the ACLU argued, the detainers implicate the Fourth Amendment because they cause extended detention "without probable cause, without judicial approval, and without due process protections." Those arguments have already convinced some federal courts that the detainer policies are illegal, and some municipalities will not detain people for ICE without judicial oversight.

Trump's motivation in punishing resistant communities may be partly informed by the challenges he faces in carrying out the magnitude of deportations he has promised. Even with his intention to hire an additional 15,000 border enforcement and ICE agents, a plan that presents significant logistical challenges, the president needs to tap the resources of local police to achieve his deportation goals. But as with at least one other Trump immigration initiative, the administration will first have to defend its order in court.

Print Citations

CMS: Carasik, Lauren. "Whom Do Sanctuary Cities Protect?" In *The Reference Shelf: The National Debate Topic 2018–2019 Immigration*, edited by Betsy Maury, 176-179. Ipswich, MA: H.W. Wilson, 2018.

MLA: Carasik, Lauren. "Whom Do Sanctuary Cities Protect?" *The Reference Shelf: The National Debate Topic 2018–2019 Immigration*. Ed. Betsy Maury. Ipswich: H.W. Wilson, 2018. 176-179. Print.

APA: Carasik, L. (2018). Whom do sactuary cities protect?" In Betsy Maury (Ed.), *The reference shelf: The national debate topic 2018–2019 immigration* (pp. 176-179). Ipswich, MA: H.W. Wilson. (Original work published 2017)

Trump Administration Sues California Over Laws Protecting Immigrants

By Evan Halper
Los Angeles Times, March 6, 2018

The Trump administration, seeking to force a defiant California to cooperate with its agenda of stepped-up immigrant deportations, went to federal court Tuesday to invalidate three state laws—the administration's most direct challenge yet to the state's policies.

Administration officials say the three laws in question, all passed by the Legislature last year, blatantly obstruct federal immigration law and thus violate the Constitution's supremacy clause, which gives federal law precedence over state enactments.

"The Department of Justice and the Trump administration are going to fight these unjust, unfair, and unconstitutional policies that are imposed on you," Atty. Gen. Jeff Sessions plans to tell a meeting of the California Peace Officers Assn. in Sacramento on Wednesday, according to excerpts of his remarks released by the Justice Department.

"We are fighting to make your jobs safer and to help you reduce crime in America. And I believe that we are going to win."

The laws make it a crime for business owners to voluntarily help federal agents find and detain undocumented workers, prohibit local law enforcement from alerting immigration agents when detainees are released from custody, and create a state inspection program for federal immigration detention centers.

Administration officials, who briefed reporters before the suit was filed, said other states that are pursuing laws similar to California's are also likely to be targeted in court.

The suit, which administration lawyers filed late Tuesday in federal court in Sacramento, considerably raises the tension between the administration and the most populous state in the country. California officials consistently have sought to stymie Trump's efforts to impose policies incompatible with the more permissive vision of the state's leaders and the liberal leanings of its electorate.

Many state and local officials in California say the administration's stepped-up deportation efforts are making communities less safe and undermining local economies.

The case will test the power of the Trump administration to force California police departments and local governments to cooperate with deportations and other aggressive enforcement actions targeting people who entered the country illegally or overstayed their visas. It reflects the administration's limited tolerance for state's rights when states want to go in a sharply different direction than the administration.

In a statement, Gov. Jerry Brown called the federal suit a "stunt."

"At a time of unprecedented political turmoil, Jeff Sessions has come to California to further divide and polarize America," he said. "Jeff, these political stunts may be the norm in Washington, but they don't work here. SAD!!!"

California officials were preparing for the suit even before it was filed. After the Justice Department announced Sessions would be making a major announcement in Sacramento, state leaders expressed confidence that Washington's legal attacks would fail.

"We'll see what the courts say," said Sacramento Mayor Darrell Steinberg, a former legislative leader.

"So far the administration's record there is not stellar," he said, referring to the administration's repeated losses in court. "We didn't pass these laws to protect people with serious criminal backgrounds. We are protecting our communities from immigration agents intimidating people and overreaching in very serious ways."

State Senate leader Kevin de León struck a similar note: "If U.S. Atty. Gen. Jeff Sessions is suing California because we refuse to help the Trump administration tear apart honest, hardworking families, I say bring it on. Based on the U.S. Department of Justice's track record in court, I like our odds," he said.

The administration, however, could be in a stronger position in this case than in previous court battles over immigration issues, including court rulings against early versions of Trump's travel ban and against efforts to cut off some federal money to cities with so-called sanctuary policies.

In many other cases, the administration has been trying to swiftly unravel or reshape well-established environmental, workplace or immigration regulations that were grounded in years of case law or voluminous administrative proceedings. In this case, it is California that is arguably in uncharted legal territory, imposing barriers aimed at undermining federal law enforcement efforts.

Administration officials charge that the state measures not only hinder their ability to carry out federal law, but also put immigration agents and communities at risk.

The suit includes a declaration from Immigration and Customs Enforcement Acting Director Thomas Homan, who said that the inability of ICE officers to go to local lockups to pick up immigrants who have been detained by local police agencies forces them to hunt down suspects in more dangerous settings.

SB 54, one of the three challenged state laws, prohibits state and local police agencies from notifying federal officials in many cases when immigrants potentially subject to deportation are about to be released from custody.

When the law was under consideration in the Legislature, former Atty. Gen. Eric H. Holder Jr., who headed the Justice Department in the Obama administration and now represents the state Senate, wrote a letter defending the measure's constitutionality. The federal government has the authority to enforce its immigration laws, but doesn't have the power to draft California officials into helping, he said.

California Atty. Gen. Xavier Becerra said Tuesday that the state would use a similar argument to defend its law in court.

"We are doing what we believe is best to make sure the people of California are safe," he said. "We are doing nothing to intrude on the work of federal government to do immigration enforcement."

"When people feel confident to come forward to report crimes in our communities or participate in policing efforts without fear of deportation, they are more likely to cooperate with the criminal justice system."

Justice Department officials cited several instances in recent weeks in which, they said, the new law prevented federal immigration agents from taking custody of people arrested for serious crimes.

Officials in Ventura County, for example, refused to turn over a suspect arrested for sexual abuse of a minor, they said. A request to transfer custody of a car-theft suspect was declined by Sacramento County jail officials, and Alameda County jail officials refused to turn over a convicted drug dealer arrested for felony drug possession while armed, they said.

State officials say those suspects are the exception and do not reflect those the law is designed to protect, who are primarily people jailed for low-level offenses.

> Many state and local officials in California say the administration's stepped-up deportation efforts are making communities less safe and undermining local economies.

California officials have been unflinching in enforcing the new laws, despite warnings from the Trump administration that they would create a confrontation.

In January, Becerra put employers on notice that they would be prosecuted if they did not follow the state's new Immigrant Worker Protection Act, AB 450, which prohibits businesses from voluntarily sharing information about workers with federal immigration agents. The law also requires that employers alert workers if their records are going to be inspected by federal officials.

Business owners who voluntarily assist with federal immigration operations will face fines of up to $10,000, Becerra warned. The Trump administration lawsuit says state officials have acknowledged that such threats are designed to frustrate immigration enforcement actions and that the law puts private businesses in an impossible situation: They are being required by the state to rebuff federal agents.

The third law under challenge, AB 103, imposes state inspections on federal detention facilities. The measure passed in response to reports of rampant mistreatment and abuse in federal detention facilities, many of which are run by private companies that act as federal contractors. Since the law took effect, the state has been conducting inspections at the facilities and demanding access to inmate documents that the administration says the state has no authority to review.

"California has chosen to purposefully contradict the will and responsibility of the Congress to protect our Homeland," Homeland Security Secretary Kirstjen Nielsen said in a statement in which she thanked Sessions for his efforts to "uphold the rule of law and protect American communities."

Print Citations

CMS: Halper, Evan. "Trump Administration Sues California over Laws Protecting Immigrants." In *The Reference Shelf: Immigration*, edited by Betsy Maury, 180-183. Ipswich, MA: H.W. Wilson, 2018.

MLA: Halper, Evan. "Trump Administration Sues California over Laws Protecting Immigrants." *The Reference Shelf: Immigration*. Ed. Betsy Maury. Ipswich: H.W. Wilson, 2018. 180-183. Print.

APA: Halper, E. (2018). Trump administration sues California over laws protecting immigrants. In Betsy Maury (Ed.), *The reference shelf: Immigration* (pp. 180-183). Ipswich, MA: H.W. Wilson. (Original work published 2018)

Municipal Suffrage, Sanctuary Cities, and the Contested Meaning of Citizenship

By Kenneth Stahl

Harvard Law Review, January 19, 2018

In November 2016, the city of San Francisco enacted a ballot initiative that was somewhat overshadowed by other election results. It permitted noncitizens with children in the public school system to vote in school board elections. Though it is unclear whether the measure will have much practical impact on the city schools, the measure has enormous symbolic significance because it helps clarify why local policies regarding immigrants, including noncitizen suffrage but especially the decision of cities like San Francisco to declare themselves "sanctuary cities" and limit law enforcement cooperation with federal immigration authorities, have become perhaps the most contentious set of issues on the national political stage. In short, local policies regarding immigrants have steadily eroded the distinction between citizens and noncitizens and raised the fraught question of who is a citizen.

As the immigrant population in the United States has exploded in the last few decades, the line between citizens and noncitizens has increasingly blurred, with noncitizens often being granted benefits previously reserved for citizens. Several cities have been at the forefront of this trend, issuing municipal identification cards to undocumented immigrants, prohibiting discrimination based on immigration status, and barring law enforcement from inquiring about individuals' immigration status. As such, participation in the political process has taken on special significance as the mark of what distinguishes citizens from noncitizens. Though noncitizens had the right to vote in many states prior to the twentieth century, no state today permits noncitizens to vote in state elections, and Congress enacted a law in 1996 that prohibits noncitizens from voting in federal elections. The Supreme Court has upheld the exclusion of noncitizens from political participation, writing that "[t]he exclusion of aliens from basic governmental processes is not a deficiency in the democratic system but a necessary consequence of the community's process of political self-definition." Yet, San Francisco is the latest of several cities, including Chicago and a few small municipalities in Maryland, to grant noncitizens the right to vote in certain local elections, and other cities have debated doing the same.

It is surely not coincidental that San Francisco enacted this measure at the same moment Donald Trump was elected President on a wave of anti-immigrant and anti-urban sentiment. In fact, this confluence of events is evidence of a broader phenomenon that illuminates the volatile politics of our present moment: citizenship is not distributed solely by the nation-state but exists at multiple scales simultaneously. Furthermore, each scale may define citizenship differently—local citizenship, for example, is generally distributed based on residence and interest, whereas national citizenship is distributed based on identity and allegiance. Usually these different meanings can co-exist with little difficulty, but during times of demographic change and economic turmoil, conflict can erupt between the different scales over who qualifies as a citizen.

As an initial matter, our political system features distinctive conceptions of local and national citizenship, or what Yishai Blank refers to as "spheres of citizenship." Suffrage is an instructive example. At the federal level, voting rights are contingent almost entirely on American citizenship. With a few exceptions, all adult citizens are entitled to vote in federal elections even if they do not reside in the United States, and noncitizens may not vote in federal elections even if they do reside in the United States. Citizenship is conferred by birth or lineage, or through naturalization, which requires an extensive residency period and a demonstration of fealty to national civic ideals. At the local level, however, and usually the state level as well, voting rights are tied to residency. Moving from one municipality to another generally means that an individual loses a right to vote in the former municipality and gains it in the latter. States and localities are prohibited from requiring a minimum duration of residence or imposing other prerequisites on the right of local residents to vote, but are not required to enfranchise anyone who is a nonresident. All state constitutions today bar noncitizen residents from voting in state elections, but local governments generally have the authority to expand the municipal franchise to include noncitizen residents, as San Francisco has done.

The contrast between a birth, lineage or naturalization standard and a residency standard marks an important conceptual distinction between local and national citizenship. Insofar as citizenship is based on residence, it is something consensual and rational. According to an influential theory known as the "Tiebout" model after the economist Charles Tiebout, individuals are perceived as "consumer-voters" who have a variety of options of where to reside within a metropolitan region, and make that choice based on which community offers the most attractive package of municipal services—low taxes, quality schools, and so forth. The consumer-voter is a shopper who votes with his or her feet, and municipalities are essentially firms that compete to attract residents who contribute to the fiscal bottom line. "Citizenship" is a market transaction, a private contractual relationship between the resident and the locality.

A logical endpoint of the consensual idea of citizenship is the enfranchisement of all local residents regardless of nationality. In principle, under the Tiebout model, membership in the community is determined by interest rather than identity, and one's interest can be determined entirely by the choice of where to reside. In the debate leading up to the Maryland City of Takoma Park's decision to enfranchise some noncitizens in municipal elections, one noncitizen resident made the case for noncitizen suffrage in exactly those terms: "I have as much interest in the community as anyone. . . . We're not asking for a voice at the national level or in foreign policy. . . . But in local matters, we're no different than somebody who has moved to Takoma Park from California." Cities have a strong financial incentive to confer citizenship on immigrants because, in our age of globalization, immigrants have become perhaps the ultimate footloose consumer-voters. Cities around the world are competing for the massive economic benefits that accompany concentrations of immigrant labor, and the enactment of policies like noncitizen suffrage and sanctuary city ordinances is one way for cities to attract immigrants.

In contrast to local citizenship, the federal idea of citizenship is rooted in nationality rather than residence, and therefore reflects a primordial conception of the citizen as deeply embedded in the territory. As Yael Tamir writes, the federal idea of citizenship "sees social roles and affiliations as inherent, as a matter of fate rather than choice." The notion that citizens can choose their state or a state can choose its citizens in the manner of a market transaction is hostile to this conception. For that reason, many lawmakers and others have expressed a preference for welcoming immigrants with cultural and linguistic ties to the United States and object to basing immigration policy on immigrants' financial contributions.

The distinction between local and national citizenship is a logical consequence of those institutions' respective evolutions. Cities have long depended on foreign trade to survive and could never rely on borders to buffer themselves against global forces; as a result, they have generally made membership in the urban political community available to those who reside or do business in the city. The modern nation-state, on the other hand, is entirely a creature of its borders, predicated on the idea that the state's sovereign authority extends the full length of the territory it controls. Thus, it has been considered essential to the very idea of the nation-state that the government must be able to differentiate members from non-members based on their connection to the territory.

Until recently, the tension between the two modes of citizenship remained latent because they were perceived as complementary rather than mutually exclusive. Closure at the national level facilitated openness at the local level. According to Michael Walzer's formulation, communities

can be open only if countries are at least potentially closed. Only if the state makes a selection among would-be members and guarantees the loyalty, security, and welfare of the individuals it selects, can local communities take shape as 'indifferent' associations, determined solely by personal preference and market capacity.

Today, however, globalization is causing the local and national modes of citizenship to come more directly into conflict. The global economy is steadily eroding the borders that defined nation-states, subjecting them to the vicissitudes of the same global forces that shaped the city. Both labor and capital can now "vote with their feet" in choosing nation-states in which to locate, placing pressures on states that wish to succeed in a global economy to cater to their demands. As this occurs, the very nature of national citizenship is changing to resemble local citizenship. Many nation-states have begun shifting in the direction of a de facto residence standard for citizenship. Increasingly, civil rights and access to social benefits are conferred on the basis of residence rather than citizenship, moving toward what Yasemin Soysal calls a "postnational" version of citizenship rooted in the individual rights of the person rather than nationality.

Needless to say, the emergence of a postnational standard of citizenship has been profoundly destabilizing for many people. Although this standard strips away the accident of birth as a privileged status, it substitutes a new privileged status, that of mobility. "The freedom to move, perpetually a scarce and unequally distributed commodity, fast becomes the main stratifying factor" in our global age. Those with mobility are moving away from declining rural and manufacturing areas towards the urban areas that are the hubs of the new global knowledge-based economy. The ones left behind resent those who have benefitted from mobility, especially the immigrants who are the most visible symbols of a mobile society, and their reaction is to retrench a definition of citizenship based on place. The city, with its open borders and flexible approach toward citizenship, appears as the embodiment of the evils of globalization. The re-awakening of a nostalgic vision of citizenship rooted in "blood and belonging" thus leads to the demonization of cities, with the "sanctuary city" becoming the pivotal flashpoint in a reckoning over the meaning of citizenship.

> **Local citizenship is generally distributed based on residence and interest, whereas national citizenship is distributed based on identity and allegiance.**

Print Citations

CMS: Stahl, Kenneth. "Municipal Suffrage, Sanctuary Cities, and the Contested Meaning of Citizenship." In *The Reference Shelf: The National Debate Topic 2018–2019 Immigration*, edited by Betsy Maury, 184-187. Ipswich, MA: H.W. Wilson, 2018.

MLA: Stahl, Kenneth. "Municipal Suffrage, Sanctuary Cities, and the Contested Meaning of Citizenship." *The Reference Shelf: The National Debate Topic 2018–2019 Immigration*. Ed. Betsy Maury. Ipswich: H.W. Wilson, 2018. 184-187. Print.

APA: Stahl, K. (2018). Municipal suffrage, sanctuary cities, and the contested meaning of citizenship. In Betsy Maury (Ed.), *The reference shelf: The national debate topic 2018–2019 immigration* (pp. 184-187). Ipswich, MA: H.W. Wilson. (Original work published 2018)

Bibliography

"2016 Campaign: Strong Interest, Widespread Dissatisfaction." *Pew Research*. Pew Research Center. Jul 7, 2016. Web. http://www.people-press. org/2016/07/07/2016-campaign-strong-interest-widespread-dissatisfaction/.

Aguiar, Angel and Terrie Walmsley. "Economic Analysis of U.S. Immigration Reforms." 2009. Center for Global Trade Analysis. Purdue University. http://ageconsearch.umn.edu/bitstream/49302/2/Aguiar_AAEA.pdf.

Alonso, William and Paul Starr. *The Politics of Numbers*. New York: Russel Sage Foundation. 1986.

Applestein, Donald. "The Three-Fifths Compromise: Rationalizing the Irrational." *Constitution Center*. The National Constitution Center. Feb 12, 2013. Web. https://constitutioncenter.org/blog/the-three-fifths-compromise-rationalizing-the-irrational/.

Barclay, Eliza and Sarah Frostenson. "The Ecological Disaster That Is Trump's Border Wall: A Visual Guide." *Vox*. Vox Media. Oct 29 2017. Web. https://www.vox. com/energy-and-environment/2017/4/10/14471304/trump-border-wall-animals.

Bhattacharya, Ananya. "Trump Administration Targets H-1B Visas—Again." *Quartz*. Quartz India. Mar 21, 2018. Web. https://qz.com/1234029/h-1b-visas-trump-administration-suspends-premium-processing-putting-indian-it-on-edge/.

Blakemore, Erin. "How the U.S. Census Defines Race." *Smithsonian Mag*. Smart News. Smithsonian Institution. Nov 9, 2015. Web. https://www.smithsonian-mag.com/smart-news/how-us-census-defines-race-america-180957189/.

Brusk, Steve and Gregory Wallace. "Commerce Department Says Citizenship Question Will Be Reinstated in 2020 Census." *CNN Politics*. CNN. Mar 27, 2018. Web. https://www.cnn.com/2018/03/26/politics/census-citizenship-question/index.html.

"Build a Wall, and Make Mexico Pay for It." *Politifact*. Politifact. Jan 16, 2017. Web. http://www.politifact.com/truth-o-meter/promises/trumpometer/promise/1397/build-wall-and-make-mexico-pay-it/.

Chinchilla, Norma Stoltz, Hamilton, Nora, and James Loucky. "The Sanctuary Movement and Central American Activism in Los Angeles." *Latin American Perspectives*. Issue 169, Vol. 36, No. 6 (Nov 2009). http://sanctuaryweb.com/Portals/0/2017%20PDFs/Sanctuary%20Movement/2009%20Chinchilla%20The%20Sanctuary%20Movement%20and%20Central%20American%20activism%20in%20LA.pdf.

"City of Chicago v. Jefferson B. Sessions III, Attorney General of the United States." *US Courts*. United States Court of Appeals for the Seventh Circuit. Apr 19, 2018. http://media.ca7.uscourts.gov/cgi-bin/rssExec.

pl?Submit=Display&Path=Y2018/D04-19/C:17-2991:J:Rovner:aut:T:fnOp:N:2
142410:S:0.

De Haldevang, Max. "Trump's Bureaucracy Is Nearly as White, Male, and Unequal as His Cabinet." *Quartz*. Quartz Magazine. Oct 23, 2017. https://qz.com/1109087/trumps-bureaucracy-is-heavily-white-and-male-like-his-cabinet/.

De Pinto, Jennifer, Backus, Fred, Khanna, Kabir, and Anthony Salvanto. "Most Americans Support DACA, but Oppose Border Wall—CBS News Poll." *CBS News*. CBS. Jan 20, 2018. Web. https://www.cbsnews.com/news/most-americans-support-daca-but-oppose-border-wall-cbs-news-poll/.

De Pinto, Jennifer. "Where Americans Stand on Immigration." *CBS News*. CBS. Aug 9, 2017. Web. https://www.cbsnews.com/news/where-americans-stand-on-immigration/.

Dickerson, Caitlin. "What Is DACA? Who Are the Dreamers? Here Are Some Answers." *The New York Times*. The New York Times Co. Jan 23, 2018. https://www.nytimes.com/2018/01/23/us/daca-dreamers-shutdown.html.

"Fact Sheet: The Secure Fence Act of 2006." *Georgewbush-Whitehouse*. Oct 26, 2006. Web. https://georgewbush-whitehouse.archives.gov/news/releases/2006/10/20061026-1.html.

Foner, Eric. "What the Fugitive Slave Act Teaces Us about How States Can Resist Oppressive Federal Power." *The Nation*. Feb 8, 2017. Web. https://www.thenation.com/article/what-the-fugitive-slave-act-teaches/.

García, María Cristina. "America Has Never Actually Welcomed the World's Huddled Masses." *The Washington Post*. The Washington Post Co. Nov 20, 2015. Web. https://www.washingtonpost.com/opinions/america-has-never-actually-welcomed-the-worlds-huddled-masses/2015/11/20/6763fad0-8e71-11e5-ae1f-af46b7df8483_story.html?utm_term=.2e075ad24247.Gjelten, Tom. "The Immigration Act That Inadvertently Changed America." *The Atlantic*. The Atlantic Monthly Group. Oct 2, 2015. Web. https://www.theatlantic.com/politics/archive/2015/10/immigration-act-1965/408409/.

Gonzalez-Barrera, Ana. "More Mexicans Leaving Than Coming to the U.S." *Pew Research*. Pew Research Center. Nov 19, 2015. Web. http://www.pewhispanic.org/2015/11/19/more-mexicans-leaving-than-coming-to-the-u-s/.

Graves, Allison. "Is Trump's Cabinet More White and Male Than Any First Cabinet Than Reagan?" *Politifact*. Politifact. Apr 26, 2017. Web. http://www.politifact.com/truth-o-meter/statements/2017/apr/26/center-american-progress/true-trumps-cabinet-more-white-and-more-male-any-f/.

Guthman, Edwin. "Underground Railroad, 1980's Style." *The New York Times*. The New York Times Co. Sep 25, 1988. Web. https://www.nytimes.com/1988/09/25/books/underground-railroad-1980-s-style.html.

Gzesh, Susan. "Central Americans and Asylum Policy in the Reagan Era." *MPI*. Migration Policy Institute. Apr 1, 2006. Web. https://www.migrationpolicy.org/article/central-americans-and-asylum-policy-reagan-era.

Hartmann, Margaret. "Trump's Census Change Could Give the GOP an Advantage for Years to Come." *New York Magazine*. Daily Intelligencer. Mar 27, 2018. Web.

http://nymag.com/daily/intelligencer/2018/03/trumps-census-change-could-boost-the-gop-for-years-to-come.html.

"Here's What We Know about Trump's Mexico Wall." *Bloomberg*. Bloomberg Politics. Dec 11, 2017. Web. https://www.bloomberg.com/graphics/2017-trump-mexico-wall/will-a-wall-be-effective/.

Hingston, Sandy. "Bullets and Bigots: Remembering Philadelphia's 1844 Anti-Catholic Riots." *Philly Mag*. Philadelphia Magazine. Dec 17, 2015. Web. https://www.phillymag.com/news/2015/12/17/philadelphia-anti-catholic-riots-1844/.

"History." *Census.gov*. United States Census Bureau. 2018. Web. https://www.census.gov/history/.

"Immigration." *Gallup*. Gallup Poll. 2017. http://news.gallup.com/poll/1660/immigration.aspx.

"In First Month, Views of Trump Are Already Strongly Felt, Deeply Polarized." *Pew Research*. Pew Research Center. Feb 16, 2017. http://assets.pewresearch.org/wp-content/uploads/sites/5/2017/02/17094915/02-16-17-Political-release.pdf.

Katz, Josh. "How a Police Chief, a Governor and a Sociologist Would Spend $100 Billion to Solve the Opioid Crisis." *The New York Times*. The New York Times Co. Feb 14, 2018. Web. https://www.nytimes.com/interactive/2018/02/14/upshot/opioid-crisis-solutions.html.

Kertscher, Tom. "Were the Founding Fathers 'Ordinary People'?" *Politifact Wisconsin*. Politifact. Jul 2, 2015. Web. http://www.politifact.com/wisconsin/article/2015/jul/02/founding-fathers-ordinary-folk/.

Kessler, Glenn. "The Debate over DACA: A Guide to the Numbers Used by Politicians." *The Washington Post*. The Washington Post Co. Jan 23, 2018. https://www.washingtonpost.com/news/fact-checker/wp/2018/01/23/the-debate-over-daca-a-guide-to-the-numbers-used-by-politicians/?utm_term=.687a215d6a80.

Kilgannon, Corey and Joseph Goldstein. "Sayfullo Saipov, the Suspect in the New York Terror Attack, and His Past." *The New York Times*. The New York Times Co. Oct 31, 2017. https://www.nytimes.com/2017/10/31/nyregion/sayfullo-saipov-manhattan-truck-attack.html.

Kirby, Jen. "Trump Blasts 'Diversity Visa Lottery Program,' after NYC Terror Attack." *Vox*. Vox Media. Nov 1 2017. https://www.vox.com/policy-and-politics/2017/11/1/16590166/trump-tweet-diversity-visa-lottery-program.

Kopan, Tal. "What Are Sanctuary Cities, and Can They Be Defunded?" *CNN Politics*. CNN. Mar 26, 2018. Web. https://www.cnn.com/2017/01/25/politics/sanctuary-cities-explained/index.html.

Kurtzleben, Danielle. "What the Latest Immigration Polls Do (and Don't) Say). *NPR*. National Public Radio. Jan 23, 2018. https://www.npr.org/2018/01/23/580037717/what-the-latest-immigration-polls-do-and-dont-say.

Law, Anna O. "The Irish Roots of the Diversity Visa Lottery." *Politico Magazine*. Politico. Nov 1, 2017. https://www.politico.com/magazine/story/2017/11/01/diversity-visa-irish-history-215776.

Light, Michael T., Miller, Ty, and Brian C. Kelly. "Undocumented Immigration, Drug Problems, and Driving Under the Influence in the United States, 1990-2014."

AJPH. American Public Health Association. Apr 23, 2017. https://ajph.aphapub-lications.org/doi/abs/10.2105/AJPH.2017.303884.

Litke, E. "Yes, We Are Experiencing a Net Outflow of Illegal, Undocumented Workers from America Back to Mexico." *Politifact*. Politifact. Apr 26, 2017. Web. http://www.politifact.com/wisconsin/statements/2017/apr/26/ron-kind/yes-experiencing-net-outflow-illegal-undocumented-/.

López, Gustavo and Kristen Bialik. "Key Findings about U.S. Immigrants." *Factank*. Pew Research Center. May 3, 2017. Web. http://www.pewresearch.org/fact-tank/2017/05/03/key-findings-about-u-s-immigrants/.

Malkin, Michelle. "Immigration and the Values of Our Founding Fathers." *National Review*. Dec 11, 2015. Web. https://www.nationalreview.com/2015/12/immigration-founding-fathers-view-michelle-malkin/.

Matthews, Dylan. "Polls Show Americans Are Closer to Democrats Than Donald Trump on Immigration." *Vox*. Vox Media. Feb 12, 2018. https://www.vox.com/policy-and-politics/2018/2/3/16959458/immigration-trump-compromise-public-opinion-poll-dreamers-wall.

Matthews, Dylan. "The Republican Tax Bill Got Worse: Now the 1% Gets 83% of the Gains." *Vox*. Vox Media. Dec 18, 2017. Web. https://www.vox.com/policy-and-politics/2017/12/18/16791174/republican-tax-bill-congress-conference-tax-policy-center.

Minkel, J.R. "Confirmed: The U.S. Census Bureau Gave Up Names of Japanese-Americans in WW II." *Scientific American*. Smithsonian Institution. Mar 30, 2007. Web. https://www.scientificamerican.com/article/confirmed-the-us-census-b/.

Miroff, Nick and Erica Werner. "First Phase of Trump's Border Wall Gets $18 billion Price Tag, in New Request for Lawmakers." *The Washington Post*. The Washington Post Co. Jan 5, 2018. Web. https://www.washingtonpost.com/.

Misra, Tanvi. "Immigrants Aren't Stealing American Jobs." *The Atlantic*. The Atlantic Monthly Group. https://www.theatlantic.com/politics/archive/2015/10/immigrants-arent-stealing-american-jobs/433158/.

Myrick, Gayle. "You Can't Make Me Perform Same-Sex Marriages." *News Observer*. Feb 14, 2018. Web. http://www.newsobserver.com/opinion/op-ed/article200224229.html.

"Naturalization, [3 February] 1790," *Founders Online*. National Historical Publications & Records Commission." 2002. Web. https://founders.archives.gov/documents/Madison/01-13-02-0018.

Newport, Frank. "Democrats Racially Diverse; Republicans Mostly White." *Gallup*. Gallup Org. Feb 8, 2013. Web. http://news.gallup.com/poll/160373/democrats-racially-diverse-republicans-mostly-white.aspx.

Nichols, Alex. "You Should Be Terrified That People Who Like 'Hamilton' Run Our Country." *Current Affairs*. Current Affairs. Jul 29, 2016. Web. https://www.currentaffairs.org/2016/07/you-should-be-terrified-that-people-who-like-hamilton-run-our-country.

Nichols, Chris. "No, Californians Do Not Overwhelmingly Oppose Sanctuary

Policies." *Politifact*. Politifact. Jan 9, 2018. Web. http://www.politifact.com/california/statements/2018/jan/09/travis-allen/no-californians-do-not-overwhelmingly-oppose-sanct/.

O'Hanlon, Michael E. and Raymond Odierno. "Assimilation Is Counterterrorism." *Brookings Institution*. Apr 19, 2016. Web. https://www.brookings.edu/blog/order-from-chaos/2016/04/19/assimilation-is-counterterrorism/.

Ottaviano, Gianmarco I.P., Peri, Giovanni, and Greg C. Wright. "Immigration, Offshoring and American Jobs." *NBER*. The National Bureau of Economic Research. Working Paper No. 16439. Oct 2010. Retrieved from http://www.nber.org/papers/w16439#fromrss.

Peri, Giovanni. "The Impact of Immigrants in Recession and Economic Expansion." *MPI*. Migration Policy Institute. June 2010. https://www.migrationpolicy.org/research/impact-immigrants-recession-and-economic-expansion.

Popovich, Nadja, Albeck-Ripka, Livia, and Kendra Pierre-Louis. "67 Environmental Rules on the Way Out Under Trump." *The New York Times*. The New York Times Co. Jan 31, 2018. Web. https://www.nytimes.com/interactive/2017/10/05/climate/trump-environment-rules-reversed.html.

Preston, Julia. "Newest Immigrants Assimilating as Fast as Previous Ones, Report Says." *The New York Times*. The New York Times Co. https://www.nytimes.com/2015/09/22/us/newest-immigrants-assimilating-as-well-as-past-ones-report-says.html.

Pritchett, Lant. "The Cliff at the Border." In Ravi Kanbur and Michael Spence, *Equity and Growth in a Globalizing World*. Washington, DC: Commission on Growth and Development/World Bank, 2010, 263.

"Public Trust in Government: 1958-2017." *Pew Research*. Pew Research Center. May 3, 2017. Web. http://www.people-press.org/2017/05/03/public-trust-in-government.

Ruiz, Neil G. "Key Facts about the U.S. H-1B Visa Program." *Factank*. Pew Research. Apr 27, 2017. Web. http://www.pewresearch.org/fact-tank/2017/04/27/key-facts-about-the-u-s-h-1b-visa-program/.

Stagg, J.C.A. "James Madison: Life Before the Presidency." *Miller Center*. UVA. Miller Center. 2017. Web. https://millercenter.org/president/madison/life-before-the-presidency.

Sterman, Adiv. "Two-Thirds of Israelis Support Peace with Palestinians That Ensures Security, Polls Find." *Times of Israel*. Dec 31, 2012. Web. https://www.timesofisrael.com/two-thirds-of-israelis-support-peace-with-palestinians-that-ensures-security-polls-find/.

Tharoor, Ishaan. "What Americans Thought of Jewish Refugees on the Eve of World War II." *The Washington Post*. The Washington Post Co. Nov 17, 2015. Web. https://www.washingtonpost.com/news/worldviews/wp/2015/11/17/what-americans-thought-of-jewish-refugees-on-the-eve-of-world-war-ii/?noredirect=on&utm_term=.0de0aa7925a7.

Thomsen, Jacqueline. "Trump Waives Dozens of Environmental Rules to Speed Construction of Border Wall." *The Hill*. The Hill. Jan 22, 2018. Web. http://

thehill.com/latino/370202-trump-admin-waives-dozens-of-environmental-rules-to-speed-up-construction-of-border.

"Title 13, U.S. Code." *Census Bureau*. U.S. Census Bureau. Web. https://www.census.gov/history/www/reference/privacy_confidentiality/title_13_us_code.html.

"Trump is Intelligent, but Not Fit or Level Headed," *Quinnipiac University*. Jan 10, 2018. Web. https://poll.qu.edu/images/polling/us/us01102018_uss771.pdf/.

"U.S. Immigrant Population and Share over Time, 1850-Present." *MPI*. Migration Policy Institute. 2016. Web. https://www.migrationpolicy.org/programs/data-hub/charts/immigrant-population-over-time.

Valverde, Miriam. "Border Fence in Israel Cut Illegal Immigration by 99 Percent, GOP Senator Says." *Politifact*. Politifact. Feb 13, 2017. Web. http://www.politifact.com/truth-o-meter/statements/2017/feb/13/ron-johnson/border-fence-israel-cut-illegal-immigration-99-per/.

Valverde, Miriam. "Donald Trump's Team Misleads in Tying International Terrorism Report to Immigration." *Politifact*. Jan 22, 2018. http://www.politifact.com/truth-o-meter/article/2018/jan/22/donald-trumps-team-misleads-tying-international-te/.

Valverde, Miriam. "Will a Border Wall Stop Drugs from Coming into the United States?" *Politifact*. Politifact. Oct 26, 2017. Web. http://www.politifact.com/truth-o-meter/article/2017/oct/26/will-border-wall-stop-drugs-coming-united-states/.

Wagner, Alex. "America's Forgotten History of Illegal Deportations." *The Atlantic*. The Atlantic Monthly Group. Mar 6, 2017. Web. https://www.theatlantic.com/politics/archive/2017/03/americas-brutal-forgotten-history-of-illegal-deportations/517971/.

Wang, Hansi Lo. "Chinese-American Descendants Uncover Forged Family Histories." *NPR*. National Public Radio. Dec 17, 2013. https://www.npr.org/sections/codeswitch/2013/12/17/251833652/chinese-american-descendants-uncover-forged-family-history.

Waters, Mary C. and Marisa Gerstein Pineau. "The Integration of Immigrants into American Society." *The National Academies Press*. National Academies of Sciences. 2015. https://www.nap.edu/download/21746.

"Why We're Reinstating Census Citizenship Question." *USA Today*. Mar 27, 2018. Web. https://www.usatoday.com/story/opinion/2018/03/27/census-question-editorials-debates/33340397/.

Wolf, Z. Byron. "Trump Basically Called Mexicans Rapists Again." *The Point*. CNN. April 6, 2018. Web. https://www.cnn.com/2018/04/06/politics/trump-mexico-rapists/index.html.

Ye Hee Lee, Michelle. "Do 80 Percent of Americans Oppose Sanctuary Cities?" *The Washington Post*. The Washington Post Co. Mar 28, 2017. Web. https://www.washingtonpost.com/news/fact-checker/wp/2017/03/28/do-80-percent-of-americans-oppose-sanctuary-cities/?noredirect=on&utm_term=.fe46550cbe47.

Yurkevich, Vanessa and Alexander Rosen. "Not Just Trump's Idea: A Short History of Famous Walls and the Environment." *CNN Politics.* CNN. Feb 13, 2018. Web. https://www.cnn.com/2018/02/13/politics/history-of-walls/index.html.

Websites

American Civil Liberties Union (ACLU)

www.aclu.org

The American Civil Liberties Union (ACLU) is an organization dedicated to identi-fying and attempting to address threats to civil liberties and civil rights. The ACLU addresses immigration and immigrant rights in several ways and the ACLU website provides information on the civil rights issues affecting the immigrant population.

American Immigration Council

www.americanimmigrationcouncil.org

The American immigration council is a nonprofit advocacy organization that pro-vides information to the public on the contributions of immigrants to the United States and on the civil rights issues facing immigrants in the country. On the organi-zation's website, the American Immigration Council provides information on recent administrative and political changes to immigration law and policy as well as data on immigrants in the United States.

Center for Immigration Studies (CIS)

www.cis.org

The Center for Immigration Studies is an anti-immigrant organization and collects, funds, and produces information designed to promote reducing immigration num-bers and rates. Because the organization's research furthers an agenda, some of the data produced and promoted by the organization has been found to be misleading and inaccurate. On the organization's website, the CIS provides articles and links to other anti-immigration groups and information.

Federation for American Immigration Reform (FAIR)

www.fair.org

The Federation for American Immigration Reform is a nonprofit organization that advocates for reducing both legal and illegal immigration rates. Often cited by anti-immigration pundits and politicians, the organization is controversial because of connections with white nationalist organizations.

Migration Policy Institute

www.mpi.org

The Migration Policy Institute (MPI) is a Washington, D.C. think tank that funds, supports, and produces research and data on immigrants and immigration. Their research is used by politicians, journalists, and researchers studying the issue and the organization studies immigration issues worldwide, rather than focusing only on US immigration policy and can therefore provide helpful data to compare US policy to other nations.

Pew Research Center

www.pewresearch.org

Pew Research Center is a nonprofit, nonpartisan think tank based in Washington, D.C. The organization conducts public opinion polling and compiles and funds demographic research. Pew Research has produced numerous studies and conducted many opinion polls on immigration and related issues, available free through the organization's website.

The United States Citizenship and Immigration Services (USCIS)

www.uscis.gov

The United States Citizenship and Immigration Services is a branch of the federal government, under the auspices of the Department of Homeland Security, responsible for the bureaucracy of the naturalization and immigration process in the United States. The USCIS can be either anti-immigrant or pro-immigrant, depending on the priorities set out by each US presidential administration. Under the Donald Trump administration the USCIS has adopted a strongly anti-immigrant agenda.

VDARE

www.vdare.com

VDARE one of the most prominent anti-immigration groups in the United States funding and supporting politicians who support an anti-immigration and anti-multiculturalist agenda. Critics have labeled VDARE a hate group because some of the organization's leaders, including founder Peter Brimelow, have expressed support for white nationalist or supremacist philosophy.

Index